DATE DUE FOR RETURN

EDUCATION AND EDUCATIONAL RESEARCH

General Editor: DR. EDMUND KING

Secondary School Administration

A Management Approach

Second Edition

Secondary School Administration

A Management Approach

Second Edition

Edited by Meredydd G. Hughes
Faculty of Education, University College, Cardiff

Foreword by Professor Andrew Taylor
Dean of the Faculty of Education, University College, Cardiff

PERGAMON PRESS
OXFORD · NEW YORK · TORONTO · SYDNEY

Pergamon Press Ltd., Headington Hill Hall, Oxford

Pergamon Press Inc., Maxwell House, Fairview Park, Elmsford, New York 10523

Pergamon of Canada Ltd., 207 Queen's Quay West, Toronto 1

Pergamon Press (Aust.) Pty. Ltd., 19a Boundary Street, Rushcutters Bay, N.S.W. 2011, Australia

First edition 1970

Reprinted 1973

Second (enlarged) edition 1974

Library of Congress Cataloging in Publication Data
Hughes, Meredydd G
Secondary school administration.

(The Commonwealth and international library.
Education and educational research)
1. High schools—Administration. I. Title.
LB2822.H84 1974   658'.91'373   74–4453
    ISBN 0–08–018010–8
    ISBN 0–08–018011–6 (pbk.)

Printed in Great Britain by A. Wheaton & Co., Exeter

CONTENTS

FOREWORD

THIS book represents the contribution of a variety of sources of experience, focused on the problems of the emerging pattern of secondary education in England and Wales. It takes account of the growing realisation that professionalism in education extends beyond the sphere of the classroom, the subject and the pupil, and that it properly includes the study of the administrative and organisational aspects of school management, together with a deeper appreciation of the school's role in community life, not only as an instrument of conservation but also as an instrument of change.

Today there is a general appreciation of the fact that educational problems, like all other social problems, are many faceted. In arranging the in-service course for secondary school Heads and senior members of staff which has resulted in the present volume, the Faculty of Education has been greatly aided by the ready and wholehearted co-operation of the following: the Head of the Department of Industrial Relations at University College, Cardiff, and members of his staff, who provided both lectures and tutorial assistance; lecturers from other universities, including Professor C. H. Dobinson, formerly of Reading University, and Professor S. J. Eggleston of Keele University; the Chief Inspector of Schools (Wales) of the Department of Education and Science, and his colleagues; and the Heads of schools who provided an essential ingredient by outlining their own approach to the problems of school management.

That the course itself was a success is in no small measure due to the participants themselves, whose active contributions gave substance to the points discussed, and to the general planning carried out by the editor, Dr. Meredydd G. Hughes, Senior Lecturer in the Cardiff Faculty of Education. Co-operative efforts such as these can only augur well for the promotion of sound educational thought and practice in an area of high responsibility and developing competence.

ANDREW TAYLOR
Professor of Education and Dean of the Faculty
of Education, University College, Cardiff

EDITOR'S PREFACE

In the original planning of the present volume—and the in-service training course for Heads and senior members of staff, on which it was largely based—a basic assumption was that, if progress is to be made in developing a new approach to school management, a genuine partnership is necessary between theorists and practising school administrators.

In Part 1 the editor's introductory survey takes account of both practical and theoretical aspects. We begin with the broad changes in the context of secondary school administration which have led to a general appreciation of a need for managerial training for those with administrative responsibilities in secondary schools. Recognising that educational administration not only gives scope for practical expertise but is also rapidly emerging as a field of academic study, we then discuss the case for turning to the social sciences for assistance in developing new perspectives within which the managerial problems of the schools can be tackled. Limiting factors which affect the application to education of general organisational theory are considered, leading to a discussion of the techniques available to relate theoretical concepts to the 'real' world. This completes the editor's general introduction to the field.

Professor Thomason, in Part 2, introduces the basic concepts and perspectives of organisational theory and proposes an adaptation of these ideas to the particular case of the school. The sensitivity which Professor Thomason shows to the special characteristics of service organisations and those employing professional personnel should quickly dispel the notion that a management approach involves the imposition on the schools of a structure of management principles which are inflexible and universally applicable. A monolithic view of management is obsolescent even in the industrial context.

Part 3, written by four comprehensive school Heads, is concerned with the operational aspects of school management. The first contributor, Raymond Jones, overtly takes account of management concepts in his discussion of objectives and administrative structure; while Mrs. Davis's description of the consultative and decision-taking organisation of a large school shows, in greater detail, how such an approach works out in practice. Michael Tucker has contributed a realistic account of an experiment in organisational change at his former school, the change being a progressive process of unstreaming, starting with the first year. Accepting for himself the role of 'change agent', he shows how the change was accomplished with the co-operation, in varying degrees, of staff, pupils, parents and community. In the final chapter of this section, Dr. Harry Judge, while still at Banbury, analyses the perplexing problems of change at the upper end of the secondary stage; he considers the factors to be taken into account in defining objectives and implementing them, and in involving staff and students in these processes, whether in a large comprehensive school or in a sixth-form college.

From the wealth of lectures on operational topics on our various Cardiff courses and other Faculty of Education occasions, it would have been easy to include a dozen or more additional chapters in Part 3. Unfortunately this would have overloaded the volume, and it was felt that four representative contributions would·show more clearly the relevance of concepts developed in the previous section.

The selection of case-study material in Part 4 gives the reader a further opportunity of considering how far the approach and ideas presented are likely to be helpful in tackling difficult situations resulting from secondary school reorganisation. The first 'Neighbourhood School' study, included by permission, is an abridged version of an article in *New Society*, while the apocryphal extension which follows was prepared for use on our Cardiff course in conjunction with a lecture by C. J. Gill of Keele University on 'Guidance and Counselling: Implications for School Organisation'. Peter Webb's three-part study, 'Westwood Comprehensive', published by permission of the late Mr. Wynne Ll. Lloyd, C.B., H.M. Chief Inspector of Schools for Wales, has been used on a number of the Courses on Organisation and Management arranged by the Department of Education and Science. The case studies make specific such problems as the reassessing of aims and objectives in changed circumstances, the organisational structure appropriate to large schools and the need for pastoral, as well as academic, provision for the whole range of pupils. These are some of the issues discussed in the final chapter of this section in comments on the case studies by two experienced Heads who attended the course.

Part 5 consists of two chapters. In the first, Peter Webb identifies and discusses a number of criteria which are relevant in the planning and evaluation of both academic and pastoral organisation. He thereby provides a framework within which empirical experience, as presented in Parts 3 and 4, can be organised and assessed, while amplifying, in a school context, the previous discussion of direction and control. This is followed by a chapter, new to the Second Edition, in which the editor argues for a restructuring of instrumental and expressive aspects of the Head's role, to take account of increasing organisational complexity and the involvement of others in decision-making. A necessary corollary is that new criteria of evaluation become relevant as the old image of benevolent autocracy is eroded and the Head becomes primarily a promoter of participation, a catalyst of co-operation.

In the concluding chapter, which has been expanded in the Second Edition, the editor comments on the common elements of the analytical and operational contributions, and considers the training implications of the approach to school management which emerges with remarkable consistency as the several ingredients are brought together. This provides further support for the basic theme of the volume—the interdependence of theory and practice in a period of rapid change.

PART 1

A NEW APPROACH

Meredydd G. Hughes

CHAPTER 1

THE CHANGING CONTEXT OF SECONDARY SCHOOL ADMINISTRATION

1

"You say that you are frightened at the prospect before you, in view of your ignorance of many practical problems of school management" (Thomas and Bailey, 1927). The words are those of an experienced Headmaster of the 1920s—Jenkyn Thomas, Head of Hackney Downs and, previously, of Aberdare Grammar School— and were ostensibly addressed to a young man who has appealed to two senior colleagues for advice and guidance on his sudden translation from classroom and staffroom to Headmaster's study. The young Head's predicament is not unusual even today.

Thomas's reply is clear and comforting. "Be of good cheer", he writes. "You understand boys and you have common sense. These are the only essential qualifications. If you have these, everything else will be added unto you." He goes on to suggest that the novice Headmaster will be able to learn on the job. "You have the capacity, too, of profiting by experience—there are plenty of men who have no such capacity."

In the same volume a second adviser, Charles Bailey, Head of Holt Secondary School, Liverpool, provides further reassurance. "If the heart of the school is sound," he observed, "the details of government will come right. Mistakes may be made but they will not be vital." In his next letter he will "discuss a Headmaster's duties as a member of a teaching staff and not as an educational managing director or a publicity manager or a school shop walker".

In spite of their disapproval of any attempt to apply management ideas to schools, the two writers agreed that a Headmaster should be 'business-like', while criticising those "who think themselves business-like but really are not". In a passage which shows school administration then to have been a far less complicated process than it is today, Thomas declares that "the business-like Headmaster gets the machine running smoothly by the end of the first morning". The metaphor is instructive and seems to suggest that, after the first morning, the 'machine' is expected to function in a routine manner with very little further attention. Paradoxically there is here an echo of the mechanistic view of organisation which was general at that time and which had found its clearest expression in the scientific management movement (Taylor, 1911). But the purpose of efficient methods in the school was to be quite different. "The whole object of being business-like is to save time and energy and thought for the vital duties"—which are, firstly, to teach, and secondly, to provide pastoral care and firm guidance to both staff and boys. These priorities are, of course, firmly rooted in what has been called 'the supremo tradition' of the nineteenth-century public school Headmasters (Rée, 1968).

The *Letters to a Young Head Master*, from which the above quotations are taken, contain many shrewd comments which are still relevant today (e.g. "It is very easy to overdo addresses to the whole school. Boys are a very deceptive audience. Often when we think we are deeply impressing them we are boring them stiff.") But the underlying theme, that the ability to teach and a store of "common sense", uncontaminated by any knowledge or experience of management, are the only essential requirements for successful secondary school headship, is a proposition that, in today's circumstances, cannot be taken seriously. The schools have changed; so also, with the growth of the social sciences, have the concepts and theories of management.

The sustained weekly attendance of over sixty secondary school Heads and senior staff for a whole term at the course which inspired the present volume, together with similar activity at universities ranged, alphabetically, from Bath and Bristol to York, is cogent evidence of the growing belief among those best qualified to judge, that organised and systematic courses can be of value in developing the administrative skills and leadership qualities which are required, not only by Headmasters but also at intermediate managerial levels, in the secondary schools of the future. Parry Michael (1967) and Raymond Long (1969) are among those who have argued that learning informally from senior colleagues (who themselves may be fully occupied adapting to change) and 'profiting by experience' (i.e. learning by making mistakes) are no longer adequate forms of initial or inservice training for Headmasters. After a sabbatical term making a study of management in relation to large secondary schools, Long declares:

> It is no longer possible to believe that practical experience alone constitutes valid management training. Too many costly mistakes can occur while experience is being acquired and, in any case, the quality of experience can vary widely. Moreover, the man who learns solely from practical experience will normally begin with sets of assumptions which may be right or wrong.

The College of Preceptors was early in the field in providing short courses, and various local education authorities and voluntary bodies have since made similar provision. University institutes of education and polytechnics are increasingly involved, while Professor George Baron and Dr. William Taylor are among those who have pioneered more extensive courses and the theoretical studies which are necessary if the study of educational administration in the United Kingdom is to proceed beyond the folk-lore stage (Baron and Taylor, 1969).

The rapid growth of interest in a hitherto neglected field of study was given official recognition by the Secretary of State for Education and Science, Mr. Anthony Crosland, in 1967 when he announced that he was asking H.M. Inspectorate to give high priority to the development of courses in school organisation and management for Heads and senior staff. Dr. Michael Birchenough, the first chairman of the H.M.I. panel on school management which was then established, foresaw (1967) that the Department would extend its own programme of short courses while encouraging university institutes of education and other bodies to provide longer courses. Addressing the Annual Conference of the Headmasters' Association (1968), he added that "we have much to learn from management education, provided we are not led astray by false analogies with industrial and commercial situations and I hope that those concerned with management education in universities, polytechnics and business schools will increasingly interest themselves in problems of school organisation". Five years later Raymond Long (1973), commenting as H.M.A. President on government proposals to expand the in-service training of teachers, called for all who are promoted to positions of responsibility in schools to have opportunities to develop insights into the nature of their managerial role.

Such views are indicative of a significant change of attitude within the education service, which is also exemplified in other ways. Most notable has been the formation in 1971 of a British Educational Administration Society, affiliated to the Commonwealth Council for Educational Administration, which brings together practising administrators, whether in schools, colleges or L.E.A.s, and those engaged in management teaching and research. The first two annual conferences were devoted to staff development (Pratt, 1973) and the management of resources, topics directly relevant to the theme of the present work. B.E.A.S has also established a journal, *Educational Administration Bulletin*, edited by the present writer, which contains research reports and seeks to encourage the discussion of basic issues and new approaches to training and development.

In 1974 the Open University's Faculty of Educational Studies ventures for the first time into the area of educational administration with a course on decision-making in British educational systems. The aim is to examine the determinants of educational policy, comparing the available theoretical models with the actual reality of educational decision-making, and bringing the two into a closer relationship to each other.

Nowadays it is generally recognised, at least "in theory", that a theory/practice polarisation is liable to be counterproductive. As Taylor (1972) has observed: "The tired old dichotomy between theory and practice in education ought to have been dead long ago." It is thus encouraging that the present volume is only one among several responses to the challenge to establish effective communication between the exponents of management theory and practising administrators in schools and other educational systems.

2

In a period of relative tranquillity and continuity, with change occurring but slowly, Jenkyn Thomas's advice to the novice Head-master to be guided by common sense may be reasonably safe. Even then there is an element of uncertainty about the conditions which have to be satisfied for propositions put forward, perhaps with un-warranted assurance, to be reliable as predictors for the future. When change is rapid and a new and unfamiliar situation arises, the distillation of past experience, which is concentrated in the precepts of common sense, may become a very misleading guide to action. In a striking passage in *The Prince* (trans. 1640), Machiavelli refers to a man who, "having always prospered, walking such a way, cannot be persuaded to leave it", and warns of the rigidity of outlook which past success in different circumstances can produce. "But if the times and affairs change, he is ruined, because he changes not his manner of proceeding . . . but if he could change his disposition with the times and the affairs, he should not change his fortune." He concludes that "he proves the fortunate man, whose manner of proceeding meets with the quality of the time; and so likewise he unfortunate from whose course of proceeding the times differ".

It is thus relevant to our theme to review briefly the main changes in secondary education which have occurred since the publication of *Letters to a Young Head Master* in 1927. Perhaps the most obvious change is that all schools have increased in size and that there are now several hundred schools in England and Wales of over a thousand pupils. The special problems which these large schools pose are considered later in this volume (see particularly Chapters 7 and 8). Machiavelli's warning, noted above, is clearly apposite when the Headmaster of a large school finds it difficult to relinquish an administrative style which he had found to be effective when the school was much smaller (see the case study, "Westwood Comprehensive"). It is likewise difficult for the staff, both senior and junior, to make the adjustments necessary to work together effectively in the new context.

Basic to a whole group of changes is the complete transformation which has taken place in the concept of secondary education in little more than a generation. The year 1927 saw the Hadow Report, *The Education of the Adolescent*, from which we learn that, according to the latest available figures, only 7·2 per cent of the children between 11 and 16 were in secondary schools while 83 per cent of the children between 11 and 14 were in elementary schools. Of the children over 11 years of age in elementary schools only 5·4 per cent were in central schools, higher elementary schools or some other form of "advanced classes". Secondary education was the privilege of the few, largely determined by social class, while the majority of those in the elementary schools were "marking time", as Hadow puts it, rather than being educated. The process by which the Hadow proposal of a second stage of education, beginning at 11 for *all* children, "not merely because their parents have the means to pay for it, or because they are of such unusual capacity that the community thinks it worth while to provide it for them" (par. 89), gradually influenced practice in different parts of the country, was further elaborated in the Spens Report of 1938 and received statutory recognition in the Education Act of 1944—all this is familiar educational history. But the full implications of the change to "secondary education for all", in terms of new aims, objectives and organisation, are still painfully being worked out a generation later.

In the post-war period an initial tendency towards more systematic differentiation was overtaken by a contrary trend towards unification (see Rubinstein and Simon, 1969). Within the tripartite framework excellent pioneering work had been done in some of the new secondary modern schools, as described by Dent (1958) and others. In spite of official disapproval there was also the development of a variety of courses in preparation for public examination, consonant with Olive Banks's view (1955) that "it is only by this route that parity of esteem between the three corners of the tripartite system will be finally secured". Even for the best of the secondary moderns, however, parity of esteem proved an elusive goal, and, in retrospect, it is easy to see that it was an unattainable ideal. As Taylor has convincingly argued (1963), "the occupational implications of secondary education will always set a limit on the extent to which a school can secure parity of esteem on its own terms rather than those dictated by society".

The trend towards unification, which gained strength in the early sixties, continued the process of change in the concept of secondary education. Selection procedures at 11 + were becoming increasingly a target for criticism on both technical and ideological grounds, and accounts of the experience of multilateral and comprehensive schools established during the previous decade led a number of local education authorities to conclude that there was a viable alternative to the tripartite system. In 1965 the Labour Government's Circular 10/65 declared that it was government policy to end selection at 11 +. Profiting from experiments in Leicestershire and elsewhere, the paper outlined a number of two-tier patterns which were considered acceptable as alternatives to the single-tier comprehensive school for pupils aged 11–18.

With the change to a Conservative Government in 1970, the commitment to a comprehensive system was withdrawn in Circular 10/70. Decisions were to be left to local education authorities, but subject to the Secretary of State's declared intention to consider proposed changes to existing schools on their individual merit. Subsequent ministerial decisions led to some slowing down of comprehensive reorganisation, but it was estimated by Benn in 1972 that, as a result of the implementation of schemes previously approved, about a half of the secondary age group in England and Wales would be in comprehensive schools by 1975.

9

In 1974 the national policy has again been reversed, following the return of a minority Labour Government. Circular 4/74 requires local education authorities to submit reorganisation plans by the end of the year, but holds out no hope of special building allocations for new schools. The Secretary of State is therefore prepared to consider "proposals for a school to function, as an interim measure, on more than one site" unless they are "manifestly unsuitable", and places his main emphasis on the fullest possible use of existing resources.

The case study, 'Neighbourhood School', in the present volume portrays some of the administrative and human difficulties which arise when reorganisation proceeds in circumstances such that the limitations of the existing and available buildings become a major constraint, thereby heightening the managerial problems. As noted in the subsequent comments, such matters provide scope for legitimate objection, on grounds of viability and timing, to particular schemes of reorganisation, and it would be unwise to assume that non-educational considerations—giving the word 'educational' its widest possible connotation—do not occasionally influence the resolution of these issues. However that may be, the point to be made here is that the move towards a comprehensive system, including the controversies over single and two-tier systems, the use of divided premises, streaming, providing for the early leaver, pastoral care, co-education, sixth-form units and sixth-form colleges, all require new thinking about fundamental aims and objectives in secondary education (cf. Halsall, 1973). At the Cardiff course Professor C. H. Dobinson spoke of the inadequacy of a formulation of school objectives which puts academic achievement above all else. In widening our objectives, however, it is desirable—as McMullen has frequently pointed out (e.g. 1968)—to try to express them in operational terms, and it will be seen that contributions to Part 3 of the present volume are relevant in this context. It can also be argued that it is by insisting on the need to clarify objectives that management education can be of most effective help to Headmasters and their senior colleagues.

Closely related to changes in the concept of secondary education are those which have resulted, particularly during the last decade, in curriculum reappraisal and revision within both primary and secondary education. In England and Wales these developments now come within the ambit of the Schools Council, with teachers centres increasingly playing a part at local level; but it is salutory to remember that they are also a part of a world-wide movement of curriculum improvement, involving not only the scrutiny and reform of subject syllabuses but also a wide view of the general problem of content and distribution of subject-matter in education. Partly this represents a shift from a concept of learning as the exploration of a large, but finite, amount of knowledge which could, in theory, be stored in a massive encyclopaedia or within a computer, to a concept that knowledge is limitless and capable of indefinite expansion (see O.E.C.D., 1966). Such a change of outlook implies a transfer of attention from the assimilation of factual information to be memorised to the identification of key concepts to be used in developing a selective structure of knowledge (Young, 1971). It is of the essence of this more dynamic view that curriculum renewal is a continuing process.

Another implication is that significant curricular change in a school cannot be regarded as a matter for concern only to the individual teacher, acting in isolation from his colleagues (Hoyle, 1972). Inevitably teachers will be involved in groups, whether as a subject department, an interdisciplinary group working on a team teaching project, or a whole staff working together (see Jones, Chapter 7; Davis, Chapter 8; Tucker, Chapter 9). Decisions vital to the administration of the school have to be made. The Headmaster and the heads of department have to decide to what extent they are consciously to act as 'change agents' among their colleagues, enacting a role which, in the American context, has been strongly advocated for the High School Principal by J. Lloyd Trump (1961). For the writer the administrative implications of curricular innovation were brought sharply into focus by attendance at the 1967 International Curriculum Conference at Oxford. The conference, while revealing

11

in plenary session deep differences concerning the level of abstraction required for dealing with curriculum development, gave attention in seminar groups both to specialist discussions on a subject basis and also to wider administrative issues such as "Rational Planning in the Curriculum", introduced by Professor Philip Taylor, and "Organising the School and its Resources", introduced by I. McMullen (Maclure, 1968). Discussions of this kind, beginning with a formulation of objectives, have to take cognisance of the technological changes taking place in education, ranging from audio-visual aids to computer-aided education. Subject to economic considerations, the new facilities provide means, not previously available, for achieving curricular change and also establish the effective limits within which change occurs. To this extent, at least, the McLuhan over-simplification, "The medium is the message", finds a response among the technologists of educational communication.

Lastly, in our review of changes relevant to secondary school administration, we have to take account of subtle changes which affect the position of schools in society. These involve changes in the attitudes of the public at large, of parents and pupils and of the staff themselves. Rée (1968) writes of the transformation of authority which, he suggests, took place in the inter-war period.

> Eventually even the most isolated and cloistered school began to feel the effects of people's waning belief in justification by rank.... Although, even today, Heads can be found who cling to certain outworn assumptions, fearful or unaware of the revolutions which have caused these to wither away, the fifties in fact completed what the First World War began—the transformation of authority.

At our Cardiff course Professor S. J. Eggleston described the "client context" for school administration which he saw emerging, and he has subsequently developed the theme (1969, 1970; cf. Musgrove and Taylor, 1969). Demands for student autonomy and parent participation are only the most publicised of many manifestations of the new outlook. In education, as elsewhere, there is an increasing tendency for the wishes of the 'customers' to be made articulate and to influence administrative decisions. Later in this

12

volume David Howells suggests (Chapter 11), in the context of disciplinary problems, that the influence of the neighbourhood should be felt in the school, "a comprehensive school being by its very nature a microcosm of the community which engenders it". It may be noted that another contributor, Michael Tucker, in Chapter 9 takes a somewhat different view of the relationship between community values and those of the school.

In this chapter we have reviewed the changed context of secondary school administration since the 1920s. We noted the increased size of schools and the more explicit formulation of organisational structure which this entails. We discussed some implications of secondary education for all and the changes which have occurred in seeking to achieve it. Reorganisation, in practice, often occurs in circumstances which are far from ideal and makes high demands on the school's administrative leadership; requiring from the Headmaster and his senior colleagues both a broad view of long-term aims and operational objectives and an ability to handle the pressing problems of day-to-day survival. The various forms of two-tier arrangements involve additional problems of co-ordination and articulation between autonomous parts.

Other important changes have also been noted. The drawing together of a number of different aspects of educational thought has resulted in the curriculum reform activities which, in England and Wales, are now mainly sponsored by the Schools Council. In responding to experimental schemes and pilot projects, the schools have to take account of the new technical resources which are becoming available to facilitate individual learning and instruction in groups, both large and small. It appears that school administration requires a flexibility of approach which is willing to question traditional assumptions and practice without uncritically accepting half-baked notions dressed up as significant innovations.

Finally there are far-reaching changes in social attitudes, notably to authority, which lead to questions concerning community-school relations and the involvement of the 'clients', both pupils and parents, in the affairs of the school. Reference has been made to "the trans-

13

formation of authority". In discussing simulated situations on school administration courses with which the writer has been associated, it has generally been found to be more profitable to consider the influence and leadership functions which a Headmaster might exert in a given situation than to mark out the limits of his formal authority. The question which arises, using Weberian terminology, is whether *charisma* has become a more relevant managerial concept than authority defined in legal or traditional terms. This is an issue, redefined in terms of sapiental and organisational authority systems, to which Thomason gives considerable attention in Part 2 of the present volume.

REFERENCES

BANKS, O., *Parity and Prestige in Secondary Education*, Routledge, London, 1955, p. 219.

BARON, G. and TAYLOR, W., *Educational Administration and the Social Sciences*, Athlone Press, London, 1969.

BENN, C., *Comprehensive Schools in 1972*, Comprehensive Schools Committee, London, 1972.

BIRCHENOUGH, M., Introduction to HUGHES, MEREDYDD G., Simulated Situations, in *Trends in Education* (7), 1967.

BIRCHENOUGH, M., Training for headship, *Report of Headmasters' Association 76th Annual Conference*, 1968.

DENT, H. C., *Secondary Modern Schools: an Interim Report*, Routledge, London, 1958.

D.E.S., The organisation of secondary education, *Circular 10/65*, H.M.S.O., London, 1965.

D.E.S., The organisation of secondary education, *Circular 10/70*, H.M.S.O., London, 1970.

D.E.S., The organisation of secondary education, *Circular 4/74*, H.M.S.O., London, 1974.

Educational Administration Bulletin, Journal of British Educational Administration Society (D. PARKES, F.E. Staff College, Coombe Lodge, Blagdon, Bristol), twice yearly from 1972 onwards.

EGGLESTON, S. J., Convergence in the roles of personnel in differentiated educational organisations, in MATTHIJSSEN, M. A. and VERVOORT, C. E., *Education in Europe—Sociological Research*, Mouton, The Hague, 1969.

EGGLESTON, S. J., Education for the 21st century—a national perspective, in BROWN, G. N. and EGGLESTON, S. J., *Towards an Education for the 21st Century*, The University, Keele, 1970.

HADOW REPORT, *The Education of the Adolescent*, H.M.S.O., London, 1927.

HALSALL, ELIZABETH, *The Comprehensive School: guidelines for the reorganization of secondary education*, Pergamon, Oxford, 1973.

HOYLE, ERIC, Educational innovation and the role of the teacher, *Forum*, Spring 1972, pp. 42–44.

LONG, RAYMOND G., Management of large secondary schools, in *Trends in Education*, (15), H.M.S.O., London, 1969; also in *Headmasters' Association Review*, July 1969.

LONG, RAYMOND G., H.M.A. Presidential Address, *Headmasters' Association Review*, July 1973.

MACHIAVELLI, N., *The Prince*, 1513; trans. DACRES, EDWARD, Tudor Translations, London, 1640.

MACLURE, J. STUART, *Curriculum Innovation in Practice*, H.M.S.O., London, 1968.

McMULLEN, I., Flexibility for a comprehensive school, in *Forum*, Spring 1968, pp. 64–67.

MICHAEL, D. P. M., *The Idea of a Staff College*, Headmasters' Association, London, 1967.

MUSGROVE, F. and TAYLOR, P. H., *Society and the Teacher's Role*, Routledge, London, 1969, Chap. 7.

ORGANISATION FOR ECONOMIC CO-OPERATION AND DEVELOPMENT, *Curriculum Improvement and Educational Development*, O.E.C.D. Pubs., Paris, 1966.

PRATT, SIMON (ed.), *Staff Development in Education*, Councils and Education Press, London, 1973.

RÉE, HARRY, The changed role of the Head, in ALLEN, B. (ed.), *Headship in the 1970's*, Blackwell, Oxford, 1968.

RUBINSTEIN, D. and SIMON, B., *The Evolution of the Comprehensive School, 1926–1966*, Routledge, London, 1969.

SPENS REPORT, *Secondary Education with special reference to Grammar Schools and Technical High Schools*, H.M.S.O., London, 1938.

TAYLOR, F. W., *Shop Management*, Harper, New York, 1911.

TAYLOR, WILLIAM, *The Secondary Modern School*, Faber, London, 1963, p. 55.

TAYLOR, WILLIAM, *Theory into Practice*, H.T.V. Publications, Bristol, 1972.

THOMAS, W. JENKYN and BAILEY, CHARLES W., *Letters to a Young Headmaster*, Blackie, London, 1927. (The writer is indebted to Dr. D. G. D. Isaac, Rector of Mar College, Troon, Ayrshire, for drawing his attention to this volume.)

TRUMP, J. LLOYD and BAYNHAM, D., *Guide to Better Schools*, Rand McNally, Chicago, 1961.

YOUNG, MICHAEL F. D. (ed.), *Knowledge and Control, New Directions for the Sociology of Education*, Collier-Macmillan, London, 1971.

CHAPTER 2

THE RELEVANCE OF ORGANISATIONAL THEORY*

THE diversity in the provision of courses, conferences and workshops, which has arisen in response to the growing demand for specific preparation for administrative responsibility in schools, strongly suggests that there are basic differences of view as to the nature and magnitude of the challenge to educational leadership which is posed by the educational and social change briefly reviewed in the last chapter.

Many of the early courses were empirical in content and prescriptive in their approach, concentrating on providing answers to immediate 'nuts and bolts' questions of organisational maintenance and legal responsibility. One such course, typical of many, included lectures by a practising Head on applying for a headship, stock and capitation, detailed organisation, discipline, staff meetings, the school office and new trends (see Hughes, 1968).

Recently there has been some reaction against this kind of approach. Parry Michael (1967), for instance, has given a warning against the almost inevitable superficiality of short courses. "All over the country", he observes, "it will be possible in six easy lessons to hear how to be a top person." Apart from the temptation to try to do too much in too short a time, there is the possibly more insidious danger of encouraging the development of what may be termed 'technician's myopia'. An exclusive preoccupation with the day-to-day technical problems of management is liable to produce

* Adapted, by permission, from the writer's article, Theory and practice in educational administration, *Education for Development* (1), Cardiff University College Faculty of Education, 1970.

obsolescent solutions of limited applicability, whereas it is the under-lying assumptions which often need to be questioned. As an American text puts it, "Not only may experience in one situation be un-representative of another, but it may close alternatives and become so technique-oriented that the broader *principles* of administration are never fully realised" (Lane, 1966).

However necessary the routine housekeeping functions of school management may be—and large schools need bursars and registrars to carry out these duties—it is basic to the approach of the present volume that a more urgent need is to encourage the development of the administrative statesmen who will take a broad view and provide imaginative and stimulating leadership to the school com-munity. According to Selznick (1957), the primary task of institu-tional leadership is to set goals, to define the mission of the enter-prise. It is arguable that, in a school—as in other service organisa-tions staffed by professionals—this task should be performed as a co-operative exercise (see Thomason, Part 2), but this does not lessen the force of Selznick's warning that "a retreat to technology", i.e. a concentration on ways and means without attempting to define objectives, is an abdication of leadership. Thomason makes essenti-ally the same point (p. 78) when, in his reference to 'Gresham's Law of Planning', he observes that "routine administrative work will drive out non-programmed decisional activity".

The paradox, then, is this. In order to achieve a wider utility, we must be prepared to be theoretical, seeking a conceptual framework within which practical experience can be understood and evaluated. This is a hard saying for Heads and others who, in more settled times, have found it possible to come to terms with a diversity of events in a limited time without too fine a regard for logical con-sistency. Griffiths (1959) has commented on the anti-theoretical bias of many practising educational administrators in the United States ("Say, do you believe this or is it just research?"). It has to be recog-nised that, in the United Kingdom also, the word 'theoretical', though of high esteem among physicists, has a distinctly pejorative connotation for many educationists. Headmasters, whether coping

17

with sudden crises or under the constant press of administrative responsibility, often pride themselves on being inveterate empiricists and improvisers. They are unlikely to be persuaded, without due cause, of the relevance to them of John Dewey's famous dictum (1929) that "theory is in the end . . . the most practical of all things".

As a former Headmaster, the writer is well aware of the danger of the growth of a false dichotomy between theory and practice, which could seriously impede the development of educational administration as a subject of study in the United Kingdom. An analogy from the field of medicine, developed by Homans (1951), may be helpful in this context:

> In action we must always be clinical. An analytical science is for understanding but not for action, at least not directly. . . . When progress is rapid, clinical and analytical science help one another. The clinicians tell the analysts what the latter have left out. The analysts need the most brutal reminders because they are always so charmed with their pictures they mistake them for the real thing. On the other hand, the analysts' generalizations often suggest where the clinicians should look more closely.

In the social sciences, as in medical science, what theory can do is to provide a simplified model which will help the practitioner to understand the relationships of the real world.

At different levels and using different methodologies, the social sciences are concerned with man in society and as a member of groups, with social systems and social interaction. Formal organisations and the sophisticated and complex behaviours resulting from management activities are of interest within several disciplines and sub-disciplines: organisational theory, which includes all theories concerned with organisations, is a multi-disciplinary study which draws on the sociology of organisations, social psychology, systems theory, group dynamics, political science, economics and even anthropology.

Through extensive field work in industrial organisations over several decades, social scientists in many countries have contributed to the development of a body of management theory which commands a healthy respect among captains of industry, and to which some captains of industry have themselves contributed, e.g. Henri Fayol (1949), Chester Barnard (1938), Wilfred Brown (1960). Governmental, military and other organisations have also been studied, particularly in the United States, and it has been claimed (Halpin, 1958) that it was during the Second World War that social science research came into its own and developed a new maturity. In the late fifties the contribution which the social sciences could also make to the understanding of educational administration began to be recognised in the United States, largely through the conferences and publications of the University Council for Educational Administration (e.g. Halpin, 1958; Campbell, 1960; Willower, 1964; Culbertson et al., 1973). Similar developments have followed in Canada, Australia, New Zealand and, latterly, in the United Kingdom (see Baron, 1969a). Baron and Taylor's Educational Administration and the Social Sciences (1969b) and Glatter's Management Development for the Education Profession (1972) are major contributions to this movement.

There is clearly a considerable potential for further growth and co-operation in this field. It is therefore relevant to seek to make explicit the kind of assistance which organisational theory can give, and the kind it cannot give, to those who are engaged in educational administration, whether in schools or education offices. It is suggested that there are at least four boundary conditions which help to define the domain of applicability. These are as follows:

1. *Organisational theory cannot be directly applied to provide solutions to specific managerial problems.* The usefulness of the social sciences to the administrator, as Downey has observed (1962), is not so much that they generate answers for him as that they order phenomena "in such a way that the administrator can see alternatives clearly, can anticipate consequences accurately and can, in effect, deal wisely with his world". From a similar viewpoint, Taylor (1969) discounts the importance of the acquisition of factual information about administrative procedures on courses for school admini-

19

strators. He continues, "What the study of educational administration provides for the administrator is not 'facts' but an understanding of the *kinds* of facts that are relevant to his task. . . . To teach within this field is to offer the student new ways of structuring his perceptions within a familiar educational and social landscape." The metaphor of perceiving structure in a landscape naturally leads to the idea of a map and, following Getzels (1960), we may regard administrative theory as a mapping of the territory within which the administrator is operating. If one has no map, a set of detailed itineraries can be useful but, as with all empirical prescriptions, the instructions become dated if conditions change. If a road is blocked or a bridge is swept away, the itinerary, taken by itself, may be useless. A map of the whole territory, however, enables the traveller to choose his route according to his assessment of the circumstances of the time. In the same way administrative theory seeks to identify a pattern of relationships within which empirical experience can be better understood.

2. *Organisational theory, in so far as it is a science, is value-free and cannot be used to validate 'ought' statements.* In an attempt to define "the nature of administrative science", Simon (1947) pointed out that "propositions about administrative processes will be scientific in so far as truth and falsehood, in the factual sense, can be predicted of them". From this viewpoint, which is now generally accepted, values are regarded as variables rather than as fixed and given in the theory. Thus the social scientist may be in a position to indicate consequences which are likely to follow from the adoption of one organisational goal rather than another or one administrative style rather than another. He cannot, as scientist, legitimately offer an opinion as to which goal or mode of proceeding is morally better.

The practising administrator, however, with problems to be solved in the 'here and now', cannot be value-free. He has constantly to commit himself to specific goals and definite courses of action which imply value judgements. If his leadership is to be consistent and authentic, the flexibility of approach which organisational theory has given him, has to be exercised within a well-developed and coherent value system (see Ostrander, 1968, for an elaboration of this point in an American setting). Selznick (1957) has stated the proposition that the institutional leader "is primarily an expert in the promotion and protection of values". Whether or not that is an over-emphasis, it is generally accepted that the administrative leader will not find the values of his system within the fabric of organisational theory. (For a differing viewpoint see Simey, 1968.)

3. *There are differences in outlook and terminology between the theorist and the practitioner which effectively limit communication and interaction.* The main interest of the theorist is in achieving understanding, but the practitioner wants to get something done, often several things, in a limited time. A statement of the academic viewpoint, made by J. A. Passmore (1953), is quoted by Tope (1965) as follows: "When the social sciences are called trivial, sometimes all that is meant is that they fail to tell us many of the things we should particularly like to know. This, of course, is not a serious objection." Such extreme detachment from the workaday world diverges sharply from the approach of most administrators and is liable to discourage their participation in the time-consuming research activities on which the advance of administrative theory itself depends.

Differences of perspective result in communication difficulties. "The language of the practitioner", observes Goldhammer (1963), "is the language of action, while that of the scientist is academic and abstract." An example of the contrast occurs in the final section of the case study, 'Westwood Comprehensive', in the present volume, in which a consultant's recommendations on administrative structure elicits a vigorous rejoinder from the Headmaster. In reacting to the case study Miss Eluned Jones (p. 211) perceptively comments that there would have been a better chance of the consultant's suggestions being accepted if they had been expressed in more traditional terms. It is also pertinent to note that some social scientists have themselves criticised fellow academics for excessively developing esoteric interpretations of language which make their work unintelligible to the uninitiated (e.g. Mills, 1959).

While such strictures are sometimes well deserved, it also has to be recognised that a technical and precise use of language is a necessary requirement in all fields of study. The hasty condemnation of unfamiliar terminology as 'meaningless jargon' often creates an unnecessary barrier to understanding and is no substitute for the effort a serious reader may properly be expected to make in a field which is new to him. The practitioner may even find that the technical terminology of organisational theory provides him with a language in which he can refine and communicate ideas of which he was intuitively aware but which could not be easily and un-ambiguously expressed in ordinary language. The clarification of thought concerning the curricular structure of a large school, made possible by the notation developed by T. I. Davies (1969) and his colleagues in the Welsh Inspectorate, provides an excellent example of this process at work.

4. *General theory has to be adapted to the special characteristics of educational administration.* In making this statement we are not claiming that there is some mystique about school management which sets it apart as a process different in kind from the administration of other organisations. It is generally accepted today that "administration is basically the same in all organisations, whether they be educational, industrial, governmental, military or ecclesiastical" (Walton, 1959). Nevertheless, as Campbell has pointed out (1958), there are characteristics relating to the nature of the educational enterprise which make it, to some extent, a special case. These include the following:

(1) distinctive objectives as a particular kind of service organisation;

(2) an especially close relationship with a primary clientele (the pupils) and, potentially, with a secondary clientele (the parents);

(3) a lack of competition for clientele in the public sector, though some exceptions can be cited;

(4) a staff of professionals, who are given—and expect to be given—a high degree of discretion in their work;

(5) the different expectations held for a school administrator (e.g. that he should be highly visible, easily accessible and affectively related to the primary clientele) from those held of administrators in other contexts;

(6) an organisational output which has largely eluded quantitative evaluation.

These points will not be elaborated further here, but they clearly form the background for Thomason's contribution in Part 2, and it will be noted that he gives particular attention to the implications of the school as a professional organisation. Less acceptable at first sight may be his treatment of the pupils in applying an input-output model to the school: "they serve as the raw material to be processed by the system, and it is the system which is of main concern" (p. 42). An abstraction of this kind, reminiscent of Galileo's seemingly absurd decision to ignore friction in formulating laws of motion, illustrates the point that a theoretical model achieves clarification by deliberately leaving out important aspects of the total situation. It is then possible, as Thomason observes, to bring the theory into closer relation to reality by building on to the basic structure "a more or less complex edifice".

We have already referred to the 'client context' of school administration, and it is only as a first approximation, as Thomason would probably agree, that it is possible to regard the pupils as the passive 'through-put' of a processing system. The peculiar nature of the raw material of the school system is well described by Wengert (1962):

> Unlike the potter who does what he pleases with his clay, the administrator finds not only resistances he did not expect in the human materials he uses, but his materials also talk back to him; his materials—that is, the members of the school community—also have power generated outside the organisation he is building; he finds that statistically adequate answers fail to comprehend the particular situation; he cannot in many cases dismiss the exception as irrelevant. His materials are more than a mere passive condition of action.

23

Without referring to the considerable American literature on the subject, there is ample evidence in Britain of the ways in which the pupil-clients are able to modify the goals of the organisation, whether overtly—e.g. through subject and course decisions in the middle school or in the sixth form (see Dainton, 1968)—or covertly through the norms of the student sub-culture (Hargreaves, 1967). A possible influence on the *structure* of the organisation is mentioned by Judge in Chapter 10 when he comments that a move to develop formal machinery for pupil participation makes it desirable also to redefine the role of members of staff in the decision-making process of the school. "Any apparent alliance of Head with students against staff will be resented bitterly and with good reason." Providing organisational leadership, while giving opportunities for participation, as appropriate, to the professional staff of the organisation and to the living material being processed, is the unique and formidable assignment of the educational administrator.

The foregoing discussion of some of the special characteristics of educational administration is relevant to a question raised by the growth of organisational theory and allied disciplines. As administrative science becomes more sophisticated and comes to rely on the specialised techniques of linear programming, queuing theory, simulation models, cybernetics, network analysis and computer science, will a new breed of professional manager emerge, freely interchangeable between different kinds of organisation, able to administer, with equal confidence and versatility, great industrial undertakings, vast regional hospitals and large school complexes? In the foreseeable future this prospect seems unrealistic as far as schools are concerned; neither, it will be argued, is it desirable.

In his classic text on administrative behaviour, Simon (1947, 1957) argues that "in almost all organisations (the administrator) has a responsibility not only to establish and maintain the organisational structure, but also to make some of the broader and more important decisions regarding the content of the organisation's work". This certainly happens in a school, and the special characteristics of the educational enterprise, as discussed above, make it particularly desirable that the Headmaster and his senior colleagues should be recognised experts in what Simon calls "the technology of the organisation". This conclusion is also implicit in Thomason's delineation of "a sapiental authority system" (p. 50). There is thus a strong case, quite apart from arguments relating to career advancement, for Heads and other school administrators to continue to be recruited from the ranks of the teaching profession rather than from a general pool of professional experts in management.

The corollary is that aspiring school administrators within the teaching profession will themselves need to become professional experts in management, and opportunities for gaining such expertise will have to be provided on a far greater scale than hitherto. Courses in educational administration are now offered at several universities within the framework of the Master's Degree in Education, and the pressure to extend the provision is likely to increase as appointing boards begin to take account of such qualifications, as already happens in the United States.

The development of appropriate courses and the exploration of promising lines of attack is still at an early stage; there is an urgent need for teaching to be supported by relevant research, which will enable the application to education of general theory to be soundly conceived (cf. Glatter, 1972). It is possible to envisage that, in the long term, the present borrowings may be repaid, at least in part, original contributions to organisational theory being initiated in the field of educational administration. For the present it seems sensible, as has happened in Cardiff and Manchester, to take full advantage of opportunities to co-operate, whenever possible, with colleagues who have experience of organising relevant subject matter in allied fields, e.g. in industrial relations, in social and public administration.

The emphasis earlier in this chapter on the multi-disciplinary character of organisational research suggests that social scientists from a number of disciplines have a contribution to make to extended courses in educational administration. It would be unwise, however, to follow Wengert (1961) all the way when he suggests that the study of administration involves the mastery of *all* sciences "in order to discern how knowledge can replace judgement in the ordering of human affairs" (see Goldhammer, 1963, p. 14). Hoyle (1969) has pointed to the dangers of an approach to educational administration which, through uncritical and indiscriminate borrowings, "falls between the interstices of the disciplines and adds nothing solid", thereby producing "an invertebrate eclecticism". In contrast to Culbertson (1965), he suggests that the multi-disciplinary character of the field of study should emerge rather than be aimed at directly, and supports his argument by showing the distinctive contribution which can be made by adopting a sociological perspective.

The other essential component of an adequate scheme of management education for preparing school administrators—and this is implicit in our previous discussion of the role of theory—is the achievement of a creative and dynamic relationship between academic study and the actual job of organising a school. This is the crucial connection, but a glance at the American literature shows that the articulation is by no means easy. Halpin (1958), among others, is a theorist who has shown an awareness of the problems involved:

> We must guard against castigating the practitioner as 'purely empirical'. The general run of practitioner is no more purely empirical than many social scientists. There are scientists so utterly empirical that their research never gets off the ground. On the other hand there are scientists and administrators, too, who consistently soar in the clouds. They forget that every theory must be rooted in the actual world of experience. In cloud-soaring, the scientist has an advantage: he can get away with flights into space for a longer time than the administrator; he is not as promptly called to account. But he, too, must eventually relate his theory to the 'real' world.

Continuing the metaphor, there are problems both of flight control and of effecting a safe return to earth.

Through their membership of advisory committees for management courses and research projects, and also informally, it should be possible for the practising administrators, without taking over the controls, to be satisfied that serious and continuing attention is given to their difficulties as they see them and to the conflicts and stresses to which they feel that they are exposed. The sustained 'feed-back' from week to week at our Cardiff course, together with the informal consultations which preceded it, made the whole enterprise a valuable learning experience for the course organiser as well as for the participants. In this connection it is a happy augury that the *Review* of the Headmasters' Association, published each term, which until recently consisted largely of committee reports and official documents, has become an important source of ideas and a forum for discussion among Headmasters which is highly relevant to the subject-matter of this volume. As Heads and their staffs become more familiar with the language and perspectives of management theory, they will increasingly contribute ideas and advice on method to those engaged in the study of schools as organisations. It may also be speculated that they will provide a more sophisticated and more critical practitioner readership of the literature of organisational research than has hitherto been the case. A stimulating and challenging prospect lies ahead.

The need to effect a safe return to earth, i.e. to relate concepts and theories to the practice of administration, has given rise to a number of facilitating techniques and procedures, including case studies, simulated situations, role playing and management games. In relation to instructional materials developed by the University Council for Educational Administration, Culbertson (1962) writes:

> Cases and simulated situations offer students unique opportunities for developing competence in perceptive generalization. They also offer opportunities for utilizing social science concepts as students practise skills essential to decision-making. Such practice can be gained without adversely affecting actual practice in school districts.

The present writer has reported on the use of these materials on courses for school principals in the United States (Hughes, 1966, 1967a). Taylor (1966), one of the pioneers of similar developments in the United Kingdom, has made the point that "simulations can help to bridge this gap between teaching and action; they have many of the attributes of the 'real', yet have a controlled conceptual vocabulary that permits a gradual assimilation and the progressive grasp of principle".

Simulated situations, with realistic documentation, tape-recordings and in-tray exercises, are particularly helpful in handling the managerial and "human relations" aspects of the administrator's role, and can be given greater flexibility by using projective techniques. The less structured case-study approach, of which examples are given in the present volume, has been found useful in handling substantial long-term issues such as evaluating a total situation, formulating new objectives and working out appropriate strategies for their achievement. There is scope for further development, and it is interesting to note that Walker of the University of New England has compiled a book of case studies (1965) and a set of in-basket exercises (1969) related to Australian schools, which provide an interesting comparative exercise in educational administration. Participant response to both simulation exercises and case studies on the Cardiff course was very favourable.

Whereas the methods discussed above bring the reality of administration into the lecture theatre and seminar room, an alternative, or additional, procedure is to send students of management into actual administrative settings to carry out studies or to take responsible administrative action. Such field work, to make an effective contribution to management education, needs careful planning. In this respect much may be learnt from the use within the higher degree structure in the United States of 'the administrative internship', involving placement in schools and district offices under university supervision (see Hencley, 1963; Walker, 1969). According to an 'Action Guide' approved by the American Association of School Administrators (Conner, 1964), "The internship is a significant way of participating in administration and facilitating self-actualisation as an administrator. As the intern learns more about administration and about himself through practice, the meaning of administrator accountability comes to life."

The internship concept was further developed by the U.S. National Association of Secondary School Principals, which, in a project directed by J. Lloyd Trump, deliberately emphasised innovative experience rather than the conservation of traditional practices (Hughes, 1967b). The aim was to encourage strong educational leadership "through on-the-job training in certain schools, chosen for their advanced instructional programmes and their skilled and imaginative staffs. The goal is a principal who understands the change process in secondary schools and is prepared himself to become an effective agent of change" (Trump, 1964). A later document made the point that "the interns were to furnish a bridge between the theorists of the university and the practitioners of the secondary schools, and all were to benefit from the resulting exchange of information and views" (Trump, 1969). From 1963 to 1969 the project included 443 interns, 343 secondary schools and 63 universities.

It is difficult to visualise schemes of this kind being directly transferable to the United Kingdom in their entirety, though it is conceivable that, in a large comprehensive school, there would be scope for the observation of administrative processes in operation and, possibly, some participation. The underlying principle of bringing the schools themselves into the process of management training is surely a sound one. It fits in well with Thomason's suggestion that the Headmaster should initiate a process of staff involvement in decision-taking, through what he terms 'organisational training' (Chap. 6); also with Raymond Jones's proposal that teachers should be prepared for this involvement by means of some introduction to administration and management in their professional training (Chap. 7). It would then not be unreasonable for the Head of a large school to arrange for promising younger members of staff to obtain relevant administrative experience, while engaged in the part-time study of educational administration at their local university. A logical development is the concept of a school as a learning environment not only for the pupils but also for members of staff, as they adopt new curricula and accept managerial responsibilities at various levels in the administrative structure. There have recently been interesting developments along these lines in the

United States (Schmuck and Runkel, 1970) and in Britain (McMullen, 1972; John, 1973; Briault, 1973; Richardson, 1973).

The views presented in this chapter may now be briefly summarised. We have argued that, in preparing for administrative responsibility in schools, as in many other fields of study, a premature concern with the mastery of technique has to give way to a quest for understanding. In particular, this requires a dispassionate consideration of the contribution which the social sciences, and especially the multi-disciplinary study of organisations, can make to our understanding of educational administration. We discussed four limiting factors: that theory provides a perspective rather than a panacea; that administrative theory is value-free and cannot generate 'ought' statements; that theorists and practitioners have different priorities and terminology; and, finally, that educational administration is, to some extent, a special case.

While rejecting the suggestion that school administration might be handed over to managerial experts from outside the teaching profession, we suggested that those who seek administrative responsibility should be prepared to undertake appropriate studies in management, normally in a university context. We have argued that there is a need for fundamental research and curriculum development in management studies, which will strengthen the link between educational administration and the general body of social scientific knowledge relating to organisations. Thomason, in the following section, gives an indication of the kind of theoretical framework within which the operational aspects of school management may be considered and provides a basis for further theory construction and application.

Later sections of the volume serve to illustrate our final point, namely, that a fruitful inter-relation between theory and practice can only be achieved through well organised consultative arrangements and an instructional strategy which supplements the use of case studies and simulation techniques with carefully planned on-the-job experience. The gap between theory and practice is finally closed when the school itself, among its other functions and with proper safeguards, becomes a learning laboratory in school management and staff development.

REFERENCES

BARNARD, CHESTER I., *The Functions of the Executive*, Harvard Press, Cambridge, Mass., 1938; 2nd ed., 1964.

BARON, G., COOPER, D. and WALKER, W. G. (eds.), *Educational Administration: International Perspectives*, Rand McNally, Chicago, 1969a.

BARON, G. and TAYLOR, W., *Educational Administration and the Social Sciences*, Athlone, London, 1969b.

BRIAULT, E. W. H., Staff development in the institutional setting, in PRATT, S. (ed.), *Staff Development in Education*, Councils and Education Press, London, 1973.

BROWN, W., *Exploration in Management*, Heinemann, London, 1960 .

CAMPBELL, R. F., What peculiarities in educational administration make it a special case?, in HALPIN, A. W. (ed.), *Administrative Theory in Education*, Midwest Administration Center, Univ. of Chicago, Chicago, 1958.

CAMPBELL, R. F. and LIPHAM, J. M., *Administrative Theory as a Guide to Action*, Midwest Administration Center, Univ. of Chicago, Chicago, 1960.

CONNER, F. E. and CULBERTSON, J., *The Internship in Administrative Preparation: Some Action Guides*, University Council for Educational Administration, Columbus, Ohio, 1964.

CULBERTSON, J. A., New perspectives: implications for program change, in CULBERTSON, J. A. and HENCLEY, S. P., *Preparing Administrators: New Perspectives*, University Council for Educational Administration, Columbus, Ohio, 1962.

CULBERTSON, J. A., Trends and issues in the development of a science of administration, in *Perspectives on Educational Administration and the Behavioral Sciences*, Center for the Advanced Study of Educational Administration, Univ. of Oregon, Eugene, 1965.

CULBERTSON, J. et al., *Social Science Content for Preparing Educational Leaders*, Merrill Pub. Co., Columbus, Ohio, 1973.

Dainton Report, H.M.S.O., London, 1968.

DAVIES, T. I., *School Organisation: A New Synthesis*, Pergamon, London, 1969.

DEWEY, JOHN, *Sources of a Science of Education*, Liveright, New York, 1929.

DOWNEY, L. W., Administration as a field of enquiry, *Canadian Public Administration* (5), 1962.

DOWNEY, L. W. and ENNS, F. (eds.), *The Social Sciences and Educational Administration*, Div. of Educational Administration, Univ. of Alberta, Calgary, 1963.

FAYOL, HENRI, *General and Industrial Management*, trans. STORRS, C., Pitman, London, 1949.

GETZELS, J. W., Theory and Practice in educational administration: an old question revisited, in CAMPBELL and LIPHAM (1960).

GLATTER, RON, *Management Development for the Education Profession*, Harrap, London, 1972.

GOLDHAMMER, KEITH, *The Social Sciences and the Preparation of Educational Administrators*, Div. of Educational Administration, Univ. of Alberta, Calgary, 1963.

GRIFFITHS, D. E., *Administrative Theory*, Appleton–Century–Crofts, New York, 1959.

HALPIN, A. W., *Administrative Theory in Education*, Midwest Administration Center, Univ. of Chicago, Chicago, 1958.

HARGREAVES, D. H., *Social Relations in a Secondary School*, Routledge, London, 1967.

HENCLEY, S. P. (ed.), *The Internship in Administrative Preparation*, University Council for Educational Administration, Columbus, Ohio, 1963.

HOMANS, GEORGE C., *The Human Group*, Routledge, London, 1951.

HOYLE, ERIC, Organisation theory and educational administration, in BARON and TAYLOR (1969).

HUGHES, MEREDYDD G., Preparation for a headship, *The Times Educational Supplement* (2687), 1966, p. 1214.

HUGHES, MEREDYDD G., Simulated situations, *Trends in Education* (7), H.M.S.O., 1967a, pp. 34–39.

HUGHES, MEREDYDD G., Training for headmastership: the American experience, *The Headmasters' Association Review* (65), 1967b, pp. 45–47.

HUGHES, MEREDYDD G., Training for headship, *The Head Teachers' Review*, Spring 1968, pp. 23–26.

JOHN, DENYS, Senior staff roles in secondary schools, *Trends in Education* (30), H.M.S.O., 1973.

LANE, W. R., CORWIN, R. G. and MONAHAN, W. G., *Foundations of Educational Administration*, Macmillan, New York, 1966.

MCMULLEN, TIM, Countesthorpe College, Leicester, *Forum* (14), 1972.

MICHAEL, D. P. M., *The Idea of a Staff College*, Headmasters' Association, London, 1967.

MILLS, C. W., *The Sociological Imagination*, Oxford University Press, New York, 1959, pp. 217–22.

OSTRANDER, RAYMOND H. and DETHY, RAY C., *A Values Approach to Educational Administration*, American Book Co., New York, 1968.

PASSMORE, J. A., Can the social sciences be value-free?, in FEIGL, H. and BRODBECK, M. (eds.), *Readings in the Philosophy of Science*, Appleton–Century–Crofts, New York, 1953.

RICHARDSON, E., *The Teacher, the School and the Task of Management*, Heinemann, London, 1973.

SCHMUCK, R. A. and RUNKEL, P. J., *Organizational Training for a School Faculty*, Center for the Advanced Study of Educational Administration, University of Oregon, Eugene, Oregon, 1970.

SELZNICK, P., *Leadership in Administration*, Harper, New York, 1957.

SIMEY, T. S., *Social Science and Social Purpose*, Constable, London, 1968.

SIMON, HERBERT A., *Administrative Behavior*, Free Press, New York, 1947; 2nd ed., 1957.

TAYLOR, WILLIAM, The use of simulations in the in-service training of school administrators in England, *J. Educ. Administration*, (4) 1966.

TAYLOR, WILLIAM, Issues and problems in training the school administrator, in BARON and TAYLOR, 1969.

TOPE, D. E. *et al.*, *The Social Sciences View School Administration*, Prentice Hall, Englewood Cliffs, New Jersey, 1965.

TRUMP, J. LLOYD and KARASIK, L., *Design for Leadership*, National Association of Secondary School Principals, Washington, D.C., 1964.

TRUMP, J. LLOYD (ed.), *A Report on the N.A.S.S.P. Administrative Project*, National Association of Secondary School Principals, Washington, D.C., 1969.

WALKER, W. G. (ed.), *The Principal at Work*, Univ. of Queensland Press, Brisbane, 1965.

WALKER, W. G., Trends and issues in the preparation of educational administrators, in Baron, Cooper and Walker, 1969.

WALKER, W. G. *et al.*, *Schools of Mapleton, Inbaskets 1–6*, Univ. of Queensland Press, Brisbane, 1969.

WALTON, J., *Administration and Policy Making*, Johns Hopkins Press, Baltimore, 1959, p. 35.

WENGERT, E. S., The social sciences, in WENGERT, E. S. (ed.), *The Study of Administration*, Univ. of Oregon, 1961, p. 79.

WENGERT, E. S., Preparing school administrators: some problems and issues, in CULBERTSON and HENCLEY, 1962, p. 41.

WILLOWER, D. J. and CULBERTSON, J. A., *The Professorship in Educational Administration*, University Council for Educational Administration, Columbus, Ohio, 1964.

33

PART 2

ORGANISATION AND MANAGEMENT

George F. Thomason

INTRODUCTION

Our purpose in this section of the book is to consider the foundations on which we must judge the Headmaster's role, together with supporting managerial roles, in the context of the evolving secondary school system. We are not concerned to provide a list of techniques which a Headmaster in such a position might use, although mention will be made of some which are more fully considered in Part 3. The main aim is rather to identify the criteria which may be applied to the assessment of how apposite and how effective the Head's management role is in this context.

We must recognise at the outset, however, that we are faced with certain constraints in attempting this:

Firstly, there is very little empirical data on the Headmaster's role within the school system. More is available on teachers' and pupils' roles (Kob, 1961; Parsons, 1961); there are a number of commentaries by Headmasters on their work (Allen, 1968); but so far, few empirical investigations have been made of this role (Westwood, 1966). This makes it difficult to draw inferences of a practical sort about it either in the pre-existing school system or in the present one.*

Secondly, the literature on organisation and management is dominated by consideration of the business organisation (Ottaway, 1961). This has included both intuitive and empirical work in the field, and most of the explanation about what happens in a managerial context is coloured by this. In considering management in the context of a service (as distinct from a business) organisation, there

* Though it still may not be easy to draw firm conclusions in 1974, the research position has improved since the above was written by Professor Thomason (Cohen, 1970; Bernbaum, 1970; Hughes, 1972, 1973). Further relevant references are given in Chapter 13 (*Editor*).

are obviously situational differences to be taken into account. (Cf. Blau and Scott, 1963.) Whilst an attempt is made to do this here, it is practically impossible not to draw one's hypotheses (at least) from the world of business management (e.g. Brech, 1963 ed.).

Thirdly, as indicated by Hughes (Chap. 1), the secondary school system is itself undergoing far-reaching changes, as it switches from a base of recruitment and instruction according to academic ability in separate locations, to one of comprehensive recruitment and instruction according to age in single locations. This at once provides the justification for new courses (cf. Higgin, 1968; Hughes, 1968; Gray, 1972), and books relevant to the management of secondary schools (e.g. Barry and Tye, 1972; Taylor, 1973), and renders it difficult to comment confidently on what kind of situation *will* provide the context of the Head's managerial role in the future. (Cf. Chap. 13; also Bidwell, 1965.)

Nevertheless, we make some attempt in the next four chapters to set the scene for school management/administration by the Head and his specialist staff in the next decades. The point of view adopted in this essay is that whatever else may happen, the school Head will be required to adopt a more systematic approach to his managerial problem than perhaps he has hitherto. By this we mean to imply only that in the past the problem of managing a school was one which was usually capable of resolution by a professional Head (i.e. a Head with professional training as a teacher) using the knowledge, understanding and insight which his training and successive teaching experiences gave him; in the future he is more likely to be required to have a knowledge and understanding of the processes and principles of administration or management, regarded as a body of professional knowledge in its own right. Society will require him to take a stance as a professional administrator rather than, or at least in addition to, one as a first amongst equals in his vocation of school teaching.

It then follows from this that what the Head needs in this transitional period is an introduction to the basic concepts and perspectives of the administrator. Of course, these are obtainable in any management textbook. But since most of these are written for the business managers, this essay seeks to link the principles and precepts to the peculiar situation of the school as a service organisation. This is done by treating four broad aspects of the problem of managing.

Firstly, in Chapter 3 we look at a simple conception of the school as an input–output system with dual objectives, differentiated resources and dual principles legitimating authority: it contains two broad types of theory or philosophy of how it should operate, of resource measured in terms of contributory roles, and of principles of distributing authority to influence and control others. This duality provides a necessary framework for considering more detailed aspects of the Head-as-manager's role.

Secondly, we look in Chapter 4 at the general question of what is involved in any managerial role and attempt to relate this to the peculiar circumstances of the school system, depicted as in Chapter 3. This part relies heavily for its basic ideas upon the management textbook, but tries to relate them to the detail of the Head's everyday tasks, in order to give this role situational definition, and to identify the kinds of decision which the Head is called upon to take.

Thirdly, we examine the organisation of decision within an organisation. This entails a consideration of what is involved in a process of decision-taking and of how judgement enters into this. The rest of Chapter 5 is then taken up with the question of what special problems are thrown up for the Head as a decision-taker by the fact that his staff are professional persons.

Fourthly, we offer some thoughts in Chapter 6 on some of the accommodations which the professional organisation (meaning that organisation which brings together roles which are definable as professional ones) may have to make in order that a viable system of decision and action may develop within the newly emerging context of the secondary school. For want of a better term, we have referred to this set of ideas by the generic title of "organisational training" but in essence it is an attempt to integrate (a) the constraints of the school situation as-it-is, with (b) the constraints which a developing educational system is likely to impose upon it.

What emerges from all this is not, therefore, a blueprint for the future, but a set of conceptual tools which the Head can use in working out the dimensions of his new role. One does not have to be a Marxist to recognise that it is at this practical level, rather than at the level of academic theory, that the definition will be provided. But neither does one have to be an ivory-towered academic to recognise that an ounce of theory may go a long way in facilitating this practical process.

CHAPTER 3

THE INPUT–OUTPUT MODEL

THE starting-point for a discussion of any purposive system of work organisation is the description of the main elements of the conceptual model of how that system works. At base, this model will require that something be put into the system and that something come out of it, the difference between the two yielding a measure of the productivity or even efficiency of the system. The 'purpose' of the system is then related to the realisation of whatever change is indicated by this comparative measure. Onto this basic conception a more or less complex edifice of theory can be built, dependent upon how close to reality the final product of the exercise has to be. (Cf. Mather, 1968, p. 201.)

The bare skeleton of the model of the system which we are to use in this section may be stated in the following terms. The school as a productive system involves the purposive organisation of certain resources (mainly professional manpower) for the modification of some 'raw material' with the objective of producing an improved end-product. On the face of it, however, the designation of the system in input–output terms appears to dehumanise the people and processes of the school. However, this rather bald statement can be amplified by translating the abstract concepts into the more human and realistic terms of the school. Figure 1 summarises the concepts and relationships involved.

Firstly, the 'raw material' involved is seen as composed of the pupils who are recruited into this system simply on the basis of age —plus a certain minimum attainment intellectually and morally. Regardless of the basis on which allocation takes place within the school (cf. Webb, Chap. 12), the pupil is required to attend the

Stylised Representation of the Organisation of an Educational Process

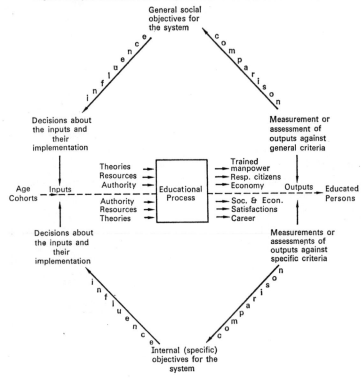

FIG. 1.

school on reaching a certain age. Because past performance and past attainments have little bearing upon whether he enters or not, the role of the pupil in the system has been described as a 'recruitment role' (Nadel, 1957). Although these persons and roles are vitally involved in the process of education, we are not particularly concerned with them in the present context: they serve as the raw material to be processed by the system, and it is the system which is of main concern.

Secondly, the 'improved end-product' which is sought is given by the objectives of the school system as these are defined principally by society at large. At the highest appropriate level of generalisation, it is possible to describe the secondary school system's objectives as the technical and moral socialisation or education of a particular age group—11 to 18 years. If this use of the term 'socialisation' seems unnecessary, it may be countered by suggesting that the school *is* concerned to "prepare its students for adult status, by training them in the knowledge and skills, and by indoctrinating them in the moral orientations, which adult roles require" (Bidwell, 1965, p. 973). This is a role which is given by the relationship of the school to the wider society. The school is, as it were, licensed by the wider society to take in 'non-social' persons, and to 'socialize' them (i.e. make them social) (Ottaway, 1953, pp. 2–3). The 'end-product' thus becomes a mature adult and the inherent time-lapse involved in this definition of purpose has its own implications, of course, for the measurement of the system's performance.

Thirdly, the definition of the input to the system requires us also to see the educational process as a compound of knowledge or belief (*theory*) about how to turn this raw material into a finished product; *resources* in the form of knowledge and skill of persons or embodied in a technology; and of a particular kind of *authority* distribution amongst persons which will be both acceptable and effective as a means of bringing about the results sought from the system. (Cf. Stinchcombe, 1967, pp. 156–7.) These may all focus on the role of the teacher as a person. Although we know that persons are the key element in this input situation, it is nevertheless useful to see these persons both as carriers of knowledge (and therefore as resources which can be employed to facilitate socialisation of the young) and as licensed (i.e. given an authority) to do so under certain identifiable constraints.

These constraints, in turn, arise out of the theories which relate not merely to the question of how naïve persons are turned into mature persons, but rather to the question of how this can be done efficiently and equitably for any and every cohort of young persons who must pass through the system. It is not, after all, merely a question of educating the best or the most amenable, but of educating *all* who, in the above sense, fulfil the conditions of the recruitment role.

Therefore, whatever licence may be given to the individual teacher to develop a relationship with an individual client, this must always be constrained by these wider considerations, and these are particularly pertinent to the definition of the role of the 'Head' as distinct from the role of the teacher. The general social objectives of achieving both economy and equity in the utilisation of resources are to be recognised as existing alongside the 'simple' objective of socializing the young. Furthermore, they must be recognised as not necessarily compatible with the realisation of this other objective in the individual case. From this we develop the concept of 'duality' in theories, resources and authority systems—in this as in any other organisational framework.

THEORIES: THE METHODS OF EDUCATION

Duality is to be found in the theories which guide action. These are, at one level, nothing more than the beliefs which we hold as to (a) the best technical methods of educating the young, and (b) the best methods of organising scarce resources to secure this end. This is not the place to review the theories of education, but it is necessary to link these to the major concern which we have with the role of the Head within a system which rests upon theories of these two types.

Some of these theories *are* purely educational concerned with the sheer feasibility or possibility of educating the young. They are 'technical' theories of instruction. They hold, generally speaking, that certain adults, whose competence to instruct is certified, can be institutionally related to these non-social persons in such a way that the objective of producing mature adults will be facilitated more than if the non-social individuals are left to acquire maturity on their own. Such theories merely state what is humanly or technically possible if certain purposive steps are taken. This would allow that a one-to-one relationship, *or* a one-to-a-hundred relationship, between teacher and pupil(s) might equally serve as a method. Resolution of *this* problem depends upon yet other theories of a non-technical sort.

These theories relate to wider questions of equity, social costs and social benefits. In these, consideration is given to problems of (a) ensuring that not only will some people benefit, but that all of a given class of person will benefit equally from an arrangement in which society invests its resources; and (b) ensuring that just because something is technically feasible it will not be done regardless of the cost of doing it (and therefore of the cost to 'society' at large of licensing certain adults (i.e. teachers) to carry out certain instructional roles). On the basis of these considerations, all children are to be educated—without fear or favour—and children are to be grouped in what the particular society at the particular time will accept as an optimum-sized group per teacher, or per school. As ideas change these numbers might well fluctuate.

Yet other theories relate the roles which involve decisions to those which entail action. In our culture, we tend to believe that there are considerable economic advantages in specialisation, and more particularly, that economy of effort is achieved if decision-roles are specialised and separated from action roles. From these follow the establishment of specialised teacher roles (e.g. specialised by subject or age group taught) and of 'Head' roles, which are conceived essentially as decision roles. The 'theories' involved in these beliefs and the organisational arrangements which flow from them will, of course, receive more consideration below, since they also involve beliefs about authority systems (e.g. the relative distribution of authority between decision and action roles).

In fact, there are so many theories involved that it might have been preferable to talk of a multiplicity of theories rather than to have characterised them as dual. However, there are two *categories* of theory which are relevant here: firstly, those which have to do with the prime task of educating the child; and secondly, those which have to do with the organisation of the process for all children in a given age cohort. Whether there is agreement within each category or not, the operational objectives which flow from each of these two categories are not necessarily or easily compatible with one another: there are circumstances in which the objectives in the one pull against the objectives in the other.

When, therefore, either teachers or Headmasters state what they see as their objectives (and therefore as the justification for any action that they contemplate) they may give more or less weight to one or other of these sets of theories: "A non-streamed school is bound to act against academic achievement amongst the brighter children" reveals a different perspective in terms of objective and theory from that which states: "There are social benefits to be derived from the equality of opportunity provided in the comprehensive school". All of us have to develop some perspective (accept some theory) or other if we are to do any effective work at all, but which we adopt will have different consequences for the kind of work we do. In our simple duality, greater weight to purely pedagogic principles than to administrative ones will tend to make us a better teacher and a poorer team member (because we will probably be impatient with 'authority' or 'paper-work' or rigid time-tables).

RESOURCES: THE ROLES OF EDUCATORS

This is also of relevance to the question of resources used in education. In the most generic sense, the resources applied to the attainment of purpose are the knowledge and skill which are either possessed and applied directly by people carrying out certain roles or embodied in a technology (e.g. schools as buildings and equipment). It is, however, realistic to discount the technological aspects for present purposes and to recognise the dominance of human performance in the educational process. This focuses our attention upon the roles created within the system with the objective of attaining the purposes, and in this case too it is possible to recognise a duality or a dichotomy amongst the roles within the system.

These roles can be divided into two broad categories which may be described as primary and secondary, or direct and indirect. All that is implied by this is that some of the roles are *directly* associated with the prime purpose of the system (e.g. those which are concerned with the teaching of pupils) whilst others are only *indirectly* associated (e.g. the administrative or secretarial roles which are more directly associated with the secondary purposes of the system). The former might also be described as 'action' roles in that their prime orientation is towards the action necessary to realise the main objective; the latter might equally be described as 'decision' roles since their main orientation is towards the decisions required to hold together the larger system.

Since our prime concern is with these resources and their organisation, it is necessary to include a few more words of introduction in relation to them, and to indicate the problem of allocating authority to them.

Firstly, there are many different ways of organising the primary roles involved. Accepting the general statement of educational purpose above, we might still recognise the organisational variants implicit in the following primary role relationships: the governess and the rich child; the hedge-schoolmaster and his small group of pupils; the class teacher and his formally constituted class of pupils; the subject teacher moving peripatetically through a number of such classes; the schools broadcasters and their 'mass audiences'; and so on. The organisation of these two primary roles within the system can clearly vary even when the same basic objective is being realised.

Such differences are associated also with a differential requirement for secondary roles. The number of such roles associated with schools broadcasting, for example, is much greater than in the case of the governess and charge. In fact, the more emphatic the demand for economy in the system as a whole (e.g. not every parent can afford a governess for his children) the greater the likelihood that the secondary role system will be highly developed.

Secondly, in the nature of the prime tasks of the school system (those concerned directly with the intellectual and moral instruction of the young) those persons who are called upon to carry them out are likely to need relatively high levels of discretion. Discretion in this sense implies that the role incumbent will be able to decide for himself in the light of the immediate circumstances, and without reference to some other (e.g. higher) authority, how to tackle a given 'problem'. In the nature of the 'raw material' such problems will be many and varied in their form and intermittent or spasmodic in their occurrence. If the teacher is to cope with this 'blooming, buzzing confusion' of problems he must have a degree of freedom to decide and act which is above that usually allowed to, say, a semi-skilled machine operator or even a skilled tradesman.

Work roles of this type are frequently distinguished as *professional*, and although the Registrar General does not classify it in this way, the primary role of teaching might usefully be regarded in the present context as a professional role in this sense. The utility of this categorisation lies in the implication which it must carry for the definition of the secondary administrative roles of, say, Headmaster or registrar within the school system. Since the professional roles contain high discretion to decide, the principles on which the 'Head' role is based, and the form its practical realisation will take, must be different from, say, the factory situation where the action roles do not involve so much discretion.

It is for this reason that a problem arises in the allocation of authority within the school system. The task-level requirement of high discretion for the individual teacher must detract from the opportunity to designate authority to decide to the Head. Any division of labour in this context must rest upon the potentially conflicting bases of authority which can be distinguished as polar types.

THE SCHOOL AS A DUAL AUTHORITY SYSTEM

It often happens that when teachers are impatient with their Headmasters and Headmasters impatient with their teaching staff, the root cause may be found in the difference in purposes or objectives assumed or in the 'priorities' which each attaches to alternative courses of action. It often happens also that these differences are explained in terms of personality, focusing either upon personal qualities or personal qualifications to do the job that the individual exhibits or the job title implies. In reality, the differences may lie in the different premises which each accepts as the foundation for carrying out a role.

All the ingredients for such tensions are to be found in the following problem case which one Headmaster presented for discussion with his colleagues.

The Head of a large co-educational school decided that he needed more information about each child than the usual examination marks. This amounted to a personality profile to be recorded for each child. How then was this information to be collected? There was no counsellor available. The job could not be given to one man or woman, as they would not know *each* child sufficiently well to obtain the information needed about a child's personal qualities and his background. Yet the staff would have a store of very useful knowledge about the children.

But this would mean more work for staff without a grant of additional payment, and the success of the scheme would depend very much on the 'morale' of the staff as a whole. An attempt was made to glean information during a 15-minute period of 'pastoral care' held once weekly. Some form teachers did a reasonably good job, others provided information which was unreliable or useless.

A degree of correlation may exist between what the form teacher in this case regarded as a legitimate demand upon him and the utility of the results which he produced from the exercise. In the first instance, the 'Head decided' on what was required, and in doing so responded to the cues provided, not by the primary objectives, but by the secondary ones concerned with overall control. The premises on which he took the decision were neither obvious nor necessarily acceptable to the staff. The responses of the staff were mixed and provided the Head with grounds for arguing that staff are awkward, reluctant helpers or 'not what they used to be'. But behind the 'difficulty' may well lie the conflict of the two systems of authority in the school.

These two systems of authority might be described generically as systems of *sapiental* authority and *organisational* authority. These derive from the primary and secondary objectives of the system respectively and may be defined in the following fashion:

Sapiental authority rests upon the legitimation of one person's power to influence the thinking, feeling and behaviour of another person by virtue of the first person's possession of superior 'wisdom' or 'expertise' or 'competence' within a defined field. In more concrete terms, a subject teacher will permit another subject teacher to influence his actions within the subject area when he accepts that the other has greater 'wisdom' than he in relation to that area. This may also be regarded as the basis for the exercise of influence between professionals, although it can also exist between amateurs (when in the literature on 'organisations' it is usually identified as a 'charismatic' system of authority or influence). (Cf. Thomason, 1969, Chap. 7.)

Organisational authority rests upon the legitimation of this power by virtue of the one's superior position within some hierarchy of power or position. Although the person may have achieved his position (and therefore his power) on the basis of superior wisdom or judgement, there is a qualitative difference between this base and that of the 'superior' in the first case. At the simplest level, one obeys the instructions of a boss because he is the boss, and has usually a given power to manipulate rewards and punishments in such a way as to ensure that his wishes are carried out by subordinates. He has an organisational power to influence which *need* not even exist in the professional organisation based on sapiental authority. (Cf. Blau, 1956; Thomason, 1969, chap. 7.)

Both foundations for authority are to be found within the school system, and the organisation of the school tends to reflect their presence, even if, sometimes at least, it does this in a confusing way. The organisation of the school, like that of hospitals or universities, reflects in fact two overlapping methods of organising authority.

This can be represented pictorially on an organisation chart as is done below by Jones (Chap. 7) and Davis (Chap. 8).

Firstly, there is the arrangement of primary roles into a shallow hierarchy for which sapiental authority provides the base. At the leading edge of this organisation are the teachers who actually instruct the pupils, relying primarily upon their professional training to guide them in their primary tasks. However, in so far as this training can never be complete (in the sense of providing a 'programmed solution' to every instructional problem likely to be encountered) there develops a professional hierarchy of status in which the more senior, experienced or wise members of the professional group are given or permitted the power to influence the more junior, less experienced or less urbane members. The donation is essentially one from the group itself. (Cf. Blau, 1956.) This may become *institutionalised* in the form of subject headships or posts of special responsibility in relation to the prime tasks, and even the Headmaster *could*, from this point of view, be regarded as a *primus inter pares* amongst his professional colleagues.

Secondly, there is the arrangement of secondary roles into a hierarchy of specialist tasks for which organisational authority provides the base. These roles tend to be better defined at the top of the hierarchy, and the Headmaster's is usually the most fully developed. He is administratively 'in charge of', 'responsible for' and 'in command of' the school as an entity, and his role is therefore defined more in managerial/administrative terms than in those of the profession itself. But his is not the only role of this type which can be distinguished. Other organisational or administrative tasks are defined and allocated as specialist tasks to others—even if these 'others' (e.g. bursars) also have professional roles within the system. These may also become institutionalised in the form of deputy head or senior, middle and lower school head, or housemaster and class teacher roles, in which the prime emphasis is upon the element of control with its two modern elements of counselling and discipline (cf. Davis, 1968, p. 20). Organisational authority is not, therefore, something which adheres merely to the roles of the 'Heads' in the

51

limited sense, but is rather spread through many other roles whose *main* orientation may remain towards the *prime* tasks of the school system.

This inter-leaving of the two sets of 'principles of legitimacy' in systems of inter-personal influence would by itself prove sufficient to create confusion. When a person seeks to influence another within the school system, it is not always clear on what basis of principle he is doing this, and it is not always accepted by the 'other' as a legitimate attempt to influence. Davis also refers to the problem of determining which subject belongs to which system of authority.

The general development of scale and size of operations within the educational system as a means of achieving greater economy tends to impose a system of authority whose principles of legitimacy are neither traditional to the professional organisation nor acceptable to it because they limit the discretion of the teacher in serving the individual client. This then tends to focus upon the Headmaster role within the modern school, since it is he who, willy-nilly, carries the responsibility for economy and efficiency of the school system. Given the 'duality' which we have ascribed to the system, we must now see the Head as occupying a pivotal, marginal or boundary role. His is not unlike the role of the scientist-administrator in industry, nor is it any less likely to be a focus of tension (Kornhauser, 1962).

CHAPTER 4

THE HEADMASTER'S DECISION ROLE

INTRODUCTION

The distinction which we have already noted between the direct action roles of the teacher, and the indirect decision roles of the administrator-head, is widely recognised. In fact, any organisation which is established to pursue some purpose is likely in its division of labour to create a separation of decision and action for the sake of economy of time and effort, and therefore of cost. Certain roles then become 'purely' (or at least primarily) decision roles, and are labelled 'managerial' or 'administrative' roles.

The role of Headmaster belongs quite unambiguously to that category of roles which we have distinguished as 'decision' roles. In most secondary schools, the Headmaster does little teaching, and in this sense does not engage, to a substantial extent, in activities which are *directly* associated with the tasks of the school as a productive system. (His immediate colleagues, who also hold 'head'-type roles —directors of studies, heads of junior, middle or upper schools, heads of houses or subject heads—on the other hand, very often carry out roles which involve *some* direct activity and *some* indirect (decisional) activity. These roles may, therefore, be the more ambiguous or confused, but for the present, we will treat all roles (or part-roles) which have this connotation of, or association with, decision-taking as if they were purely defined.)

For purposes of this present chapter, we make the initial assumption that this decision role can be described and examined in general terms. Although we are aware of the problems of, for example, tying Headmaster roles too closely to concepts derived from mass production industry (to use the example most often quoted), and although we propose to qualify some of the derived propositions later, it is necessary for the sake of convenience of treatment to make this initial assumption. We can then develop further the rational or clinical approach started in the preceding chapter. Thus, here again, we ask the reader to accept a rather distorted conception of the school system and of the Headmaster's role in order to advance the argument, in the knowledge that this model will subsequently be modified in the light of the situation of the school.

In particular this assumption will permit us to examine the decision role of the Headmaster as if it were a role concerned with three main classes of decision: firstly, the decisions which are concerned with allocation of resources within the system—the so-called organisation function of management; secondly, the decisions which are concerned with the steering of the organisation in certain directions rather than others—the directive function of management; and thirdly, the decisions which are essentially monitoring or checking decisions—the control function of management (Cf. Tannenbaum, 1949).

THE PURPOSES OF MANAGERIAL DECISIONS

Let us start by taking as axiomatic that managers (even Headmasters) take decisions, since this is a part of their role. Let us also accept for the moment, that it is quite right and proper that they should take these decisions, since this is the way society tends to operate. We may then ask what is the purpose of decision? or to what end are such managerial decisions taken? The management textbooks are full of answers to these questions, although it would scarcely be true to say that they all answer them in the same way or with the same set of concepts. Here, however, we will employ the Tannenbaum synthesis of the manager concept which is based upon an examination of many different authors' accounts (Tannenbaum, 1949).

Before identifying these concepts or purposes, however, we must note that behind all the theorising about management functions and principles there lies the relatively simple observation that most organisations appear to strive after survival: they try to keep themselves in business in the face of challenges and pressures from their environments. At base, there is a simple observation that many organisations do survive. From this, however, the belief grows that perhaps they possess some mechanism which helps them to do this; that, for example, the social system is equipped with a means of facilitating survival. Perhaps we do not know what this process is, or at least not in the sense that we could describe it with such accuracy as to provide a blueprint. But we infer enough about it to permit us to argue that organisations do seem to have a means of maintaining an equilibrium or steady state relationship with their environments (cf. Hanika, 1965, Chap. 1).

From this we develop the further argument that this must mean that the organisation somehow responds to the demands and pressures of the environment—that somehow or other it (a) becomes aware of the environmental demand; (b) decides how it should cope with it; and (c) actually meets the demand in such a way that some sort of equilibrium is restored. In some cases this may be a highly institutionalised process, as, for example, when a customer places an order with a manufacturing company, the company puts the 'order' into production, and despatches the product and gets the cash back. In other cases, the process may be much less clearly definable, as when, for example, a political party faces a vacillating public and must interpret the undercurrents correctly if it is to survive at the polls. Certainly not all organisations survive and certainly we do not know precisely how those that do, do, but we have some ideas and it is these which underpin most of the discussions about management processes (cf. Bennis, 1966).

Managers are then seen as the immediate instrumentalities by which the response of the organisation to these environmental pressures is decided upon at the 'right' time (i.e. they receive the messages when they are sent) and in a 'correct' fashion (i.e. they are able to make the correct decisions as to what to do). In some of the shorter definitions of management, this is recognised by saying that management is concerned with taking decisions and implementing them. The function of a decision is then that of ensuring that the organisation determines on the right course at the right time in response to the circumstances. Some means must then exist for 'activating' the working end of the organisation in the light of this decision. From this, then, we derive the notion that managerial decisions are concerned with forecasting, planning, and organising, and that implementation involves commanding, co-ordinating and controlling (Fayol, 1915). Although different authors use different words, this simple distinction between decision and implementation is capable of being read into all of the more comprehensive descriptions of the management process.

Tannenbaum has attempted to synthesise the plethora of definitions of the management function, and suggests that managers are really concerned with decision-taking for three main purposes: organisation, direction and control:

Organisation. The term 'organisation' is normally employed to indicate a rather special arrangement of units or parts which can have an independent existence, in such a way that they all function together as if they constituted a single whole. This implies that each part must have a particular but related and co-ordinated function to perform within the whole. The notion of organisation, thus, involves two important elements: that of separate and possibly specialised parts which *could* be considered in isolation from one another in some meaningful way; and that of a special kind of relationship between them which serves to bring about concert or integrity in overall functioning.

This meaning of the term 'organisation' can be applied to both animate and inanimate systems. When we use it to indicate 'human organisation', however, human beings (who clearly have an existence on their own) compose the important parts: they are, therefore, considered difficult to conceive and understand, partly because we become enmeshed in ethical considerations about the 'independence' or the 'autonomy' of the person. But it is important to recognise from the outset, that the human 'parts' in social organisations are not persons, as such, but the roles (or the 'parts' in the dramatic sense) which they play within them. Persons are recruited and allocated to roles within the human organisation, and in the process of allocation some attempt is made to ensure that the playing of the role will mesh in or co-ordinate with other roles within the system.

When the term 'organisation' is used to indicate a 'function' of management (Tannenbaum, 1949), managers are then seen to have a special role which consists of *determining* what 'parts' there shall be in the system and what relationships shall exist between them. This relies upon the dictionary definition of the verb 'to organise' which describes the process as "to arrange or constitute in interdependent parts, each having a special function, act, office, or relation with respect to the whole". This is entirely consistent with the above definition of 'organisation', but the attribution of this function to managers in this more active sense must be seen as restricting 'organisation' to the category of *purposive* arrangement usually within the framework of rational organisation on 'bureaucratic' lines.

Direction and control are defined in terms of 'employing' the apparatus thus created for the 'attainment of purpose'. 'Employment' in this sense entails the use of authority to turn the static 'organisation' into a dynamic objective-achieving instrument.

'Direction' is defined as the use of authority to guide subordinates, and in this sense is not very different from the conception of influence employed by Simon (1953) or Cartwright (1965). But Simon's expansion of the definition makes it clearer that what is meant is a particular method of arranging the decision structure within the organisation: "Direction involves the devising of the purpose of action and the methods and procedures to be followed in achieving them. The decisions to be made in connection with direction, must answer the questions 'what?', 'how?', 'when?', and 'where?'." The training of the professional is likely to complicate the direct translation of this conception into the professional organisation, since it is designed to ensure that he can answer many of these questions for himself, and superordinate solutions could be extraneous, if not resented.

'Control', on the other hand, seems, at least potentially, to be defined in a rather more generic way. Control also entails the use of formal authority but "to assure, to the extent possible, the attainment of the purposes of action by the methods or procedures which have been devised." Carrying out this function involves the selection and training of individuals, the provision of incentives and the exercise of supervision. What makes this potentially a wider definition of function than a simple consideration of industrial management would support, is that different organisational situations could place differential emphasis on the means of control (training, incentives, and supervision) and thus create different climates of operation. The school system, has, for example, relied traditionally upon the use of training to ensure control, where industrial organisations have relied more directly upon incentives or supervision (the emphasis varying from time to time with the external conditions).

Direction (or influence) and control (check), in their more generic senses, may be employed as the means of organising the consideration of the management/administrative process in this section. Direction will be understood in the sense of steering the organisation in appropriate directions (however determined) and control in the sense of employing any and every means of monitoring system performance in relation to the objectives and purposes laid down (by someone).

But when we distinguish the purpose of the administrator role in this way, we are identifying something which is not necessarily fully acceptable to nor accepted by those who are more directly involved in the action system and committed to its values. There *is* a disjunction between the two sets of roles, which can be distinguished as action-oriented and as decision-oriented even if complicated by the development of differential status considerations.

The fact that in the school system, the action-system depends upon professionally trained persons to carry out the action roles, whilst the decision-system depends upon professionally trained persons switching away from their primary task concerns to embrace others which have an organisational (rather than a professional) base seems to offer an additional complication not found, say, in industry. This may be more apparent than real, more a question of confusing form with substance, since the trade union organisation of the action roles within industry might be regarded as something of a functional equivalent to the professional organisation of action roles within the school system (cf. Prandy, 1965). In both situations, it is worthwhile recognising that the value-premises (which will guide judgement) which might be applied to any decision are likely to vary as between the incumbents of the action roles and those of the decision (or managerial) roles. It is just these differences in value which lie below the tensions and criticism which exist in all of these systems. (Cf. Kornhauser, 1962, on the tensions between scientists and managers in industry.)

This defines the prime purposes of the administrator role as concerned with decision-making as a means of organising (or co-ordinating), directing and checking the activities carried out within the other sub-system of action. In carrying out this decision role, as the case quoted above illustrates, difficulties may be encountered as the value-premises underlying the decision prove unacceptable, but this does not detract from the basic definition of the administrator's purpose.

SPECIALISATION OF DECISION ROLES

Let us conclude from this discussion that *whoever* takes decisions with these purposes of organising, directing and controlling in view, and does so on behalf of the organisation as a whole, is exercising a management function on behalf of that organisation. We can then proceed to examine the degree of specialisation which creeps into the decision-taking roles. It may be that, in the past, most of these 'school-level' management decisions have been taken by the Headmaster; he alone within the school was responsible for all these types of decision. When he took these decisions he did so as the school system's decision-taker. (Although others may have taken decisions

59

about subject areas or particular pupils, it was usually the Head who either took, or took responsibility for, all the decisions at the level of the school as a unit.)

The size and complexity of the comprehensive school is most likely to change this conception of a single, generalist, decision role within the organisation. Indeed, the signs are already there and evidence is accumulating of a tendency for roles to become specialised. In Chapter 8 by Mrs. M. J. Davis, for example, there are descriptions of the bursar-administrators and the directors of studies, who already exist in such specialist-decision roles. This is therefore no crystal-ball prediction of a change. It merely extrapolates from what is already in evidence and thus suggests that the future is likely to lie with the development of ever-more specialisation in school decision-taking.

From the standpoint of defining decision-roles within such a changing system, therefore, the classificatory schemes which have been applied to other more complex (and not necessarily only industrial) organisations may prove useful in the context of the larger and more complex school system. These relate to the two dimensions of definition which may be described in terms of division along a vertical axis of decision-taking, and along a horizontal axis, the first relating to the level or breadth of decision and the second to the subject area of decision.

VERTICAL DIVISION: THE LEVELS OF DECISION

Even if all decisions are concerned with organisation, direction and control, not all of them are as far- or as near-reaching in their effects or coverage and not all of them have the same 'weight' for the organisation as a whole. In fact, when the decision-taking function of the organisation becomes divided between specialist decision-takers, it is usual for quite clearly defined levels of decision to appear. This does not deny overlap as between levels of status in organisation, nor does it deny that single individuals will take different 'levels' of decision in a day's work; but it does help to define decision roles in specialist organisations if we can conceptualise the levels of decision recognisable.

In governmental and industrial contexts the distinctions have been drawn using the terms legislative, administrative and executive to indicate a descending order of decision.

Directive (or legislative or policy-making) decisions are those decisions which determine what shall be the objectives sought in any endeavour and what standards shall be applied to the assessment of adequate performance in pursuit of these objectives. This definition is thus curtailed from that given by Tannenbaum for his term. Since these decisions are usually taken by the people at the top, the fact that the taking of these decisions must involve the 'ultimate' authority in the organisation becomes a part of the definition of directive decisions. Its import is that such decisions cannot be overturned by any higher authority. In a 'simple' hierarchical organisation, if there is such a thing, the ultimate authority might be easy to identify; in governmental and industrial contexts the association of ultimate authority with Parliament and the board of directors respectively may be a simple process. In other organisational contexts, particularly in service and commonweal organisations, the exercise may be less easy. But it may be taken as axiomatic that there will be *some* ultimate authority in the system whether it is easy or difficult to identify in practice, and it will be concerned with the setting of objectives and policies.

Once the broad, overall decisions about objectives and standards have been taken the determination of the manner of their realisation remains for decision. As methods of reaching objectives become more complex, such decisions are taken by yet other specialists who, whilst they do not possess ultimate authority, yet exercise power by virtue of their capability in deciding the manner in which others shall behave. It is this which provides both the purpose of *administration*, and the definition of the administrator's role—at least in its ideal-typical form. If the function of direction (as a level of decision) is to determine the answer to the question 'what?', that of the administrator is to determine 'how?' (cf. Chamberlain, 1948). In the school context, Parts 3 and 4 provide numerous examples of these 'how to do it' questions.

The third class, execution, is essentially the 'day-to-day' management, the decision-taking which is directly associated with the response to immediate local problems of an operating kind, but within the framework of policy and programme decided at higher levels; this is primarily the role of the supervisor as decision-taker.

As direction and administration have been described thus far, they are open-ended functions: they entail decision-taking, but not check on whether and how the decisions have been carried out. Such a 'control' function is built into every role, however, and the full definition of both roles must allow for the monitoring of the effects of a decision to ensure that it is no mere 'good idea' but a positive influence upon the operation of the system of which they form a part. Thus, whatever the level of decision involved, control as a function is built into it, even if, in practice, many routine control decisions (of a 'day-to-day' sort) are delegated to 'supervisors' or 'executives'. There may be roles within organisations which are purely executive in this latter sense (that is primarily concerned with monitoring) but this does not and cannot deny the validity of associating the control function with every other decision role in the system. The notion of difference in levels is, in other words, really a hierarchical division of Tannenbaum's conception of direction.

One important question which has to be answered in applying these concepts to the educational system is "Where does the ultimate authority lie?" One answer might be with the governmental agencies which provide the means or with the Government itself which decides the ultimate policy with respect to education (or in more local terms, with the Boards of Governors or the local education authority). But another answer, derived from the nature of teacher training in this country, might well be with 'the teachers' or the 'educationalists' all of whom, through training, are fitted to judge the rightness of educational objectives and standards as well as to teach in the more limited sense.

Even if these alternatives are not seen to apply at the level of ultimate authority, however, they are likely to have much more relevance at the level of *administrative* decision—the determination of *how* the general purposes of education are best served by the application and organisation of resources to the overall task. Most trained teachers would feel themselves equipped to take such decisions, although not all would want to do so. The administrative functions of the management textbook—e.g. forecasting, planning, organising, commanding, co-ordinating and controlling—are likely to be within the general compass of the professional in matters relating to the professional tasks involved in the system. His long training fits him to exercise judgement in these areas as well as to carry out the more routine teaching tasks.

The Head as an administrator in this system is, to an appreciable extent, therefore, merely applying a professional judgement to a range of professional problems. He is freed from the mechanistic aspects of teaching (at least to some extent) to enable him to specialise in this kind of decision role. As the size of his staff increases, he comes more and more to concern himself with standards which will be generally applied over the whole range, so that he 'makes administrative policy' and creates standards of performance 'for' the subordinates. This may, indeed, prove not to be the whole of his job, but it is the basis for the Head's administrative role. The fact that he must carry it out in a situation in which many of the 'subordinates' are also both similarly trained and highly experienced, is a complication likely to increase the strain upon him, and incidentally to differentiate him from many managerial specialists in industry (who are often recruited from a totally different background and thus 'protected' from this problem).

In addition, the Head has delegated authority from the educational system in the wider sense, and his purely professionally administrative role cannot be exercised in isolation from that other executive part of his total role which requires him to pursue the externally given objective of economy or efficiency. He is not simply required to find the best way of organising educational resources to serve the simple purposes of education, but is forced also to see this in conjunction with a search for economy of resources. He is not simply a senior professional, but also a supervisor who takes day-to-day decisions within a given framework of control whose mainspring is economy. It is this which separates his role from that of his professional colleague without the status of a 'Head'.

HORIZONTAL SPECIALISATION

Horizontal specialisation of the administrative decision tasks in industry gives separate recognition to such areas as finance, marketing, product development or production (Woodward, 1965). In the recent Fulton Committee report on the civil service we find a similar kind of distinction arising between the business-economic arm and the social and other services (Fulton, 1968). In the single school unit, scale of operations is not likely to permit much specialisation, but it is already possible to describe such specialist jobs as bursar or directors of studies, and with increasing scale, more are likely to appear. (See below, pp. 123–6.)

Our starting-point here must therefore be with the Head's own role. Our question is really what there is in the current role which is likely to provide a basis for further specialisation. This again, is to take and apply to the school the approach which has been used elsewhere. It is usual to start with a conception of an entrepreneur or owner manager in business organisations and show how, as the operation increases in size, he is forced to divest himself of many specialist aspects of his work to leave himself free to do those which he can do best (Urwick, 1951).

The same might be done with the role of the Head. Is he likely to retain the generalist role which as *the Head* he had imputed to him in the past? Two trends imply that he will not.

Firstly, the trend towards bigger schools, in which a bad decision by the Head could have severe consequences for a large number of pupils and for staff resources, will in itself increase the amount of surveillance of the Head's role, and entail a more stringent control of it. Secondly, the development of a 'body of knowledge' relating to the Head's role specifically (i.e. as distinct from that of the teacher) is likely to create a presumption in favour of one particular conception of the role: this body of knowledge will tend to generate its own set of expectations as to the role the Head will carry out.

The first of these might be regarded as a trend connected with the increased concern by society for the efficient employment of its educational resources, and therefore as likely to bring in its train a more 'bureaucratic' structure of direction and control applied to the school through the Head-role. The second, however, is more likely to develop through discussion amongst Heads themselves and the more academic analysis of what the Head's role really entails. There is evidence that both of these developments are under way, and although we have certainly not yet reached the stage where the Head-role is clearly defined, there are some indications that the administratively 'professional' definition is not far away. To see this, one has merely to read much of the current literature on the subject of the Head's role—which, in volume, is itself something of a recent novelty.

What tends to emerge from this, however, is, firstly, a conception of the Head's role as a 'boundary' role. By this is meant, simply, that the head stands on the edge of or even between different systems of authority distribution or of role allocation; he mediates the demands of the subordinate system to the wider system, and vice versa. For example, Mrs. M. J. Davis, in the opening of her paper on 'The Head in a Comprehensive' (1968), highlights the essentially boundary function of the Head:

> Externally the Head has to convey the ethos and interpret the aims of the school to the community. Internally he has to frame policy and plan the delegation of responsibility to ensure maximum efficiency, in putting theory into practice: he must attempt to create an atmosphere in which staff can work in harmony and pupils develop in security, maintaining the balance between stability and innovation (Davis, 1968, p. 18).

Secondly, the discussion is beginning to assemble a kind of package of the internal duties which are appropriately carried out by the Head of this new 'thing', the large comprehensive school. This

tends to start with curriculum planning and move through consequential questions of streaming/non-streaming, counselling staff
and pupils, and end up with a definition of the mechanics of the role
which emphasises an approach, which in industry has been termed
'management by objectives'.

For example, Mather has offered some suggestions on what type
of problem the Head is there to solve. He first recognises the school's
primary task as "providing as wide a range of beneficient learning
opportunities as possible", and after amplifying this, goes on to
argue that "the main instrument for the implementation of the
primary task is the curriculum" (Mather, 1968, p. 201). This is
perhaps a useful starting point for consideration of the Head's
administrative role, because it involves a conception which is
clearly beyond the capacity of the individual teacher to devise,
alone and in isolation. In the nature of the curriculum it is (a) bigger
than the subject or the teaching of a specific class of pupils, and (b)
integrative of the professional work of the school system as a whole.
It is—and this is particularly important—not a part of the activity
which inherently serves the limited objectives of economy and
efficiency, but is still a primarily professional activity which nevertheless extends beyond the capability of the individual professional
to devise and control.

Its 'bigness' arises out of the concept of a school as distinct from
some simpler interpersonal teacher–client relationship; the school
curriculum must inevitably bring together the diverse and specialist
teaching activities which go on within the school. But it must also
yield a 'package' in the end and this in turn implies that the separate
parts must be related to each other in a way which will effect
integrity.

Curriculum planning must inevitably embrace all other elements
in the school system to some extent and at some level of decision.
Holt has commented in this vein, with, for example, ". . . it's impossible at the moment to discuss the general pattern of secondary
education—and curriculum reform in particular—without the issue
of streaming arising" (Holt, 1969, p. 58). None would deny that

streaming is a topical issue at the moment, nor that it is a pretty important educational question to be resolved by the professionals. (See below, Tucker, Chap. 9.) It can, therefore, be brought within the general framework of curriculum planning as a question to be resolved by the Headmaster in consultation with—or possibly with the participation of—the staff of the school (H.M.A., 1972; Parkes and Williams, 1973).

Nor does the sequence of packaging end there. McMullen has carried this thought further with a 'model' of organisation which he claims to have found useful although clearly needing further expansion. Congruently with the thoughts developed in this section, he starts with a concept of objectives which he spells out in some detail and then proceeds to link other areas of administrative and professional concern to them in sequence. As he presents this, it forms a linked check-list of possibilities, running through modes of study, materials, media, time-table organisation, staff organisation, accommodation, costing and communication and review, each of which is illustrated with examples (McMullen, 1968).

Two points might be underlined in this. Firstly, that decisions are called for in each of these areas listed, since they provide alternative courses of action between which the school (or the Head) has to choose. The choice, as Vickers might indicate, will depend upon a diagnosis of the needs of the situation, and a determination, according to the standards of the judging mind, of which is best. It implies that those called upon to exercise the choice, or to share in it, will be in a position both to recognise the possibilities and to appraise them in relation to the situation. But it is perhaps important to recognise that the system does *permit* such choices to be made, and it is not merely a question of responding to the 'requirements of the educational system' in some vague and rather passive sense. This way lies the passive bureaucratic approach, with the administrator-head devolving into a mere office boy. What McMullen is suggesting with his model is that one can take arms against a sea of troubles and act professionally.

Secondly, the manner of presentation tends to under-emphasise, although not ignore, the element of 'review' in the system. This is important as the trigger mechanism which provides the 'occasion for decision' or which determines when a decision is called for. There is, therefore, a clear sense in which the whole sequence can be developed as a series of feed-back or control loops. For example, the effect (or outcome) of choosing one mode of study rather than another (e.g. independent, supervised individual, small group, large group, etc.) can be either measured or assessed against the objectives sought in the choosing. If the result of the comparison is judged to be unsatisfactory in some way, the decision process is restarted thus providing an 'occasion for decision'. This can be carried through the whole sequence, and it therefore becomes quite unnecessary to wait for some prod from a source external to the school system, to bring about decision and action.

The general question of how the Head might approach the problem of decision-taking is, however, considered in the ensuing chapter, to which these considerations form the back-drop.

CHAPTER 5

THE ORGANISATION OF DECISION-MAKING

INTRODUCTION

Thus far in this part of the discussion of the Headmaster's role, we have noted two features of the system of organisation and management of schools which have an important bearing on the question of performance. Firstly, we have noted that there are many alternative conceptions of theory, resources and authority distribution which can be polarised in the way in which we have described them in Chapter 3. Secondly, we have seen how certain general concepts which have been applied to the definition of the manager's role in other situations might be applied to the role of the Headmaster.

In the present chapter we aim to examine the mechanics of the Head's decision role. To do this we will follow a well-accepted description of the three main phases of decision, that given by March and Simon (1959). They identify three phases in a decision process:

(a) The phase of problem recognition which really raises the question of how and when problems are presented to managers for determination. This is therefore concerned with 'when' decisions have to be made by managers and the mechanisms set up to ensure that managers note the existence of problems at the right time.

(b) The phase of search for solutions which really places the emphasis upon how creative the individual or the organisation has to be in looking for solutions. In connection with this phase, therefore, we can look at the question of what activities (and therefore decisions) the Head gets himself involved in in carrying out his role.

(c) The phase of determining which of the alternatives is the best (or at least 'satisfactory') to adopt in the circumstances. This is the phase in which it is not possible to dispose of the application of human judgement (of relative value) to the decision process. As we will note *en passant* in the subsequent discussion, Vickers (1967) has argued that judgement is called for at each phase (i.e. judgement of reality, of action, and of value) but it is in connection with the exercise of this value judgement in the context of the school system that the most intractable organisational and management problems are likely to be found.

In the subsequent sections, therefore, we will follow this general conception of main phases in decision-taking, but use each phase as a foundation for consideration of such questions as the when, the what, and the who of decision.

(a) THE OCCASIONS FOR DECISION

March and Simon identify the first phase of decision as that of finding the occasion for making a decision—this involves usually some sort of trigger mechanism which indicates that something in the current state of affairs (*the reality*) is different from what is desired or desirable. The judgement of how far the reality departs from the desirable, which is Vickers' first *type* of judgement, will be called for whenever the situation is *open*—that is where there is no prior arrangement for determining when the actual departs from the desirable.

In these circumstances the occasion for decision may be determined simply "by the interests of the judging mind", in Vickers' phrase. This is essentially an appreciation of the situation in a non-formal way: it depends upon a particular relationship existing between the situation and 'the interest of the judging mind'. But situations are not always open, and in the rational organisation, it is more usual to make specific provision to ensure that as many such judgemental situations as possible are *closed* by developing mechanistic or 'automatic' means of signalling the 'error'. In the context of a normal organisation of rational authority however, the interests of the judging mind may be dictated by the system itself. An individual may not be interested in rendering a report on a particular subject at a particular time, but the system will force his mind to be interested in doing so. This may merely push the problem back because somebody presumably laid down the requirement that this report be rendered at this time, and perhaps therefore it was the interest of that judging mind which determined the aspects of the situation to be reported and evaluated. Nevertheless, it seems likely that the implication of simple volition as a basis for decisional action is a too naïve one; the objectives of the organisation or system are likely to have some major part to play in requiring decisions at certain times.

The principle of this kind of arrangement can be illustrated by a diagram of closed loop control such as is presented on p. 72. Examples might be the setting up of minimum stock levels, such that when stock falls below a certain quantity, reordering is automatic and does not require someone to 'judge' whether a reorder decision is called for; or the requirement that a report must be rendered on the first Friday in each month, thus abolishing the need for judgement as to just when it should be rendered. In this, the measurement or assessment of the output of some system (level of stock or passage of time) when compared with the target (minimum stock level or first Friday in the month) says when a decision or an action is called for. A closed-loop device of this sort then provides a basis for determining when a judgement of reality is called for and might therefore be said to provide a 'trigger' for decision and action. An error signal produced by comparing system output with objective or target, triggers off, or provides the 'occasion for' decision or action.

The basic elements in such a system of control are three. These may be expressed either in simple electro-mechanical terms (e.g.

Organisational Communications in System Terms

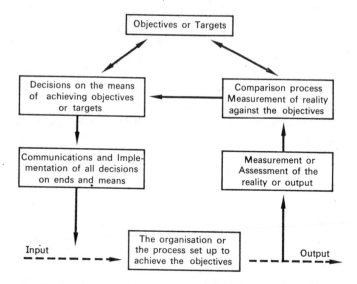

FIG. 2. Communications are represented on the diagram by the solid lines. They are necessary to control (without which we cannot talk of survival). The right-hand side represents the 'feed-back' and the left-hand side the 'feed'. Whilst both are present in a system, there may be different relationships between them according to whether management is initiating a change or whether it is responding to a change fed back via the right-hand channels from the organisation or process which management is there to run.

as in a thermostat) or linked to the concepts of management used in the preceding chapter:

    (a)   the performance to be controlled, conceived in black-box terms as having an input which can be influenced, and an output which can be measured or assessed;

    (b)   the process of influence, consisting of target setting, target communication, and target acceptance as an influence upon the input (this is recognisable as 'direction' in the Tannenbaum sense);

(c) the processes of measurement and comparison, which rely upon the assessment or measurement of performance and the comparison of the outcome against the target in order to derive the nature of the signal (this is identifiable with the control or monitoring process in management).

This implicit degree of 'control' is not always possible in a management situation, but it is entered into the discussion here to guide the subsequent examination of the kinds or styles of control exhibited by Heads. They, whether they think in these terms or not, do control in line with these underlying principles. In particular, they do have measuring devices which tell them when they must take a decision about something (a performance) in the system.

But in the reality of the school situation, the first point of some interest in this regard arises from the amount of discretion which a Head has to shape his own role to suit himself and his personality, and, therefore, to decide when told to do so by the interests and predispositions of his own judging mind. This may be linked to the concept of extensibility as used by sociologists to describe a category of role in which the incumbent has a great deal of freedom to mould the role to his own personality needs (Schneider, 1957).

In the past the Head has usually possessed a great deal of discretion to shape the school's day-to-day objectives. The 'power' of the Head has lain in this 'extensibility'. It was not, of course, unrestricted: there is a certain minimum requirement imposed upon the role, particularly by the wider educational system of authority which donates the administrative authority enjoyed by the Head. This minimum may well differ significantly from the 'average' actually met by the Head, and will almost certainly vary markedly from the maximum which they meet. In the nature and direction of the change in the wider system, however, there may well be some tendency for the minimum requirement imposed by the educational system as a whole to be increased—and in consequence the

Head's role will become increasingly administration-based and less closely linked and identified with the professional system, resting on sapiental authority.

Nor is he unusual in this—many other managerial jobs are of the same kind (Jaques, 1956). But it does mean that the translation of general objectives into specific objectives will be strongly influenced by the Head and the way in which he shapes his own role to suit his own personality and predilections. For example, there are many different day-to-day activities in the school to which managerial weight might be given.

According to his own predispositions, the Head might, for example, give greatest emphasis to one of a number of control activities:

1. *Time-tabling.* The Head in this situation pays great attention to ensuring that the time-table is set up in such a way as to minimize disruptions and dislocations, so that the flow of teaching goes on under most predictable circumstances, even including absence.

2. *Improving the technology.* The Head in this situation pays considerable attention to ensuring that the school has all the latest visual aids and other equipment deemed necessary to improve the performance of class teachers.

3. *Inspecting the standards.* In this situation emphasis is placed upon a continual check upon the standards of performance of subordinate staff, so that class teachers are, as it were, kept on their toes in professional terms. Teachers here are likely to find themselves encouraged to go on Easter Courses, and the like.

4. *Minimising the waste.* Here the emphasis is upon the costs of running the system and the need to check waste in all its forms, so that the securing of stock is often the most difficult operation for a class teacher to undertake—capable of being likened to getting blood from a stone.

5. *Housekeeping.* The Head, being somewhat houseproud, spends

a great deal of his time chasing up the caretaker and kitchen staff, to ensure cleanliness and tidiness. This may carry through to checking on state of footwear of pupils, etc.

6. *Satisfying the client.* Rather more general in its implications is the focus of activity upon the client, to whose interests everything else is made subservient, and although this does not necessarily mean 'the pupil right or wrong', it can have this implication, and act to the detriment of the teaching system as a whole.

6a. *Satisfying the parent.* This is a variant on and extension from the previous one.

Whilst this is not by any means an exhaustive list of the activities and functions which may be emphasised by a particular style of headship, it is perhaps long enough to indicate that:

(a) there can be differential emphasis on different elements in the overall control problem; and

(b) that, taking into account the differences in human predisposition which have full play in roles with a high discretionary content, there could well be a potential conflict between class teacher and Head on the subject of what ought to be given most emphasis.

If these differences in style or emphasis exist, then they suggest that in controlling a school operation, each will be capable of providing a set of objective or subjective standards against which the performance of the system or of individuals can be judged. If the Head is adamant about controlling waste, then presumably the amount of chalk or paper which a class teacher uses can be employed as a yardstick against which to judge his performance. If, however, the emphasis is upon teaching ability or performance, then presumably the Head has some subjective standard against which a particular teacher's ability or performance is measured. Such standards can be built into some systematic, closed-loop control arrangement. That it is not seen in these terms does not invalidate the principle that it could be formalised in this way. In fact, all that has been done in "management by objectives" is just this. 'Management by objectives' (see Hughes, 1965) could be described as a formalised attempt to create a condition of two-way communication about objectives and about the standards appropriate to them which will be used in assessment. The only novelty in it is the 'formalisation' of the procedures involved in communicating the objectives and the standards of the person in charge of a unit to the people he is in charge of. The more complex the system to be controlled—as in a comprehensive school—the more likely it is that such formalisation will be called for as a major means of ensuring control, which now becomes roughly equated with having some device for ensuring that the Head (or other decision-taker) is 'told' *when* a decision (or action) is called for.

(b) KINDS OF ACTION (DECISION) INVOLVED

March and Simon identify a second stage of decision as one of determining the courses of *action* which are possible and feasible as a solution to the problem thus indicated. This is sometimes referred to as a 'search' process—the searching out of ways of reducing the problem. In a routine situation, this search may take no time at all— it is merely a question of picking a ready-made solution or programme off the memory shelf and applying it. But in highly innovative situations, search may prove to be the time-consuming phase; what to do about difficult or tricky situations is a question which may take hours of consideration.

In this vein, Simon distinguishes the two polar types of decisions, programmed decisions and non-programmed decisions, with "decisions of all shades of gray along the continuum" between these poles (1965, p. 58). In this context 'programme' has the sense of "a detailed prescription or strategy that governs the sequence of responses of a system to a complex task environment" (p. 59). The two polar types are defined as follows:

Decisions are programmed to the extent that they are repetitive and routine, to the extent that a definite procedure has been worked out for handling them so that they don't have to be treated *de novo* each time they occur (pp. 58–59).

Decisions are non-programmed to the extent that they are novel, unstructured, and consequential. There is no cut-and-dried method for handling the problem because it hasn't arisen before, or because its precise nature and structure are elusive or complex, or because it is so important that it deserves a custom-tailored treatment (p. 59).

Vickers tends to discount the importance of the judgement required at this stage. For him action judgement is the least important, presumably in the sense that we usually have a repertoire of possible courses of action, but which of these is used depends upon how we read the situation and what solution we consider to be the best in all the circumstances. Action judgement is therefore "only called for by the interaction of (the other two kinds of judgement) and is only selected by the further use of the same criteria" (Vickers, 1967, p. 52). Although there is some evidence to suggest that we do use such repertories of actions as a foundation for action (e.g. Marples, 1961) nevertheless there are occasions when creative solutions must be sought and found.

Simon's second type of decision—the creative—usually receives most attention partly because these are the more difficult ones and partly because, in their nature, they cannot be blue-printed as to the manner of proceeding. But they are not necessarily the most numerous. Nevertheless, many problems are often tackled *as if they were* non-programmed decisions, simply because of ignorance or because of status considerations. Non-programmed decisions are after all 'higher status' or more important than the others, and many managers having insufficient pressure upon them to force their attention elsewhere, spend their time producing creative solutions to problems which could be solved by the application of routine procedures. This means that judgement is often applied to problems which require no more than, say, a clerical routine or a structural solution (like, for example, the setting of minimum and maximum stock levels).

This occurs for the rather human reason that it adds interest and in spite of the fact that bureaucratic organisations ideally function to pin decision-taking to the lowest possible level of skill, and therefore of position and pay. The point of making decisions a matter of clerical routine or organisational structure, for example, is that this enables people low down in the organisation, and with relatively few skills as decision-takers, to engage in a process of decision, thus freeing those scarcer resources (people with a flair for decision-taking) for those which cannot be solved in this routinised way. We often spend a lot of time and money looking for people who have a demonstrated capacity for taking decisions or for exercising judgement, when in fact we ought to have concentrated more of our attention on understanding and defining the process of decision-making itself, in order that it can be shaped to the more 'ordinary' capacities of the human being to choose between alternatives (cf. Simon, 1965, pp. 64–68).

But the corollary to this is somewhat unpalatable—it is that many so-called decision-makers will find their decision-taking function increasingly overtaken by machines or that their decision-role is really only a relatively minor one, dealing with sub-problems and sub-parts of a problem in a fairly routine fashion. They become the searchers, the providers of information required for other decisions taken by another person, and not those who are required to exercise either reality or value judgements; they report on the reality and they search out the alternative courses of action, but the judging mind is the mind of someone else.

In fact, much of the administrative decision-making, so called, in the educational system may be of this sort. This does not mean that there are no decisions to be taken by Headmasters; there are, but they are decisions of a 'political' nature. The administrative decisions may be really nothing more than reportage or search. One of the problems that this system has not yet solved is the problem which is sometimes referred to as 'Gresham's Law of Planning', which states that routine administrative work will drive out non-programmed decisional activity. Operation within the framework of someone else's structure of decision-taking (e.g. that of the local education authority) is always easier than taking innovating decisions for oneself, and the easier course is the one which people tend to accept to the disadvantage of the organisation as a whole. This is a more palatable economy of effort than that of divesting oneself of routine decisions.

In the educational system as a whole such considerations might well be relevant. But concerned as we are with the school unit in isolation, the question to be resolved is less far-reaching than this one. It turns upon the question of how much of a Head's role represents a necessary application of judgemental ability, and how far it is a role which is composited of relatively low level decision-tasks which could be taken by others with lower levels of ability.

It was in order to gain some insights into this that we asked Heads to supply us with information on what they did with their time. From this we hoped to be able to produce a categorisation of their activities, which in turn would enable us to approach answering this question. In the event, we did not receive as much information as we would have liked, but what we had enabled us to produce a crude fourfold classification of the activities of Headmasters and those others who carried out 'head'-type administrative activities. These may be described briefly as follows:

Firstly, there is that part of the Head's role which is professional in scope and content, meaning by this that he engages in those activities which are primarily those of a teacher. In carrying out such activities he is not differentiated from the teacher. Particularly for those 'Heads' who do not have actual *Headmaster* roles this can take up a high proportion of total working time. But because this is essentially non-administrative work, we are not presently concerned with it.

Secondly, there is that part of the Head's role which might be described best as concerned with public relations. Under this heading we might conveniently list the contacts with pupils, parents, and other outsiders of similar ilk. This is part professional, but in its implicit specialisation (we can visualise the Head as acting as a specialist buffer between the professional class teacher on the one hand, and the clients or the surrogates of clients on the other) it begins to approach the form and nature of a secondary role. In this capacity he acts as a 'representative'.

Thirdly, there is often a substantial part of the Head's role which is taken up with activities which only achieve integral identity under some heading like 'control'. The activities themselves range from fairly low-level clerical activity to lengthy discussions with inspectors and other Ministry and local education authority personnel over policy questions. In between these extremes are the control activities which involve contacts with school staff and whose form is given by the requirement that activities within the school be both apposite and co-ordinated.

It is useful to break down this third category into at least two sub-categories, not only because this set of activities is more directly related to the management system, but also because Heads themselves tend to recognise a sub-classification in reporting what they do. Therefore:

(i) There are those administrative (largely paper-work) activities which relate to some external system of control. Into this sub-category go the tasks of completing returns for the local education authority, the Department of Education and Science and other external educational bodies. With this might be coupled activities concerned with the administration of external examinations or with school savings (in two estimates we obtained, this latter activity took up 50 and 90 minutes per week).

There are also those activities which involve interpersonal communications with the agents of external control systems —the L.E.A., D.E.S., etc., officers of various sorts who visit or are visited to discuss policy or practice. These are difficult to estimate as a proportion of time because frequently they occur in large but intermittent episodes of time commitment. Estimates obtained varied from 15 minutes to more than 2 hours per week, on average.

(ii) There are the corresponding internal administrative activities, often involving some paper-work—internal examinations, time-tabling, canteen co-ordination, and daily mail handling. In some cases, the dividing-line between internal and external may be a fine one to draw, but it is probably convenient to try to draw it.

Similarly there are those internal communications duties which (whilst also associated with some of the activities already mentioned) probably take up the largest single slice of working time. Into this category fall the activities which involve contact with staff and prefects on an individual or small group basis, and the large-group functions (including assembly, school council meetings, speech days, and the like).

Such activities do not, of course, *occur* in categories. A Headmaster's day is made up of a succession of varied activities which *can* be classified in this way. The following table (p. 83) provides an illustration of this, although there is no way of determining whether it is typical. The Headmaster in question has sought to develop a degree of classification into the statement and has attempted to indicate what is regular and what is occasional in the distribution of time devoted to administering the school.

This suggests that the role is composed of two kinds of activity: firstly, the representative or figurehead activities (representing the school to outsiders or taking assembly as the 'Headmaster'); and secondly, the residual specialist activities which, if not done by some 'specialist' would tend to interfere with the carrying out of the prime roles of the system (teaching). The latter adds up to a 'job' in only the aggregated sense: in a larger organisation, they would tend to be carried out by specialist managers, supervisors, or clerks, but in the school, the sheer lack of scale in each activity area makes it necessary to aggregate them into a composited role. With increase in the scale of the comprehensive school, however, the distinct possibility exists that some, at least, of these activities will acquire sufficient scale to justify the creation of separate roles such as those of bursar or registrar, in addition to those of clerk or secretary.

On the assumption that this set of estimates provides a reasonable if tentative picture of the situation, two inferences may be drawn. Firstly, that it is extremely unlikely that a blue-print can be drawn up for the secondary school's organisation, without taking scale of activity into account. This is likely to be a partial function of sheer school size, but also a partial function of school objectives (e.g. denominational schools will tend to differ from non-denominational and comprehensive without streaming from grammar or modern schools). Secondly, that it is likely that increased standardisation of secondary school objectives and forms in the future will lead to increasing specialisation of decision (as distinct from professional) roles. Although these specialisations may well be tacked onto the professional roles themselves (i.e. they will not be full-time organisational roles) they are likely to develop with greater frequency in the future. This in turn would seem to have very important implications for the nature of the teaching situations. But it is also likely to force attention upon the manner in which school decision-taking is to be organised.

(c) THE ACT OF CHOOSING

The third distinguishable phase is that which entails the act of choosing the *best* or the most acceptable alternative from the possible ones discovered by search. Again, in the routine situation, this may not cause much worry, because the *value* judgement as to which is best or most acceptable may have been tried and tested beforehand, and it is merely a matter of repetition. But for the creative solution, the choice may be a time-consuming process as an apparently good solution is tested before the final decision is taken. In many 'ordinary' routine decisions, however, the process of choosing is carried out coincidentally with the process of search, some alternative courses of action being dropped as they are thought of because they are obviously not going to be good enough.

Description of activity	Time taken estimate	Regular or occasional
Preparation of Prayers and Assembly	15–20 mins.	Regular
Taking School Prayers, announcements, etc.	20 mins.	Regular
Sorting mail, dealing with matters arising, distributing information to staff	30 mins.	Regular
Dictation of letters	30 mins.	Regular
Meeting people:	2 hours +	Regular
(i) *Official* (Clerk of Works, Visiting Inspectors, Elect. Engrs., Architects Dept., Police, etc.)		
(ii) *Medical* (doctor, nurse, dentist)		
(iii) *Unofficial* (charities, parents, workmen reporting in, etc.)		
(iv) *Staff* (teachers bringing requests, suggestions or discussing problems (often personal))		
(v) *Children* (disciplinary, seeking advice, vandalism)		
Investigation:	30 mins. In some cases considerably longer	Occasional
(a) Serious cases of lost or stolen property.		
(b) Fabric in cases of damage or dealing with workmen or accompanying Clerk of Works.		
Planning: Time-tables, schemes of work in conjunction with staff. Special activities, e.g. prize-giving, sports, eisteddfod, exams, terminals (with rearranged classes)	Averaging 5 hours per week	Occasional
Answering telephone calls and making outgoing calls	30–60 mins.	Regular
School meals—overall supervision	30 mins.	Regular
Completion of forms—ministerial, L.E.A.	30 mins. +	Occasional
Completing school log and records	10 mins.	Regular
Educational bodies requiring statistics	1 hour in a term	Occasional
Cleaning staff: dealing with problems brought by cleaning staff via caretaker, problems of heating, complaints re fuel, etc.	15–30 mins.	Occasional

In this area, the 'interests' or the 'predispositions' of the judging mind are likely to play an extremely important part in determining what is the best course of action to follow in a given set of circumstances. When we speak of the 'criteria' of judgement, it is usually the value judgement we have in mind. Since different people will tend to hold different sets of values, which provide the standards for judging, there is less firm ground for consensus: as Vickers says, the correctness of a value judgement can only be determined by the exercise of another value judgement, either by the same person or by someone else. If the 'someone else' holds a different set of values from the first person, his assessment of the act of choice will tend to result in a negative judgement. That which is best in a given situation is rarely axiomatic, and room for dispute certainly exists.

Once again, however, that which is routine may be distinguished from that which is novel. When the same course of action is applied time after time, people in the situation become lulled into the belief or the acceptance that this course of action is 'the best one': they accept it as best through long familiarity and usage. But certainly not everyone will go along with this; in fact one attempt to explain the difference between the approaches of British and American managers has sought to suggest that the former are more likely to *accept* the familiar, whilst the latter are more likely to *challenge* the familiar solutions as a matter of habit.

In the context of the school, the implication of most significance in all this is that both reality judgement and value judgement will be affected by the sub-system of authority which is allowed to define the role. When the point is made that teachers and Headmasters hold different values (above, p. 46) its importance lies in what is implied for the exercise of judgement in situations which call for decisions. Where a teacher might act on a decision base which emphasised the value of giving full attention to the individual pupil's needs, the Headmaster might act on a decision base which emphasised the value of giving most attention to the needs of the largest number (or, of course, vice versa). The training and experience of those in different role-contexts is likely to emphasise different values and also different perspectives (linked with the notion of reality judgement), and where they differ, therefore, the outcomes of action are also likely to differ.

The involvement of judgement in the decision process makes it inherently difficult. It also makes it difficult to train people for decision-taking in any straightforward fashion, and therefore expensive to attempt. We know that decision involves judgement, but we do not at the present time know enough about judges or judgement to permit us to say, for example, what are the factors which make for good judges or good judgements (see Taft, 1962). Because we do not know the answers to these things, we are not able to determine how the judges ought to be trained, nor how a person's judgement might be improved. The acquisition of a good judge or good judgement by an organisation is, therefore, a question to be resolved in selection; you pick either a good judge or a bad or indifferent one, but once having done so, there seems to be little that you can do after this to effect improvement. It would seem that all that can be hoped for is that immersion in a particular cultural setting will cause the values of the system to 'rub off' on the individual, but even this is by no means a sure-fire method of improving judgemental ability (Thomason, 1968, Chap. 3).

Given this state of knowledge about judgement, and the requirement of the organisation that some people take good and correct judgements on its behalf, organisations seek to establish an arrangement to control the process of decision in such a way that the 'interests of the judging mind' are not the only criteria which determine *when* a decision shall be taken, and that the personal feelings and predispositions of the individual are not the only criteria for determining *what* is best in the circumstances.

Given the importance of value judgement in the decision-process, and the costliness of the resource which is required for the exercise of non-routine judgements, we have to ask whether the school unit is adequately organised to economise this judgemental ability. In the large complex organisation, this question usually starts in train a discussion of the problems of centralisation and decentralisation of decision. This is usually resolved in terms which suggest that a decision role should be located at that point in the system where it balances against each other those forces which pull the decision-centre towards the source of information (i.e. placing the emphasis upon the costs of search) and those which pull it towards the source of action (i.e. placing the emphasis upon the costs of implementation). The decision-centre is then a point of equilibrium in terms of relative costs of 'deciding' and of 'implementation'. (Cf. Kruisinga, 1954.)

Different types of organisation seek to accomplish this by different means. The business-type of organisation seeks to achieve this end by a high degree of *specialisation* in decision-making and a complex interlinking arrangement of 'offices' to 'hold' decisions to the required paths. The professional service organisation, on the other hand, tends to rely much more on a process of professional *training* to inculcate the 'professional values' so that these can be relied upon in subsequent operations without specific controlling or holding devices being built into the organisation itself. The period of time which elapses before a middle manager's decisions are checked by someone else is probably much shorter than that for, say, a Headmaster and more certainly a doctor, reflecting the difference in the extent to which the organisation relies upon specific control or generalised commitment as the means of ensuring that values applied to decision are the 'requisite' ones.

The interesting question which then arises for the school system is whether, with the development of larger comprehensive schools, the reliance upon such professional commitment can or will continue. This larger more complex school organisation will probably place much greater reliance upon the specialisation of roles and the interlinking of these roles into more purposively control-oriented arrangements. In the kind of terms used in the previous section, it is likely that the process of control will assume greater significance in the new school system whilst the significance of influence via professional training will be diminished. But this situation has probably not yet been reached, and the school unit continues in a transitional condition which forces us to examine that which is neither purely bureaucratic nor purely professional in form.

It would be, perhaps, all too easy to make the assumption here, that business organisations are *always* concerned with a detailed separation of direction and control roles, and that no attempt is made in that context to develop commitment to a set of organisational values. In terms of the notion of a system with which we started above, it is too easy to assume that a management process in, say, industry, is conceived only in terms of closed-loop controls. This is patently not so. On the one hand, many managers take decisions and implement them but then fail to check on their efficacy in any purposive way. On the other, industry has been led to adopt many specific devices—such as management by objectives as a currently well-publicised example—to try to rectify a situation in which this open-ended control occurs. If, on the other hand, the professional organisation, like the school or the hospital or the university, tends to institutionalise the open-endedness of the control arrangements, this makes it different in degree rather in kind from the business organisation.

CHAPTER 6

ORGANISATIONAL TRAINING

INTRODUCTION

At this point, we must honour the pledge of the introduction to bring together the propositions from the intervening chapters to present a conception of how the stresses of the developing comprehensive school and the strains imposed upon the Head's role may be accommodated and resolved.

The first step in this is to recognise the universality of what, in Chapter 3, we have referred to as duality in theories, resources and authority systems. The language used here may differ from that used elsewhere, but the same general point is often made. For example, Taylor has argued that it is no longer sensible to consider the training of school administrators in terms which are appropriate to existing roles. This, of course, merely highlights the change which is overtaking the secondary school system. But he goes on to identify 'forces' at work within the new system which seem to rest upon totally new premises. The new approach to training should result from fresh thinking about roles and the "kind of tasks that are generated by the internal and external relationships of an organisation pursuing a shifting pattern of objectives" (Baron and Taylor, 1969, p. 111). In dealing with some of the internal relationships, he quotes some of the more radical suggestions that have been made for changing the conception of the Head's role—approval of staff for Head's action, rotation of headships, staff election of Heads. This, by itself, does not illustrate duality, but it does imply that there are at least two theories of how the Head's role ought to be endowed with an acceptable authority.

Whether a Head is elected or rotated or not, the role of the Head will remain to be carried out by someone. The position—as distinct from the manner of filling it—will still remain one in which the strains of the system are concentrated. The Head will still have to exercise a boundary function, mediating the internal demands to the external relations, and the external demands to the internal organisation. Since these demands are not always compatible, the main problem for the Head is one of accommodating strain and for the educational system as a whole that of effecting an acceptable and realisable compromise between conflicting demands.

The solution of the Head's administrative problems appears to lie in the 'correct' organisation and ordering of decision within the system which has been outlined. What is 'requisite' or 'situationally correct' in this system must take into account the 'facts' of the situation which enter into the model of system functioning. That teachers are professionals demanding high levels of discretion may be taken as a fact (although this can be tested); that the educational system as a whole is interested in securing efficiency and economy in the allocation of teaching resources may also be taken as a fact (which can also be tested). The pressures which arise from their existence will tend to determine what is a correct response. It may be objected that this defines correctness in rather Macchiavellian terms—that which will prove acceptable within the system as a whole—but against this it may be countered that short of invoking a Divine Right of Headmasters, this is the only source of judgement criteria which can be used.

The question which is therefore asked in this part is "How can the Headmaster administer the new school system?" Although we make reference to certain techniques, the burden of the argument is that he does this by establishing or fostering a particular form of ordered decision-taking. We describe this as 'organisational training' because it relies essentially upon a maximum involvement of the human resources in the administrative decision process (i.e. consistently with the usual requirement of the professional role that decisions be taken by the professionals themselves as far as possible). Since in this form, the proposition might be said to apply in any circumstance, it requires qualification to the extent that such involvement must involve the resources on a 'group' rather than an 'individual' basis. Industry's 'management by objectives' approach requires translation to fit it to the situational demands of the professional organisation, but it nevertheless serves the same ends of communications improvement and increased commitment to the organisational objectives.

THE IMPOSITION OF SOLUTIONS

In the administration of any unit, the administrator always faces the problem of deciding between alternative methods of taking and implementing decisions. Either he can take the decision and impose it upon those over whom he has a 'given' authority, or he can invite the subordinate group to share in the decision and accept the decision thus arrived at in joint decision-taking. When the administrator is 'given responsibility' for something or other he has, of course, to take it and cannot simply abdicate; but it is not necessarily 'soft management' to invite participation in the decision and implementation process.

On the other hand, it may be either unnecessary or undesirable to do this. There are some circumstances in which the subordinates do not want to participate and would not, therefore, contribute anything if asked to do so. But there are, equally, other circumstances in which the subordinates do want to participate and will in fact hold back a necessary contribution of co-operation if they do not do so. The problem for the administrator is not, therefore, whether he should be soft or hard in his approach, but whether he has the right approach in the circumstances. This is really the argument advanced by Likert who declares that two different systems of this general sort exist side by side in modern society, the one (hard-line) system being applied appropriately to the mass production, assembly-line, routine operations kind of situation, and the other (soft-line) to the more varied selling organisation or research department (Likert, 1961).

The distinction which he draws is similar to that drawn by McGregor in his contrasting of two theories for managing, which he refers to simply as Theory X and Theory Y. Theory X is essentially a hard-line theory, and Theory Y a soft-line approach— as we have used these terms above (McGregor, 1960). It is often forgotten in the enthusiasm generated by the protagonists of Theory Y, that the question of relevance must be considered. In the school context, certain *facts* of the situation may make it extremely relevant as a theory, as, for example, Mather (1968, p. 231) has argued that it is—"the atmosphere of the organisation should encourage staff to exercise not only their leadership but their imagination, ingenuity and creativity in the solution of organisational problems".

The more important of these facts are:

Firstly, that the professional organisation depends for effective action upon the 'workers' in the system having a high level of discretion to decide about the day-to-day problems involved in their work (and thus creates a presumption that the system will tend to resemble Likert's second pattern).

Secondly, that the professional worker's competence to take these decisions will be certified as a result of long involvement in training (in which attention will be given not only to inculcation of method and technique, but also to the acculturation of the trainee to the values of the profession) supported by experience gained under the direction of its more senior members.

Thirdly, that the assumption of a basic equality in the ability and capacity of each trained professional renders it incongruent that they acquire differentially specialist roles related to decision-taking within a structure of formal authority.

Fourthly, that formal administrator roles on the industrial or bureaucratic basis are ill-developed and do not form a part of the traditional structure, so that the direction and control become interleaved within the conception of the professional role itself. Administrative decisions, as these have been defined and described above, must therefore be taken within this general framework of 'facts'. If this is not done, the organisation will change its general form, and come to resemble the bureaucratic organisation, in which an alienated work force will have to be directed and controlled within a framework of abstract rules and procedures determined by specialists at the top of a hierarchy and handed down with formalistic impersonality, and which is similar to Likert's first pattern. But to accomplish the aim, the only principle which can be employed (i.e. whatever the specific form it takes) is that which sees the professional group as a competent decision-taking body.

This does not, however, raise any new principle for school administration. It merely elevates it in significance, but there are many examples of its being applied, perhaps intuitively, but sometimes consciously. It takes the form of meetings of staff to discuss and decide policy with respect to streaming or non-streaming, subject-teaching and the extension of learning opportunities, time-tabling, visual aids, and teaching methods—in fact all the subjects which come within the ambit of the professional organisation's administrative function. Examples abound in the periodical literature of such meetings being used for these purposes. Whilst of course they can be used well or ill for the purpose, the *fact* of their use is not really disputable.

But neither is the alternative method of administration of the school unknown. In this, the Head takes the decision and then seeks to implement it on the strength of the authority he possesses 'as Head'. Without denying that there may be circumstances in which this is all that is necessary, it can also be asserted that in the evolution of the school system, this may often prove to be inadequate and even ineffective unless the Head can further equip himself with more devices for controlling or disciplining his staff. The problem may be illustrated in the following way:

The Head of a medium-sized grammar school considered that there was an urgent need for supervision of pupils leaving school after the four o'clock bell because of the accident hazard on the public road outside the school. When the problem and a possible solution of more supervision were put to the staff, most refused to co-operate on the grounds that they would, thereby, assume a legal responsibility for the safety of the children after the ending of the school day. About a quarter did agree to the request, accepting that they had a professional responsibility towards the children, but even they quit after a matter of a couple of months when they found that they were going to carry the can for good and that the rest of the staff were unwilling to join them.

This case raises the question of the McGregor-like assumptions which can be held by a Headmaster, as to the motivation and professional commitment of his staff. In this case an assumption of commitment to common ends might well have been unwarranted, and the only feasible solution then becomes one of imposition of a centrally determined solution, which would contribute towards changing a professional organisation into a bureaucratic one.

It could be argued in relation to this case, that better relationship between Head and the individual staff member might have been used to reduce the problem. But more realistically, this was a problem which could only be solved if virtually all the staff could be brought, in a concerted fashion, to accept the responsibility and the objective implicit in it. In a large school, the individual approach would probably not prove feasible, and to reduce a problem of this nature would pre-suppose mobilisation of the staff as a whole in a communications and objective-setting process.

This is the major disadvantage of industry's 'management by objectives' technique, which tends to reflect the specialist and individualistic situation of the bureaucratic organisation and is therefore worked out in terms of improving communications between the superordinate and subordinate *as individuals*. This does not invalidate the principles, but in considering its application to a professional organisation, it is necessary to take into account the 'group' structure of the professionals themselves.

MOTIVATING AND TRAINING THE GROUP

By this notion of 'group' in this context is meant only that a number of the objectives in the school situation can only be realised if the teachers as a whole are brought into the objective-setting implementation and control processes, for example, in curriculum planning, counselling or time-table building. Another way of stating this might be to recognise that the staff are—as a result of training and probationary experience—capable of solving these administrative problems, provided they are given the opportunity to do so, *and* that it is essential to do so if the concept of a professional labour force is to be maintained in existence within the school system (Light, 1973; Webb, 1973).

There are practical problems in the way of doing this within the school as it is now organised. Already, the newer and larger schools are experiencing difficulties of getting staff together, either on a subject basis or a school basis. The nine-to-four mentality tends to place difficulties in the way of extending the length of the formal working day and vacations tend to be sacred cows (even if they would tend to provide no real substitute for on-the-job discussion and training). Staffing ratios tend to be so tight as to make flexibility a problem, when coupled with the elements of legal responsibility in the school's role. This leads Mather to suggest that the best way to encourage this kind of planning is for the "enlightened education authority" to provide an "occasional day closure for a school staff conference", so that "the whole staff (can) spend a day working in small problem-solving groups and . . . review developments and problems inside and outside the school" (Mather, 1968, p. 231; cf. Glatter, 1973, and Dines, 1973).

But this is only feasible and realistic if the discussions in small groups are ably and purposively directed towards the solution of administrative problems within the school. To this end, it is perhaps useful to adopt the approach implicit in McMullen's model, above. This can be amplified as an extension of the 'management by objectives' technique of private industry into the realms of 'organisational training'. Management by objectives, with its emphasis on interpersonal relationships between superordinate and subordinate, is replaced by a relationship between senior and junior professionals, each contributing ideas and techniques to a common pool with the aim of satisfying organisational requirements.

In developing the allied concepts of organisational training and staff development, it is, however, necessary to bring into the discussion the same notion of the control loop which we have noted above. It is not much use relying upon the assumption that because people know something, or even understand it, they will necessarily apply what they know or understand. But we have relied very heavily upon this assumption in the past, and because it has some validity we have got away with it. In particular, in teacher training, we have used the technique of training people to know and understand the methods of teaching and examined them at the end of it to find out whether we had succeeded. Apart from the device of the inspectorate, nothing was done to check on whether the methods learned in training were being applied. This has led to the recognition of a kind of stagnant ditch between training and the classroom-as-it-is (Rée, 1968, p. 7).

If our approach can be visualised in this context, perhaps it can also be seen in the relationship between the Head's instructions or recommendations and the teacher's performance. Where the decision is taken by the Head that a certain course of action is desirable, and this course is then recommended or 'required', some attempt may be made to train or otherwise attempt to ensure that the teacher understands what is required, and in conversation, some attempt may be made to 'examine' how well the message has been understood. The model is clearly of an open-ended sort.

Of course, we can develop a more sophisticated approach to this aspect of communications to influence behaviour. We can erect some apparatus—functionally equivalent to the development of an inspectorate—to check upon whether the decisions have been carried out in the manner intended. The model now becomes a closed-loop control arrangement, and under some circumstances it can work well. But when people are involved, this may not always be so, and the effect of the method may be to create a condition of 'cycling'—i.e. the problem runs round and round the loop. This can happen when the decision-taker is in the position where he has limited means of influence available to him, and seeks to respond to the constant error signal by applying more of the same means in an attempt to solve the problem. "I've asked old so-and-so time and time again but nothing I say to him seems to produce any effect." Heads are often in this position—or at least see themselves to be—because they cannot really manipulate the rewards of teachers or influence the man's career if he has 'settled down'. The means which managers in industry seem to possess to enable them to make their decisions stick are noticeably absent. For this reason it becomes necessary to tackle the motivation problem from a totally different angle, relying upon a different authority base, and using the professional capacity of the staff themselves to solve the problem.

Professional people (whatever may be the case elsewhere) are rarely if ever completely satisfied with the situation in which they work. If asked, they would doubtless be able to pick holes in the system, and generally express some discontent with it. Where the Head takes the decisions himself or in conjunction with the people in the office, this is about as far as it will get. If, on the other hand, he is willing to 'give away' his formal authority as a bureaucratic head of a system, he can in fact use this as a means of motivation and capitalise upon the discontent usually present in such systems. Even if this discontent is nothing more than a feeling that somebody has that something or other can be done better, it exists as a resource which can be used to good effect, with the proviso above.

Thus, the concept of organisational training becomes a process of involving the 'total group' in a process of administrative or co-ordinative decision-making, starts with the inherent discontent of the members, harnesses the motivation implicit in this, and develops as a mechanism for adapting the structure and performance of the system in accordance with the basic drives represented within it. The Head, as the representative of the wider educational system, must, clearly, play a significant part in this, or the process will become unresponsive to the external objectives, but this 'part' ceases to be one of autocratic dimensions.

STEPS IN ORGANISATIONAL TRAINING

Organising to use this approach requires that the Head shall go through a series of systematic steps to secure the objective.

1. He has to find someone who can and will act as a leader or catalyst in relation to the problem. Frequently, this will be someone who expresses doubts and dissatisfaction, but he must also be someone with enough personality, drive and professional status to be able to see the exercise through—and he must have enough time to devote to it.

2. He has to find a supporting group who will be willing to assist in the planning and implementation of the task. Where the dissatisfaction is sufficiently general, this might not prove difficult, but where a man with fire in his belly wants to get moving it may be necessary for the Head to find a supporting (if also curbing) group for him. This group may also have to receive access to resources, such as secretarial assistance, if it is going to be effective. (Giving away authority might involve giving away such assistance too.)

3. He has to encourage the group thus set up to explore the reasons for dissatisfaction, and from them to develop ideas which might help to reduce the dissatisfaction, yet still meet the objectives of the system, and prove workable and acceptable within the larger system. The Head must at this stage provide encouragement, both verbal and material, to enable the group to turn destructive criticism into constructive plans of action which will still be acceptable to others as well as the planning group. In other words, the Head cannot use the avalanche principle of delegation once the group starts work; on him really rests the onus of ensuring that the working group gets sufficient access to the others likely to be affected to get a fair hearing for their ideas.

4. As the discussions proceed and the others are brought along with the exercise, the group must be encouraged to produce a plan of action, in simple, but nevertheless, detailed terms, so that others can see it, check it, consider it against all sorts of other eventualities, and really come to some decision about it. A vague idea may look

97

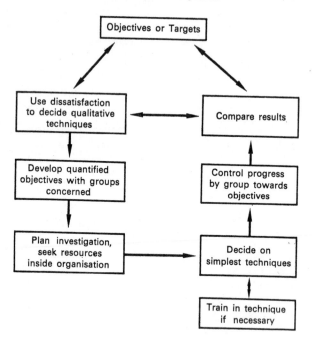

Organisational Training Model

FIG. 3.

good on paper, take up little of anyone's time in listening to it or in reading it, but it is likely to store up trouble as the 'operational' snags begin to appear on the first run through in practice.

5. When it is decided (by the system as a whole, even if still on the Head's authority) to implement the plan thus devised, there must be set up, simultaneously, a means of checking systematically on the results being obtained. There may be a lot of initial goodwill for the plan if it has been worked out in this way, but if it is implemented, and then merely assumed that it will work, it will probably create more problems than it solves. If, however, a regular means (e.g. a periodical review at least) is established to check on how it is work-

ing out, the problems which do develop are likely to be tackled constructively rather than destructively, and the modifications made as required—so that the process of decision on a system basis then begins over again.

This model differs in principles of control very little from the loops presented earlier, but it has the one major difference in that it is a system of objective-setting and performance review which is likely to prove both more relevant to the professional organisation of the school and more acceptable to professional teachers. It is also likely to prove more time-consuming and more demanding of real effort on the part of the Head and the staff to solve their administrative problems at the level of the school. But if it does, it is also likely to prove a more effective safeguard against the development of a bureaucratic system of control in the school, with all its attendant inefficiencies and problems of effective control (Merton, 1957).

REFERENCES

ALLEN, B., *Headship in the 1970's*, Blackwell, Oxford, 1968.

BARON, G. and TAYLOR, W., *Educational Administration and the Social Sciences*, Athlone Press, London, 1969.

BARRY, C. H. and TYE, F., *Running a School*, Temple Smith, London, 1972.

BENNIS, W. G., *Changing Organisations*, McGraw-Hill, New York, 1966.

BERNBAUM, G., The role of the headmaster: final report, Duplicated Report to the Social Science Research Council, London, 1970.

BIDWELL, C. E., The school as a formal organisation, in MARCH, J. G., *Handbook of Organisations*, Rand McNally, Chicago, 1965, pp. 972–1022.

BLAU, P. M., *Bureaucracy in Modern Society*, Random House paperback, New York, 1956.

BLAU, P. M. and SCOTT, W. R., *Formal Organisations*, Routledge, London, 1963.

BRECH, E. F. L., *The Principles and Practice of Management*, Longmans, London, 1963 edn.

CARTWRIGHT, D., Influence, leadership and control in MARCH, J. G., *Handbook of Organisations*, Rand McNally, Chicago, 1965, pp. 1–47.

CHAMBERLAIN, N. W., *The Union Challenge to Management Control*, Harper, New York, 1948, esp. pp. 11–48.

CLAYTON, B., Subject teaching in non-streamed comprehensive schools, in *Forum*, Spring 1969, pp. 40–42.

COHEN, LOUIS, *Conceptions of Headteachers Concerning their Role*, Ph.D. Thesis, University of Keele, 1970.

DAVIS, M. J. (Mrs.), The head in a comprehensive, in *Comprehensive Education*, Spring 1968, pp. 18–21.

DINES, PETER, Staff development in the institutional setting: a response to Dr. Eric Briault's paper, in PRATT, S. (ed.), *Staff Development in Education*, Councils and Education Press, London, 1973.

DUBIN, R., Business behaviour behaviourally viewed, in STROTHER, G. B. (ed.), *Social Science Approaches to Business Behaviour*, Dorsey Press, 1962.

FAYOL, H., *General and Industrial Administration*, Durod, Paris, 1915.

FULTON, LORD, *The Civil Service*, Vol. I, H.M.S.O., London, 1968.

GLATTER, RON, Off-the-job staff development in education, in PRATT, S. (ed.), *Staff Development in Education*, Councils and Education Press, London, 1973.

GRAY, H. L., Training in the management of education: an experimental approach, *Educational Administration Bulletin* (1.1), Summer 1972.

GREIG, D., Admin. Courses for Heads, in *Education*, **131** (1), 5 January 1968, p. 10.

HALSEY, A. H., The sociology of education, in SMELSER, N. J., *Sociology*, Wiley, New York, 1967, pp. 384–434.

HALSEY, A. H., FLOUD, J. and ANDERSON, C. A., *Education, Economy and Society*, Free Press/Collier-Macmillan, New York and London, 1961.

HANIKA, F. DE P., *New Thinking in Management*, Hutchinson, London, 1965, Chap. 1.

HEADMASTERS' ASSOCIATION, *The Government of Schools*, H.M.A., London, 1972.

HIGGIN, G., Workshops with secondary school Heads, in *Forum*, Spring 1968, pp. 28–30.

HOLT, M. J., Is unstreaming irrelevant?, in *Forum*, Spring 1969, pp. 58–59.

HUGHES, C. L., *Goal Setting: Key to Individual and Organizational Effectiveness*, American Management Association, New York, 1965.

HUGHES, MEREDYDD G., Training for headship, *The Head Teachers' Review*, Spring 1968, pp. 23–26.

HUGHES, MEREDYDD G., *The Role of the Secondary School Head*, University of Wales Ph.D. Thesis, University College, Cardiff, 1972.

HUGHES, MEREDYDD G., The professional-as-administrator: the case of the secondary school Head, *Educational Administration Bulletin* (2.1), Autumn 1973.

JAQUES, E., *The Measurement of Responsibility*, Tavistock, London, 1956.

KOB, J., Definition of the Teacher's Role, in HALSEY, FLOUD and ANDERSON (q.v.).

KORNHAUSER, W., *Scientists in Industry*, Cambridge U.P., London, 1962.

KRUISINGA, H. (ed.), *The Balance Between Centralisation and Decentralisation in Managerial Control*, H.E. Stenfert Kroese, N.V. Leiden, 1954.

LIGHT, A. J., The search for a strategy, in PRATT, S. (ed.), *Staff Development in Education*, Councils and Education Press, London, 1973.

LIKERT, R., *New Patterns in Management*, McGraw-Hill, New York, 1961.

MARCH, J. G. and SIMON, H. A., *Organisations*, Wiley, New York, 1959.

MARCH, J. G. (ed.), *Handbook of Organisations*, Rand McNally, Chicago, 1965.

MARPLES, D., *The Decisions of Engineering Design*, Institute of Engineering Designers, London, 1961.

MATHER, D. R., By process or monomania?, in *Education*, **131** (6), 9 February 1968, pp. 200–1.

MATHER, D. R., Leadership and delegation, in *Education*, **131** (7), 16 February 1968, pp. 230–1.

McGREGOR, D., *The Human Side of Enterprise*, McGraw-Hill, New York, 1960.

McMULLEN, I., Flexibility for a comprehensive school, in *Forum*, Spring 1968, pp. 64–67.

MERTON, R. K., *Social Theory and Social Structure*, The Free Press, Glencoe, Ill., 1957.

MUSGRAVE, P. W., *The School as an Organisation*, Macmillan paperback, London, 1968.

NADEL, S. F., *The Theory of Social Structure*, Free Press, Glencoe, 1957.

OTTAWAY, A. K. C., *Education and Society*, Routledge, London, 1953, 2nd edn. 1962; paper 1966.

PARKES, DAVID L., Circular 7/70 and the government of schools, *Educational Administration Bulletin* (1.2), Spring 1973.

PARSONS, T., The school class as a social system, in HALSEY, FLOUD and ANDERSON (q.v.).

PRANDY, K., *Professional Employees*, Faber, London, 1965.

RÉE, H., New school world, in *Education* **131** (1), 5 January 1968, pp. 7, 28.

SCHNEIDER, E. V., *Industrial Sociology*, McGraw-Hill, New York, 1957.

SIMON, H. A., *Administrative Behavior*, Macmillan, New York, 1947.

SIMON, H. A., *The Shape of Automation*, Harper, New York, 1965.

STINCHCOMBE, A. L., Formal organisations, in SMELSER, NEIL J., *Sociology: An Introduction*, Wiley, New York, 1967, pp. 154–202.

TAFT, R., The ability to judge people, in WHISTLER, T. L. and HARPER, S. F., *Performance Appraisal*, Holt, Rinehart & Winston, New York, 1962.

TANNENBAUM, R., The manager concept: a rational synthesis, in *Journal of Business*, 1949, p. 233.

TAYLOR, WILLIAM, *Heading for Change*, Routledge, London, 1973.

THOMASON, G. F., *Personnel Manager's Guide to Job Evaluation*, I.P.M., London, 1968.

THOMASON, G. F., *The Professional Approach to Community Work*, Sands, London, 1969.

THOMPSON, D., An experiment in unstreaming, in *Forum*, Spring 1969, pp. 56–57.

URWICK, L., *Problems of Growth in Industrial Undertakings*, B.I.M., London, 1951.

VICKERS, G., *Towards a Sociology of Management*, Chapman, London, 1967.

WEBB, PETER C., Staff development in large secondary schools, *Educational Administration Bulletin* (2.1), Autumn 1973.

WEBER, M., *The Theory of Social and Economic Organization*, trans. by A. M. HENDERSON and T. PARSONS, Free Press, Glencoe, 1947.

WESTWOOD, L. J., Reassessing the role of the Head, in *Education for Teaching* (71), November 1966, pp. 65–74.

WILLIAMS, T. A., Circular 7/70 and the government of schools: a headmaster replies, *Educational Administration Bulletin* (1.2), Spring 1973.

WOODWARD, J., *Industrial Organisation*, Oxford U.P., London, 1965.

PART 3

OPERATIONAL ISSUES

CHAPTER 7

THE APPLICATION OF MANAGEMENT PRINCIPLES IN SCHOOLS

RAYMOND JONES

1

THE school organisation is a complex of resources to achieve educational purposes. There has been an assumption that there is an acceptable size for such organisations—traditionally three or four forms in each year group. On this basis selection at 11 has ensured that no major administrative problems have been created by size. Grammar schools have been large enough to provide economic sixth forms, while modern schools have been small enough to make possible the establishment of satisfactory arrangements to meet a more complicated pattern of educational and social objectives. The administrative procedures employed have traditionally been based in the main on the personal aspects of leadership. These procedures have been informal and implicit and the concern has been to lay emphasis on the organisation as a community of people who share the same educational ideals and who have come together to work for a common purpose. The point is worth making, however, that even in small schools the administration is more formal in operation than may at first appear. An examination of the simplest school unit—the one teacher school—will reveal, if it is functioning effectively, the application of elements of management. This is illustrated by the existence of a time-table, however rudimentary, a syllabus of work, the arrangements made for delivering a lesson, the grouping of the children, and so on. Immediately there is a division of duties, even between two people, the demands on the administration become more exacting. The establishment of a common purpose becomes necessary, co-ordination becomes important and a system of communication is required. The introduction of a third person to share the duties increases the intricacy of the process of co-ordination and communication to a point where a network or pattern begins to emerge.

As a result of social pressures, schools have now increased greatly not only in size, but also in complexity with the result that the nature of the administrative functions has become a matter of concern in itself. The implications of these changes are currently receiving increasing consideration (Taylor, 1973). If an organisational pattern is not established on grounds that conform with observable principles of administration, then the system may be self-generating. Thomason (p. 38) has pointed out that it is practically impossible not to borrow hypotheses from the practice of management in organisations outside the educational system. Desirable and necessary as this may be, the problem is whether techniques of management, successful in a commercial or industrial undertaking, can be transferred to an organisation concerned with values rather than commodities. Closely related to this question is whether the skills of management seen to be necessary in the administration of a school, where the major resources and all the input material are human, are of a special kind, and whether particular training is required for them. These questions also arise from Hughes's discussion in Chapter 2 (pp. 22–23).

2

Theories of administration have obviously been extensively applied to industry and commerce and more recently theories of administration concerned specifically with educational organisation (Walton, 1959) have appeared. Nevertheless, the practising Head is unlikely to have had any special training in management and will depend to a considerable extent upon the specialist knowledge others have obtained from the study of non-educational organisations. There is a danger perhaps in these circumstances of oversimplification of the principles involved, for the preceding chapters have made it clear that these principles are in no way axiomatic. A greater danger, however, may be the failure to recognise that there are elements of management and administration common to all organisations, and that the principle for operating a typical input/output system may have a relevance for schools.

Thomason has indicated that a primary function of management must be to ensure the survival of the organisation: a response to the demands and pressures of environment. The first consideration for a school administration must certainly be to have the clearest possible conception of the educational and social purposes of the organisation and to ensure that these purposes are known to all personnel. In the stylised representation of the educational process on p. 42 the purposes are represented as both general and specific. The translation of the general purposes into specific objectives would, therefore, appear to be the next cardinal function of the administration. This process of translation will, however, be controlled by conditioning factors: these will include reference to prevailing educational theories and assumptions and the nature of local resources: environmental conditions, the catchment area, the quality and quantity of the fabric and the facilities, and, not least, the quality of the existing and potential personnel. A further function of the administration must be to identify local factors in so far as they will influence the management procedures that will be adopted to realise both general aims and specific objectives. The procedures selected must obviously be consistent with realising the aim of the system: in Thomason's model, age cohorts becoming educated persons. Conceived as a whole the procedures will emerge as a pattern or administrative structure and the establishment of such a structure on a formal basis will be a further function of the administration.

The administrative structure of any organisation must satisfy certain criteria. These criteria are well established and perhaps self-evident: the structure must be functional, i.e. it must be justifiable at all levels by what it sets out to achieve; it should make the best use of all resources both human and material; to ensure this the lines of demarcation into specialist areas should be clear and staff should be deployed within these specialist areas and their functions, in terms of actual role rather than formal position, should be sharply defined. The delegation of responsibility should be paralleled by a delegation of authority and there should be established a satisfactory co-ordinating process. The communications system within it should be horizontal as well as vertical and should establish links between groups operating in separate specialist areas. While the centre of authority should be readily identifiable and the processes employed in the exercise of it discernible, at the same time it should permit the maximum degree of individual initiative and creativity. It should provide for the most effective and economical implementation of policy decisions and at the same time provide the means for effective control of activities involved in that implementation. Finally, the structure should contain within itself procedures for self-evaluation.

3

The immediate relevance of these principles to a school organisation is clear. An assessment of the general purpose of the school, for instance, though fundamental, is not necessarily easy to make and is occasionally ignored: a comprehensive school run like a grammar school with all the syllabuses watered-down versions of the G.C.E. requirements is the result of a failure to recognise the general purpose of the school (see the case study, Neighbourhood School). This general purpose may be conceived to be social rather than academic if it should exist in a socially deprived area. Overall, the purposes of a school are established by the general will. They will in part be specific: to provide an education for each child of a certain age in a given area, but they are in the main extremely broad: to give every child an equal opportunity or to equip every child for a satisfactory career. The prescription that each child should receive an education according to age, aptitude and ability is not much more precise. The purposes for which a school is established are also variable and dependent upon the changing demands of society. If it is the communal will that a selective school should become a non-selective school then it is one of the first functions of administration to interpret what the non-selective school is intended to achieve.

It is in this concern with the general aims of the school that the administration becomes involved in external relationships. Formal links have to be established with organisations outside the school. Some will already exist: there are those with the local education authority, the governing body and the inspectorate. But the growing trend towards community and neighbourhood schools may make possible and necessary, administrative procedure for community relations: the patterns already set by schools with community colleges and some of the Bristol comprehensive schools may become general. It would be in keeping with the suggestion for extended sessions (Newsom, 1963). Appropriate machinery to establish formal contact is fundamental. A school of 2000 pupils will concern 4000 parents. A Parents Association or a Parent–Teachers Association for such a large group may not be viable. More effective contacts may be achieved through house or block. The parents' organisations would then be linked with the section of the school responsible for pastoral care. Arrangements for individual parent contact will involve the Careers Advisory Service and more than likely a counselling service. The arrangements for the operation of these within the school will need to be known by parents and links between home and school be well established and clear. A Counselling and Advisory Clinic may exist at the centre of the pattern of parent–school relationships. The whole question of reporting to parents becomes more difficult the larger and more complicated the school becomes. When a large school is organised in parallel bands or the children placed in mixed ability groups, traditional methods of measuring and reporting on children's achievements become meaningless. A form order has no significance at all. The single literal termly report may need to be replaced by a system of reporting much more comprehensive in conception and operation. The explanation of how the school is setting out to achieve its aims is the converse of the interpretation of what the general aim of the school is intended to be, and this too may make demands upon the administrative organisation. Public relations, in the strict sense, is a function of management which increasingly demands formal procedures.

The major management function must be, however, the translation of the general purposes into specific objectives and the selection of procedures to effect them. The principal objectives will initially be expressed in general terms: to satisfy the educational needs of each child—the prescription of Matthew Arnold over a century ago: to meet the economic and social needs of the community: to make the most effective use of resources and, in particular, since the major resource of the school is the knowledge, skill and dedication of the teaching staff, to deploy that staff efficiently by creating a sound system of personal relationships. Immediately these objectives must be made more precise. The pupils' needs will be divided into academic, social and communal, and personal and physical requirements. Clarifying further, academic needs will include the acquisition of knowledge and skills, the training of thought processes, the exercise of judgement and discrimination and so on. Questions concerning curricular objectives will now arise and also questions concerned with the constitution of forms and teaching groups around which the curriculum functions (see Webb, Chap. 12). Each stage of the process is the refining of the broad aims to a degree of preciseness that permits positive and, if possible, justifiable action. Under the broad term social education, the accepted objective will be to provide for the children, opportunities for responsibility for things, events and people—perhaps even policy; opportunities for service and for training in the elements of citizenship. Each child is, however, more than a sum of a set of talents and abilities or a person holding a set of school offices. There are the personal links within the school and the family, the reaction to the pressures and mores of society, the variety of emotional and physical changes that occur during a school career. A further objective of the school must be, therefore, to provide adequately for the child as a person.

The extent to which satisfying the needs and demands of society should be a major objective of the school may be debatable. Every organisation is subject to environmental pressures—local, national and international. The conditioning influences of society are present even if the school makes no formal recognition of them: a balanced curriculum must include the satisfaction of vocational desires and education for the use of leisure and these are social considerations. There can, however, be no question that teachers can be fully effective only when they recognise and accept the purpose of the whole and appreciate their part in it. The objective must be to ensure that the administrative structure provides for maximum understanding, participation and involvement. The clarification of aims and objectives is then paramount, and so is the establishment of a pattern of procedures which will be based upon observable fact as well as on value judgements.

The locale of the school must, as already indicated, have a controlling force on the structure to be set up, and so will the physical nature of the school organisation. The school established on two sites will be inhibited from employing a communications system which may be perfectly adequate for a school in one building. Large schools which are purpose-built will limit the freedom of the administration considerably: a school built in three-tier blocks of upper, middle and lower must be organised differently from a school which is established in eight house blocks. These are very obvious examples of the controlling influences of site and fabric. Less obvious is the influence on choice of procedures exerted by the nature and quality of the personnel. The amalgamation of a grammar school and modern school produces a comprehensive school of which the staff is composed of men and women whose skills by training and experience can be deployed only in certain areas of the organisation. This in fact may be a permanent problem in that teachers are trained in specialist skills and in particular subjects and at different levels. Making the best use in terms of economy, efficiency and not least

111

equity of both the physical and human resources available will also control the administrative structure that will be established. In the definition of specialist areas the lines of demarcation may, as already stated, depend upon physical factors and the qualifications of the staff or both. The existence of headship of department as an official position and the acceptance that the head of department is responsible for his or her subject suggests that the area of academic organisation must be centred around these offices. This would apply throughout the whole school, whatever the geography of the buildings. Physical and geographical factors might, on the other hand, have a conclusive influence on the arrangements made for pastoral care: a school built in house blocks would be unlikely to organise this around the year group. A campus school might only be able to make use of the house system for social and competitive purposes. The procedures adopted to achieve the same objectives would vary considerably from school to school. The common factor would be that the lines of demarcation between specialist areas should be well defined and recognisable. The next administrative function will be to deploy staff to these areas and to allocate the functions of those who are so deployed: a statement of delegated responsibilities and a statement of the levels of decision making both vertical and horizontal. As the administrative structure is delineated, the role structure of the staff becomes increasingly significant within it.

The distinction between role and position is important (Burnham, 1969). The position occupied in the school organisation by a member of staff is easily identifiable. Local authorities appoint Head teachers and assistant teachers. They are, in the secondary schools, appointed to specific subjects and only on general terms to specific positions such as heads of departments and posts with special responsibility. The definition of functions, however, is a matter for the internal organisation of the school. In practice it will mean that a single teacher, holding one official position, will assume a variety of roles. The second mathematics master will in the subject department have a part to play in the formulation of departmental policy concerning the teaching of modern mathematics: the same person, as a house-master, will be concerned with both the establishment and the operation of the links with parents if that should be one of his allocated functions. The significance of a person's role—both his conception of what it demands of him and his acceptance in the performance of his functions by his colleagues—will depend initially upon the importance the role is given in the administration through the range and level of the delegated responsibilities. These, therefore, must be specific and seen to be relevant, not only to the specialist areas into which the whole is subdivided, but also to the successful functioning of the whole.

4

An examination of the administrative structures of most organisa-tions—and this includes most schools where a structure has been established—suggests that they are hierarchical in concept and based upon the principle of chain-of-command. This will obviously be efficient in achieving many of the objectives of the school. Further-more, it is well founded on accepted practice. It has some credence in observable fact: the 'pecking order' is a fairly universal pheno-mena. Primitive and sophisticated social groups have accepted it as a principle for government and its theological basis gives it an almost divine authority. The dangers of abandoning it are expressed alarmingly by Shakespeare: "Untune that string: and, hark! what discord follows." It ought to be good enough for school organ-isations. Certainly those Heads who hold the view that the function of leadership is to decide policy and to direct the staff to the activities necessary for its attainment, would support a structure based upon chain-of-command. The existence of the hierarchical structure in small schools may not, however, be strictly relevant. The chain-of-command concept may be the accepted base of authority, but the closeness of the personal relationships and in particular the acceptance of the role of the Head as *primus inter pares* blurs the sharpness of the hierarchical divisions. The question is prompted whether in a much more complex and elaborate organisation in which the hierarchy commensurately becomes more sharply defined, the principle could and should in practice be modified. A diagrammatic representation of a school structure presented hierarchically is illustrated in Fig. 4.

Since it is a primary function of management to establish an administrative structure that is functional, i.e. with the minimum of elaboration it provides the attainment of the objectives of the organisation, then the structure should be evaluated within these terms of reference. The diagram clearly indicates the centre of authority: the areas of specialisation are defined: academic objectives within the departments, social objectives within the houses, tutorial and pastoral within the block. All are supported by the administrative personnel whose concern will be with the supply and maintenance of physical resources. The direct lines of communication represented by the continuous lines and the indirect lines of communication represented by the broken lines are clear, and the links within the chain are as short as possible. The subject teacher's immediate responsibility is to a head of department specialist in the same subject: similarly the house-tutor's immediate link will be with the housemaster/mistress. Finally delegation is made possible and in particular the importance of the middle-management emphasised.

This role of middle-management is possibly the most significant part of it. The specific delegation of responsibilities is discussed in the following chapter. The concern here is with the principles. Some of these are basic. 'Clear responsibility for' and 'clear responsibility to' is axiomatic and is a positive expression of the concept of chain-of-command. That the delegated responsibilities should help to foster both role conception and role expectations has already been mentioned. Perhaps the most important fact is that management cannot be divorced from what is being managed. The areas of specialisation within the administrative framework must be conceived not merely as subdivisions for realising aims, but also as managerial units of varying degrees of independence. The measure of independence

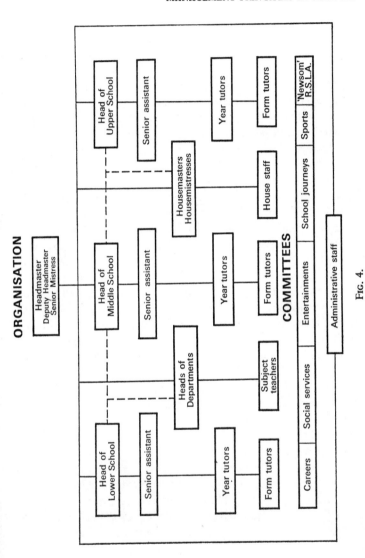

Fig. 4.

must be related to the nature of the physical and human resources available and, in turn, the level of delegated responsibility and authority must be related to the degree of independence granted. The breakdown in very large schools is often a physical factor. The first necessity is to delegate responsibilities required for the maintenance of the suborganisation. These may include discipline, behaviour, attendance, punctuality, control of public functions and assemblies: maintenance of reports and records, supervision and direction of staff, guidance and welfare of pupils and the care and maintenance of the fabric. Other responsibilities will be related to the aims of the whole. Procedures concerned with curricular objectives, operation of option groups, constitution of teaching groups and relations with outside organisations are included among these. The major difficulty is to equate the delegation of responsibility with the delegation of authority. Independence of action will be controlled by the level of independence allowed in decision-taking. To establish formally, administrative levels for decision-taking is not easy, but the effectiveness of the middle management will depend more upon this than it does perhaps on the range of responsibilities. Different kinds of decision have been distinguished by Thomason. Basically the difference is between the recurrent and routine, and the non-recurrent and those concerned with policy; furthermore, some are of limited influence, others of unlimited influence. No decision which effects the whole can be taken independently. Broadly in the school context, all routine and recurrent decisions, most decisions concerned with the implementation of policy and with the direction of activities can, and should be, delegated. Policy, procedural and judicial decisions cannot be taken independently and a system of referral is necessary. Perhaps a crucial quality of the middle manager, in a school organisation at least, is a capacity to make judgements on what needs to be referred. The conception of role once more. The more effective the administrative structure is in establishing an effective middle-management the more efficient must be the system of communication, and what is even more important the system of co-ordination.

The organisation represented in this way does, however, have certain limitations. It does not make manifest the system of co-ordination necessary—particularly if it is accepted that co-ordination is essentially collaboration, a range of reciprocal influences between individuals and groups. It is questionable whether the introduction of a formal administrative pattern of this kind into institutions which have by tradition existed as informal organisations, may in fact be a step towards bureaucracy; an intrusion into the educational world of the managerial revolution. Some of the elements of bureaucracy, as outlined by Weber, would certainly seem to be present. There is a clearly defined hierarchy of officers—heads of schools, heads of departments, housemasters, staff holding posts of special responsibility—and these are supported by the salary structure. Further, the staff holding these posts are appointed, not elected, and they are appointed on the basis of technical qualifications. They hold career appointments. Any emphasis on delegation without co-ordination contains the dangers of departmentalism. Behind it all there is the incipient growth of non-accountability. There is, however, another side of the coin. The emphasis on role rather than formal position cuts across the hierarchy of office. Apart from specialist subject teaching, technical qualifications are less important in a school than personal qualities. Schools would have to become very much larger than even the largest in existence before the independence of departments should present a problem. More significant than the dangers of bureaucracy is that an organisation functioning on strict hierarchical principles might not permit the easy expression of the innovating and creative talents of the individual staff. It might fail also to recognise the growing trend, both inside and outside the schools, towards full participation and involvement of staff. In this respect it would have limitations in meeting one of the principal objectives mentioned earlier. For in the last resort the success or otherwise of the whole organisation may depend upon the manner in which it determines such questions as how autocratic or how democratic a school can and should be.

5

The current attitude of questioning not merely the nature and source of authority, but also its need is obviously a matter of considerable concern for schools. Superficially, it is a simple matter. Authority has been accredited to the Head, and he may wield it as he will. The sources of his authority are in part contractual—derived from statute and the articles of government—in part social, conceded by the communal will both inside and outside the school—and in part personal, based upon qualities of technical competence and less tangibly as a result of possessing recognisable qualities of charisma. Put simply there is a person at the top who in turn for certain rewards accepts certain responsibilities. Parallels are easily drawn from outside the education system. But the real issue is the way authority is exercised. The universal trend, as Hughes has noted in Chapters 1 and 13, is against the expression of authority through either autocratic or paternalistic methods. This trend has come at the same time as the pressure in the schools, in terms of increased size and increased complexity, has necessitated the introduction of many more formal administrative procedures. The two must somehow be reconciled. It may be of use to recognise authority not as the source of edicts and directions, but as a flow of influence and a decision-taking function at the centre of a decision-making process. Authority as expressed in both these ways is again closely related to the conception of role. If, for instance, a head of department's authority is measured in terms of influence then it is considerable. By his influence on the methods used for teaching he will exert indirect control on facilities and staff required. The success or non-success of a subject can have repercussions throughout the whole of the curriculum.

But the real concern is the degree to which it is possible to recognise formally the desire for participation and involvement, not merely to meet the demands of 'democracy' or to maintain good personal relationships, but because it is essential to management efficiency. The problem is one of method. The procedure in the small school is built around the functions of the second master as a communication link and the regular formal meetings of the full staff. After an expression of relevant viewpoint agreement is usually reached by consensus. The system works well but with the growth of staffs to over a hundred it becomes ineffective and unrealistic. As pointed out by Davis (Chap. 8), a full staff meeting may have its purpose as a briefing session, or when matters concerned with staff welfare are under consideration; and it helps in fostering unity. It cannot, however, meet the need to involve staff. A compromise may be to set up a small group of staff, selected by virtue of experience and personal qualities, who would be regarded as representatives of the staff as a whole. Within this group, or inner cabinet, policy decisions are discussed and formulated and programmes of action decided upon. These programmes are then presented to the whole staff for comment and discussion. But unless the cabinet is elected there is the danger of establishing an 'us' and 'them' concept —the substitution of an oligarchy for an autocracy. A greater weakness is that it does not provide scope for the expression of initiative and creative impulse by individual teachers.

If the quality of the school can be no greater than the sum of the cumulative skills and talents of the staff, the administrative structure must make possible the fullest expression of those skills and talents.

Staff involvement will be most effective if it is integral to the administrative and role structure. Each functional area is the concern of every teacher in one of his or her series of collective roles. Each is a subject teacher in a department, a house tutor in a house, and a form tutor in whatever administrative or pastoral unit that has been set up. Consideration and discussion of objectives and procedures connected with the academic organisation will be centred around the subject departments. Meetings will be held at departmental and inter-departmental level. Similar procedures would operate in respect of other aspects of school life. Since every member of staff is a member of a series of groups and since every meeting is minuted and recommendations referred for further consideration or action, then participation is real, and Thomason's 'organisational training' (Chap. 6) comes to life. The dialogue between individual and individual, between group and group, and between group and the nominal authority allows every member of staff to contribute to the policy-making and decision-making process of the school. The whole question of pupil involvement can be resolved in a similar manner.

The operation of this process in practice will not limit the authority of the Head. His function is initiatory and creative. He establishes the administrative machine and lays down the lines of demarcation. He both deploys staff and allocates functions. His most important day-to-day function may consist of making qualitative judgements upon the merits of conflicting viewpoints and recommendations. He remains at the centre of the authority, but does not wield it as by prerogative.

The following diagram may represent more accurately the administrative breakdown in its operation than the hierarchical representation illustrated earlier in Fig. 4. It is consistent with the principles of management. Viewed conically it recognises the levels of authority. But the points of contact are more clear and the processes of co-ordination are implicit in the links established between groups. It may be more closely related to the conception of a school as a social organism as well as a functional organisation.

6

The acceptance of the need for formal administrative procedures and the employment of management techniques in schools again raises the question of training in administrative techniques and concepts.

The main problem is who is to receive the training and when. The respective merits and demerits of inservice and extra-service training need to be clarified (Glatter, 1973). What of the future? The case for the establishment of a staff college has been forcibly put (Michael, 1967). The essential weakness of such a college would be, perhaps, that it would inevitably limit recruitment to a few from the most able or the most ambitious teachers. But it would be wrong to

Organisation

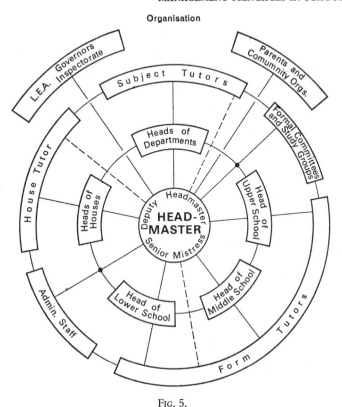

FIG. 5.

assume that what a large school requires is an administrator rather than a sound administrative system. If every member of staff must have a clear conception of role they must also possess an equally clear conception of the relationship of the role structure to the administrative procedures employed. Heads of departments are not merely subject specialists, but executives with important functions in terms of middle-management. Schools organised around the house block would demand of the housemasters the undertaking of responsibilities assumed by the Head of a small school. Further, if the

121

trend towards the greater involvement of staff is recognised and accepted, not merely as socially desirable, but in very large schools as functionally necessary, the running of these schools might well depend upon each teacher possessing a reasonable knowledge of management and administration. Professional training is the responsibility of the colleges and departments of education. If within a few years, as seems likely, the great majority of teachers will be employed in large and complex schools, it might be appropriate that every course for a Certificate or Diploma in Education should include alongside teaching methods, the sociology of education, curriculum development and so on, aspects of administration and management as they apply to schools. The main function of the teacher will always be to teach children, but to achieve the fullest level of professional competence every member of a school staff must acquire knowledge and skills that will be employed well beyond the walls of the classroom.

REFERENCES

BURNHAM, P. S., Role theory and educational administration, in BARON, G., and TAYLOR, W. (eds.), *Educational Administration and the Social Sciences*, Athlone, London, 1969.

GLATTER, RON, Off-the-job staff development in education, in PRATT, S., *Staff Development in Education*, Councils and Education Press, London, 1973.

MICHAEL, D. P. M., *The Idea of a Staff College*, Headmasters' Association, London, 1967.

NEWSOM REPORT, *Half Our Future*, H.M.S.O., London, 1963.

TAYLOR, WILLIAM, *Heading for Change*, Routledge, London, 1973.

WALTON, J., *Administration and Policy Making in Education*, Johns Hopkins Press, Baltimore, 1959.

CHAPTER 8

DELEGATION AND INTERNAL COMMUNICATION IN THE LARGE SCHOOL

M. J. DAVIS

THE Head of a large school is often asked "Has the concept of a Head teacher now become out of date? Has it become more important to be a good administrator?" No doubt most Heads would feel that both are necessary—one should be able to teach at all levels in order to appreciate the needs of the less able as well as those of the potential university scholars, and one must delegate in order to provide for the efficient working of the school and to free oneself for the complex issues and problems which demand the personal attention of the Head. As he is ultimately responsible for every aspect of school life he must see that each one is adequately covered, that the areas of responsibility are clearly defined, and that lines of communication are established in order to ensure that the Head is always well informed and that staff and pupils are not left in small pockets of isolation.

Large schools must have a bursar or the equivalent to deal with the secretarial, domestic, cleaning and grounds staff, finances and other day-to-day administrative chores. His responsibilities include the appointment and welfare of all non-teaching staff, although no doubt the Head will wish to appoint his own personal secretary. He organises the work of the school office, including arrangements for duplicating and dealing with correspondence other than that of the Head, statistical returns, and the like; he assists the Head in the preparation of estimates and is responsible for keeping accounts and

123

balancing the school budget; he deals with school lettings, he is responsible for the upkeep of buildings and grounds and the supervision of caretakers, groundsmen and their staffs; he is the chief liaison officer with the school meals service; he is concerned with transport to school in consultation with welfare education officers, and between sites if necessary, the latter involving the arrangements for availability, driving and maintenance of any school cars or buses there may be. If the bursar is also clerk to the governors he can relieve the Head of much official correspondence.

Responsibility for academic care can be directed through Head and deputy to senior members of staff who in turn organise the work of junior, middle and upper school. There are various ways of doing this, the two most popular being a straightforward division into upper and lower school, with a head of each, or a division into junior, intermediate and sixth form sections each under a director of studies. In Cirencester the triple division has been adopted.

The director of junior studies is the school's chief liaison officer with local primary schools, and in areas where there are associations of secondary and primary school Heads he is usually a member of such a body. He has the task of making contact with the pupils of the new intake by such means as visiting them in their schools, arranging for them to spend a day in their new school during the summer term, organising a meeting of parents of new pupils and conducting interviews; he receives the reports of primary school Heads and allocates new pupils to their teaching groups and houses, or other units for pastoral care, and he is responsible for passing on to house tutors or form teachers confidential information re new entrants. The curriculum of the juniors is his concern, and he should try to ensure continuity of study between primary and secondary school, so that the transition is a painless one. This can be helped by interchange of staff which he should be able to encourage.

The director of intermediate studies has to ensure that the very varied needs of pupils of this age are met by the provision of a wide variety of subject options, so arranged that they do not limit a pupil at too early an age to a narrow course of study, and the organisation of pupils into these after due consultation with house tutors or form-teachers, parents and pupils themselves; he must provide for a continuing pattern of careers guidance and visits from careers officers, and attendance at leavers' conferences, while the initiative for day release and works experience projects should come from him.

Responsibility for sixth form studies places equally heavy burdens on the director of sixth form studies, who has to deal with the complex structure of 'A' levels and general studies, together possibly with provision for one and two year 'O' level, vocational and general courses. Just as in the junior school links have to be forged with primary schools, so here approaches have to be made to colleges of education and further education, universities and the world of work. Pre-university courses, exchange visits at staff level with colleges, the continuation of provision for careers guidance, and parental contacts all come within his sphere of influence.

The delegation of responsibility for academic work goes next to heads of departments. They have the task of welding the members of staff in their departments into a team, ensuring communication and promoting understanding within the department. It is particularly important that they should establish lateral communication within their departments if working on separate sites. It is up to them to keep abreast with proposals for curriculum development, to assess their relevance to their own particular situation, and to initiate a discussion of reforms where appropriate. They are responsible for keeping within the financial estimates while endeavouring to supply the needs of members of the department. They must endeavour to maintain the quality of teaching in their subject and to ensure that staff are allocated to groups they are most fitted by temperament as well as ability to teach—they should exercise close supervision of new entrants to the teaching profession and students on teaching practice, to whom they should be ready to give help and advice if needed. Often in a large school the Head seeks the help of heads of departments in the appointment of staff.

Pastoral care is increasingly becoming the concern of houses, and the function of the house system in schools is much broader in concept now than formerly when emphasis was on the competitive element. There are, of course, other methods of ensuring that individual welfare is catered for, by the maintenance of the year group as against the house group and the retention of form teachers instead of house tutors, but the principles are much the same. In Cirencester we have adopted the house system; there are eight houses, formed by the amalgamation of a former girls' modern with a boys' grammar school house and vice versa, and in the first instance heads of houses were chosen from members of staff already holding responsibility allowances who wished to concentrate on pastoral care. The head of house is responsible for the welfare of members of his house. For this purpose a detailed file on every child is necessary, containing information on his potential, personality, background, and physical history from his primary school, records of parental contacts, progress and problems in school. The head of house may be asked to organise assemblies, he may wish to conduct school dinners, he makes provision for house clubs, and other activities in the field of drama, music or sport. Many schools now have youth leader/teachers attached to them and the house master often finds here a valuable link with the youth service to provide help and equipment for the various activities. He must promote goodwill and understanding amongst the members of his house, and can arrange for residential accommodation (particularly for first-year groups), camping, outings and the like. He allocates his house tutors to their groups in the first instance, and must endeavour to smooth over any personality conflicts between tutors and pupils. He is responsible for holding regular meetings of house staff, receiving reports from them on members of the group, and making arrangements for the smooth running of his house.

As pointed out by Jones in the previous chapter, it is essential that areas of responsibility be clearly defined and understood, and this is of paramount importance in a large school which has been formed by the merger of two or more smaller schools, and in which members of staff may be performing new roles. It is as well, therefore, to state quite clearly where responsibility lies (see Appendix 2). Equally it is important to ensure that no member of staff opts out of responsibility because he thinks that there are plenty of others to do the job for him! The most junior member of staff must always be aware that he has a responsibility as a subject teacher to his head of department or member of staff in charge of his subject to maintain a high standard of teaching and to encourage a high standard of endeavour, coupled with his duty to his head of house to be vigilant for the welfare of every child in his group. Above all he has to realise his importance as a member of staff in maintaining the standards of conduct and discipline expected by the school.

To what extent can pupils be involved in this delegation of responsibility? Many schools now believe that the status of being a sixth-former carries its own responsibilities and that the hierarchy of prefects is out of date. Senior members of staff discuss problems with them, and gain their ready co-operation and advice on how to deal with school offenders. Routine duties can be delegated to pupils of the intermediate school through the house system, and the feeling encouraged that they are expected to see that law and order and respect for school property are maintained.

How does the Head keep in touch with the ramifications of this organisation? Is he perforce in an ivory tower, a remote, impersonal figure, or can he have any closer contacts with staff and pupils? Having delegated responsibility what feed-back is there? To what extent are decisions made at the top and passed down for execution? What communication is there between members of staff and between different groups of pupils?

If delegation is to succeed, the Head must be prepared to trust those to whom he has given responsibility, and must allow them to make decisions which he must support. An efficient system of communication must therefore be established. The bursar can be left alone to cope with the day-to-day organisation of his office, but the Head will wish to check such important returns as Form 7 Schools. On the vexed question of estimates, the Head will no doubt decide departmental allocations in the light of the general financial situation, the requests of heads of departments and his own desire to give encouragement to certain new developments or to help specific needs. The deputy head is concerned with the general organisation of the school, and must be at one with the Head in all matters of policy. A daily meeting between them is essential, as are regular contacts between them and the senior master/mistress. In a large school the deputy may issue a weekly bulletin to staff, keeping them informed of day-to-day events, giving notice of courses, requests, students, visits in and out, and matters of general interest. The Head will need to meet deputy, senior master/mistress, directors of studies at regular intervals during the term to plan for the weeks ahead. At these meetings academic matters will provide the basis of the discussions—is the amount of homework fairly allocated?, what arrangements are being made for meeting of parents of each year group?, have heads or directors got complete copies of all schemes of work?, are the systems for assessment satisfactory?, when new staff are to be appointed, is there to be a change of emphasis?, has any form proved to be a disruptive element, and if so what measures have been, or are to be taken? In the light of consultations with tutors or form teachers, does any child seem to be in the wrong group and if so what action has been taken or is recommended? Have any pupils been placed on report, with what success?

The Head has direct links both with heads of departments and with heads of houses at their meetings. The former are occasions when policy is discussed and provision can be made for closer understanding by one department of the value of others. This is particularly important again when modern and grammar schools have been joined in a comprehensive system, and mutual respect must be fostered. Opinions on streaming, setting, zoning, banding, mixed ability teaching should all be aired here, so that the Head knows the force of the arguments on either side before a decision is reached. This dialogue is a two-way affair—subject teachers air their views to heads of departments, who sift and assess before in turn presenting views at this meeting. The stages in time-table construction can provide a good exercise in communication and planning—the Head and deputy may meet early in the school year to discuss policy and possible amendments, and request the time-tablers to conduct feasibility studies and draw up form structures in the light of their recommendations, for discussion. These can then be considered at one of the meetings with senior master/mistress and directors of studies, to look at the overall balance. Each director can then take the structure of the forms within his care to heads of departments to get their comments on allocations, and can settle some of the outstanding problems. Others may need the good offices of the deputy head. Revised structures can then be presented to a heads of departments meeting, and most outstanding difficulties settled by negotiation. If there are any final problems the Head must make the ultimate decision. Heads of departments can then be given the allowance of teaching periods per subject, and allocate the staff within their department, with mutual and informal discussions concerning staff connected with team teaching and interdisciplinary work. Finally Head, deputy, senior master/mistress and directors can look at the teaching pattern for every group to check that there has been an equitable distribution of the teaching force.

In some schools the houses undertake supervision duties of certain sections of the school, therefore discussions on general conduct and discipline and school uniform may form part of their agenda. The difficulties of individual pupils may be discussed, particularly if these are linked with inter-house friendships. Reports from tutors on residential courses may be available and general progress reports made, schemes for voluntary service may be mooted, and mutual co-operation arranged. As the house system as now developing in the large school is a relatively new concept, much time may be devoted to discussion of general principles and practical details, e.g. the best methods of keeping records, parental involvement, and how to introduce education in personal relationships.

Joint meetings of heads of houses and heads of departments are necessary to discuss matters of mutual concern. As each head of house is a subject teacher and most heads of departments are house tutors there is a great deal of overlap. Moreover, all are dealing with the development of the children and must unite to promote their welfare. The system of careers guidance is a case in point—in many schools the careers officer is a regular visitor and is available at certain times for consultation with house masters. The latter can consult with the director of intermediate studies to advise pupils on courses and possible careers. Another matter which affects both is the question of serious breaches of discipline. If a number of pupils misbehave in a class, to whom are they reported? If they belong to a number of different houses, the standards of punishment may vary, and moreover this may involve members of staff in attempting to deal with the classroom discipline of someone possibly senior to them, or not in their department. Open discussion of these issues can clarify the position, and show that the director of studies or head of school is the person to enforce discipline when this affects academic progress, whereas individual cases can be referred to the house master, who may know of some psychological reason for the disturbance.

If those in charge of academic and pastoral care are reporting back through their own organisation, the chain of communication should be good. It is essential that careful minutes should be kept of all meetings, that these should be published to all staff. Heads of houses keep confidential information about pupils which cannot be generally divulged. Much of this is given by education welfare officers, who visit schools daily to keep regular contact with house masters. The Head, of course, must always be kept informed—in Cirencester house communications books are kept in the Head's office in which heads of houses enter confidential comments and reports, and vice versa—and lists can be circulated to staff giving names of children about whom house masters have certain information. Heads of houses usually recommend to the Head the names of children in need of help from the Child Guidance Service, but after the official link has been made they may continue to make personal contact with the educational psychologist, again using the communications book to keep the Head informed.

However, the Head needs to have direct formal contact with the staff on some occasions. The staff meeting, when the staff numbers a hundred or so, takes on more of the appearance of a public meeting, and some schools no longer hold it. Where it does remain, it can provide an opportunity for a discussion of bursarial and other reports and general business matters proposed for the agenda by Head, deputy, or staff. It can also be the occasion for a talk on some educational topic by an outside speaker. In order to encourage the flow of ideas from those who hesitate to voice their opinions in a large meeting of this size, some Heads set up common room or staff committees. Their functions are to discuss matters informally in the staff room and act as a channel along which ideas flow from staff to Head and vice versa, arrange social functions for staff alone or in concert with parents and old students' associations, make suggestions for speakers for meetings, propose reforms to be discussed in full staff meeting, etc.

If unity of purpose is to be achieved when the staff is large, it is necessary to provide opportunities for them to meet in differing contexts, and consideration of a variety of topics by study groups can lead to greatly increased understanding and respect—staff chiefly concerned with teaching the less able may have much to contribute to a study group on the sixth form of the future, while the classicist may have some very relevant ideas on content and teaching method when devising a curriculum for those who will be affected by the raising of the school-leaving age. This understanding is essential, too, in another context, for individual members of staff must know to whom they can turn for help in their difficulties, where they can find a sympathetic ear amongst their colleagues. This applies to the day-to-day irritations and worries, while for serious problems or personal difficulties they should always be able to confide in the Head.

The more formal methods of communication must be efficient— some schools use a tannoy system, others prefer to rely on telephonic communication for immediate contact. A central place must be found for staff pigeon-holes—which should be large enough to hold circulars, catalogues, etc., without overflowing. A major problem is how to manage the bulk of paper communications, i.e. staff bulletins, minutes, memos, and the like, and to ensure that what is written is also read. Notice-boards need to be large enough to hold notices, and divided into sections so that staff know where to look to find the information they need—including a section marked 'Urgent'! Memos from Head and deputy head can be printed on different coloured paper, as can minutes of meetings, to make them more easy to distinguish. The larger the school, the more imperative it is to make sure that any changes in routine are notified through the proper channels—when pupils are taken on an educational visit staff otherwise concerned in teaching them need to know, as it does not promote good staff relations to race from a considerable distance away to take a class which may be visiting London Airport, nor does the cook-supervisor take kindly to having thirty surplus lunches. Time-table changes must be kept up to date so that one can be sure of finding Miss X in room 15 if that is where the time-table says she is, instead of any one of the other rooms scattered over the campus.

Pupils, too, need to be informed and involved in the affairs of the school. There is now an encouraging growth in the number of pupil councils, representative of different age-groups. They can allocate school funds and discuss with interested staff and Head their own suggestions for improvements and reforms. Such topics as vending machines can excite vehement comment, but more often the discussion is a considered give-and-take of opinion. The head girl and head boy, and head pupils of other sections of the school, usually meet frequently with the senior master/mistress and/or deputy head, and at regular intervals with house captains and sports captains. Those holding house responsibilities consult regularly with heads of houses. Pupils throughout the school meet and communicate with each other in a variety of ways—in tutor or teaching groups which may be mixed in ability, in house groups, and teams. House activities —music, drama, clubs, voluntary service—provide the basis for a wider involvement in school choirs and orchestras, plays, activities and local versions of 'Task Force'.

However streamlined may be the pattern of organisation and

communication, there will always be much value in informal conversations and groupings. Corners can be cut, individual initiative encouraged, provided no one is inconvenienced thereby. The delegation of responsibility should leave the Head free to attend to staff problems, to be about the school sensing the atmosphere, to be seen to be available. Far from being dehumanised or remote, if the chain of communication is working efficiently, he should be relieved of the burden of administration in order to be seen and known as a person, not dismissed as a mere business manager.

APPENDIX 1. DIAGRAM

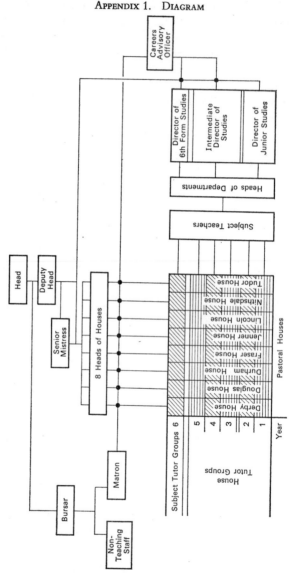

Cirencester School: Organisation Structure

Cirencester School

Position	Responsible to	Area of responsibility
Head	Governors and L.E.A.	EXTERNALLY, determining the ethos and interpreting the aims of the school to the community. INTERNALLY, framing policy and creating an atmosphere in which pupils can develop in security, staff can work in harmony; retaining the final decision in matters of policy; maintaining a balance between stability and innovation; appointing staff; delegating responsibilities as shown below.
Deputy Head	Head	Deputising for Head as required. Welfare of male staff, supervision of male students in liaison with heads of departments and directors of studies, supervision and counselling of prefects; co-ordination of all departments of academic studies and consultation with directors of studies. Structure of curriculum. Welfare and discipline of boys in liaison with heads of houses (general) or directors of studies (academic) as below. Administration of sites and general administrative duties.
Senior Mistress	Head	Welfare of female staff. General welfare and discipline of girls in liaison with heads of houses or directors of studies. Supervision of women students in liaison with heads of departments. Co-ordination of house matters. Organisation of public functions and social occasions. Supervision and counselling of prefects. Site administration and general administrative duties. (*continued over*)

APPENDIX 2 (cont.)

Position	Responsible to	Area of responsibility
Directors of Studies	Deputy Head	Working of curriculum and maintenance of professional standards within the areas under their control.
		Consultation with heads of departments on matters relating to balance of subjects within time-table structure. Organisation of internal examination time-tables, homework time-tables, and day-to-day staffing contingencies. Promotion of inter-disciplinary understanding.
Heads of Department	Directors of Studies	Organisation and internal standards of efficiency within departments, including dispositions of staff.
		Keeping abreast of new developments in teaching of subject.
		Holding regular meetings of departmental staff.
Heads of Houses	Senior Mistress	General welfare of all children in house, oversight of tutor groups, liaison with parents.
		Discipline outside classroom (including uniform).
		Social education, with E.P.R.
House tutors	⎧ Directors of Studies	Academic progress of form or group.
	⎨ Heads of Houses	Pastoral care of form or group. Informing head of house of matters reported by subject teachers.
Subject teachers	Heads of Departments	Academic standards in own subject. Class discipline. (Form teacher or house tutor to be kept informed.)

CHAPTER 9

ORGANISATIONAL CHANGE: THE PROCESS OF UNSTREAMING*

MICHAEL TUCKER

LIKE the rest of the population, teachers form three groups on matters of opinion—they are 'for', 'against' or 'don't care'. On many important issues, streaming for example, the 'don't cares' are likely to be fewer, but there is no doubt that some teachers care so little for their work that they remain cool in the face of burning issues. (I speak of teachers in other schools than my own, of course!) When a Head wishes to take up a position incompatible with the *status quo*, if he changes a policy, if he introduces any new ideas, he is likely to seem to be threatening the security, integrity and well-being of some sections of his staff. In each case he must judge the state of opinion: he is likely to find that nothing pleases everyone and whatever he decides will be opposed in some quarters. His problem, then, is to see how to minimise any harm done and balance this against the supposed gain. In making this calculation he may find the risks too great and decide to wait for, or work for, a change in the disposition of opinions. It helps if the initiative has come from among the staff. He may use the section already supporting the change to lever the rest into a more favourable frame of mind; or he may use them to isolate the opposition and compel its acquiescence—a dangerous, but sometimes necessary tactic. If he has a majority of 'don't cares' on the staff on any given

* Written in 1970, this chapter is largely a participant account, from the viewpoint of the Head, of a major organisational change taking place in a particular school. The author was Head of Settle High School, 1964–72.

137

issue he may simply notify them of the new order by pinning a memorandum to the staff notice-board; this may be acceptable and wise on a minor issue on the fringe of teachers' concern, but for a proposal for a reform that will entail major changes in class room practices, syllabuses, methods and in the school ethos in general, a good deal of work must be done to ensure *active* support; active because the teachers must decide *how* to implement the reform, what changes to make in their work. They are not merely passive receivers of new arrangements; they are required to create new teaching practices; even if they are not entirely sympathetic to the new idea, they must at least grasp its purpose and know what the new objective is. In my experience, the school that has complete backing and understanding for its stated objectives is non-existent, so the innovating Head can console himself when opposed, in the knowledge that he is likely to be merely changing the persons in opposition and that, as T. S. Eliot said, "it's good for us to change our ways of being wrong".

Comprehensive schools have been established usually because a local education authority has been influenced by vaguely egalitarian notions about the evils of selection and the need for equality of opportunity; but in rural areas, a scattered population makes it difficult to keep separate sorts of secondary schools and comprehensives have been established for expediency rather than principle. The comprehensive argument has been about selection or rejection, about segregation or integration, but in relation to social and political beliefs rather than pedagogic actualities. The confusion of ideologies that lies behind the school structure and the plain lack of any systematic discussion about aims, ends and values have created conflicts about what should be done with the children in the schools. If they are graded at 11-plus and educated accordingly in the secondary school, then selection and rejection is operating within the school and opportunity, to that extent, is reduced. Many teachers have felt for years that comprehensive schools should not "ape the grammar schools" (Pedley, 1956; *Forum, passim*) that the top 25 per cent should not form an elite within the school, the bottom 75 per cent being rejected. What Hargreaves (1967) and Partridge (1968) have found in secondary modern schools can be found in comprehensive schools and in the past few years teachers have been looking for ways to avoid stratification of pupils and to promote individuality in co-operation instead of competition. The practice of streaming is obviously obstructive of progress to these ends and its abolition has been recognised by many as a necessary preliminary to the proper development of comprehensive schools.

One of the difficulties in the way of such organisation is to agree on the common curriculum that all the children are to follow. If there are no separate streams, with their own separate regimen (languages, specialist science, etc.), then there must be a set of subjects or, at any rate, a group of staff available equally to all children. In most secondary schools this *will* mean subjects because secondary schools are usually staffed by subject specialists. Many comprehensives will have to modify their curriculum and reallocate staff resources if they change to mixed ability grouping. This, in my view, is one of the best reasons for changing, but there is a real danger that scarce skills will be spread too thinly, or that subject-oriented staff, deeply and immovably committed to training pupils for "academic" examinations, will be required to adopt methods whose rationale escapes them. One of the ways to get over this is to adopt team teaching by which pooled staff resources can be made available to all children, regardless of whose form they happen to be in. Charity James (1968) argues with immense conviction for the abolition of streams as a corollary to the introduction of interdisciplinary inquiry. Staff may find that a change in what is being learnt, a move away from the uniformity of class teaching, will make the question of streaming irrelevant. The more children learn as individuals the less attention need be given to the range of supposed ability in any groups.

Another objection to streaming is the more technical one, that it is not *possible* accurately to stream children on transfer to secondary school, leaving aside the whole question whether it be *desirable* or not. Primary schools differ in their standards and in their methods and curriculum; to line up the children on a single scale of achievement or assessment is not possible, this being the standard argument against 11-plus examinations; to assess them shortly after transfer is unlikely to give a fairer view as children often under-perform before settling down in the new school. In my own school, the children come from twenty to thirty different primary schools and a number of staff who were unmoved by the ideological arguments about streaming none the less believed it necessary to postpone the streaming for a year in order to 'sort them out properly'. However much he may be out of sympathy with this sentiment, a Head wishing to introduce mixed ability groups will recognise this as a chance to get his foot in the door, bringing the ideological forces with him. At Settle High School this was very much the position; the starting-point for reform was a high degree of agreement that first-year streaming must go, although for several different reasons. There were some who appreciated these reasons, or some of them, but considered the opposing case to be, on balance, the stronger. These were a minority and they came, in due course, to accept an obligation to go along with the others. Behind many teachers' objection to classroom reform is a real insecurity about their teaching. Most of us collect our own particular bag of tricks over the years and if we find ourselves faced with a teaching situation in which these tricks are clearly not appropriate, we are inclined to retreat behind dogma—though some, more helpfully, will accept the new situation as a challenge to their competence and see how they can meet it. The head of mathematics at Settle High School was quite sympathetic to the ideological arguments (Clayton, 1967), but felt sure that it just was not possible to teach serious mathematics to mixed ability groups. As a serious mathematician, however, he was willing to wrestle with this problem and look for possible solutions. He carried his colleagues with him and, taking small steps, they moved towards the abolition of streaming and successfully taught mixed ability classes in first forms and then in second forms.

The Mathematics Department was encouraged to take its first tentative steps by the promise that they could revert to streamed classes (i.e. cross-setting) when they needed to. They were not irrevocably tied to an untried organisation. Had they approached the innovation with ill-will, they would quickly have found it unsuitable ('I told you so'), but their stakes were not so high that they felt threatened, but were high enough to excite them to new thinking. The smaller departments had to commit themselves to a year at a time, lacking the staff to 'set' independently across the whole four forms of entry. Inevitably this entailed a good deal of compromise but there was general agreement to trying it experimentally. The argument for mixed ability groups was clinched by the support of staff of the practical subjects who had for some years taught mixed ability groups; they tended to be rather superiorly aloof from the argument as if they could not see what there was to disagree on! The social arguments weighed strongly with them and it was widely felt that because there were urgent social reasons for abolishing streaming we *had* to find ways of teaching mixed ability groups.

It is likely, however, that, in any particular situation, some will be opposed to change. At Settle High School the French Department sympathised with the social arguments but could see little advantage in trying to teach French to *all* the children. There was no alternative, however, as we did not have the staff to make independent cross-setting possible. We time-tabled French and Mathematics as sets so that if ability grouping were resorted to by the Mathematics Department the French classes would share the same grouping. In the event, the Mathematics Department did not ask for re-grouping.

The French Department's problems were reduced to some extent by two factors; one was an additional full-time teacher, the local education authority accepting my case for sufficient staff to enable a common curriculum to be offered to the new intake; the other was the introduction of an audio–visual system, because it was expected that an oral approach to French would make the subject accessible, in its first stages, to children of all abilities, including non–readers.

It is difficult to assess the value of this innovation in French teaching; one of the criteria is children's inclination to continue the study of French when they have the chance to drop it. So far we have not been short of clients for a G.C.E. course; quite the contrary in fact. Under the former arrangement of streaming, all the top stream took French willy-nilly, many nilly. This year, 1969/70, the second forms are in mixed ability groups in French, on the initiative of the Department.

The introduction of new methods of teaching can only be successful if the staff concerned are *at least* acquiescent; but it is doubtful if a Head could push this through without willingness from a good many colleagues because once the question, "Why unstream?" is answered, the question "How?" arises. A Head can recommend general guiding principles for Departments, but he cannot prescribe any detailed methods or materials and any Department can shelter from innovation behind its own specialist mystery. When the head of mathematics agreed to try mixed ability groups he prepared half a term's lessons for the first forms and provided his three colleagues with lesson notes; after that they preferred to make their own approach to the material agreed on. In this way, the whole Department was drawn actively into the experiment. After the first term, they decided to continue to the end of the year; in the summer, they decided to continue into the second year.

The impetus in the first year of the change came largely from converts and zealots and most of those keen on mixed ability groups were given them to teach and some of those opposed to the reform were kept away from the first year. Now that the new organisation is established, most staff have had a hand in teaching in mixed ability groups and some of the Hawthorne effect is wearing off. But when new staff are recruited their willingness to work with mixed ability groups and their sympathy for the idea are looked for.

As well as some conviction among the staff, the school that innovates must try to keep (or gain) the confidence of parents. Comprehensive schools are almost always creamed by selective schools and their pretensions to academic standing are suspect; their general lack of tone, style, tradition and the vague institutional solidity of older establishments make it harder for comprehensives to break new ground, especially when the change suggests egalitarianism and other communist notions! At Settle High School, the locality served by the schools is widely scattered, lacking a centre, so the parts do not cohere as a whole and it is, above all, conservative by inclination. There is little predisposition to support the idea of a comprehensive school and the more progress, as I see it, that the school makes, the more the worst fears of the pessimists are confirmed! Some parents see school as a prolonged and arbitrary interruption to the children's earning; others see school as a place where natural childish waywardness should be cured. A good deal of thrashing goes on in many of the homes. One parent at first sent his boy to a fee-paying school; he did not prosper and his father (who thought a school day well spent only when his boy came home thrashed), thought he might as well send him to the comprehensive to be not beaten for nothing, as pay for him to be not beaten! The general air of liberal, progressive egalitarian reform at Settle High School has to be continually justified to parents, so the Parents Association and the school work constantly to keep parents informed of and in sympathy with, all that is going on. Our success in these tasks is only partial.

Most comprehensives can point to equivalent disabilities in carrying the parents with them. One of the most confusing things for parents is to gauge their child's standard in relation to his age group, a perfectly proper thing to wish to do; some answer (although a misleading one) is given when a child fails or passes the 11-plus examination. If he did not take the 11-plus, then his stream at the secondary school is an indicator. Many comprehensives now take children without selection; if they then put children in unstreamed classes, the parents will lack guidance as to what to expect for their child. It is not easy to persuade parents to keep an open mind on this question and be willing to accept tentative and provisional judgements.

If, as at Settle, some children take the 11-plus examination and some do not the problem is aggravated. Some children come to Settle High School because they pass the 11-plus and are therefore not allocated to the local secondary modern school (about 25 per

143

cent of the intake); others (about 10 per cent) come because they have failed 11-plus; yet others come without selection because their parents opt for a comprehensive school (usually on the advice of the primary school that, if they opt for selection, they will fail) and the majority come without any selection procedure. Parents whose children have passed the 11-plus examination may still regret that their child is not going to a grammar school; when they find him in class with roughs and scruffs of all abilities, not even in a separate stream, their confidence is threatened. In the short term, schools can do little to convince parents; the best they can do is to get them to reserve judgement. If, after a year or so, they can see their child still happy and busy, visibly growing academically, then they will be reassured. At Settle, the parents of in-coming children visit the school during the summer term and, while their children are being shown round, I speak to the parents and deal specifically with the school's policy on streaming; it is also referred to in Notes for Parents sent to newcomers before the meeting:

> In their first year children go to a Form—1 North, 1 South, 1 East or 1 West. In this group of about 30 they take their lessons in the first years; later, children go to sets for some lessons, groups are arranged according to progress. Special arrangements are made to help children with serious learning difficulties.
>
> So children are not 'streamed' on entry at 11-plus. It is hardly possible to do this justly. Children have such diverse abilities and interests, it is wrong to grade them at an early age and try to foretell their future development. Furthermore, children must learn a good deal more in school than information about subjects. They must learn to value and understand others; clever or foolish, weak or strong, good or bad, children must have the chance to come to terms with human diversity. It is diversity that is encouraged in mixed ability classes (as opposed to 'streams' or 'sets').

The Parents Association held a meeting about streaming after the first year of change. This was because I knew some parents were unconvinced and suspicious that this new arrangement was a part of the Socialist Government's plot to snatch their children's rights from them. Many were genuinely confused and had not grasped that,

because children take their lessons together, they are not all limited
to the same level of achievement. I do not think the meeting changed
anything greatly. It was valuable simply because it demonstrated a
willingness to explain, a willingness to be questioned and scrutinised.
But the proof of a pudding is in the eating: of the 1965 intake nearly
80 per cent chose to stay on after the age of 15 years and much of
their work, particularly in C.S.E. courses, is of a high standard.

Other areas have other problems and, where neighbouring schools
compete for parental support, the balance between the traditional
and the expected on the one hand and the new and original on the
other hand is very hard to strike. An insecure, rising middle-class
parent body is likely to be difficult to move along progressive lines;
if the clients simply vote with their feet, the school will have to take
account of this.

An advantage we enjoyed at Settle was that all the children came
without exception from unstreamed primary schools; none of them
is big enough to be streamed. So the children were used to a degree
of individual work and to sharing activities with children of all
abilities. On the whole, I think the children at the High School
prefer the unstreamed classes on social grounds, but this is hard to be
sure about as they cannot make valid comparisons. The second forms
have been grouped for French, but the children prefer their 'normal'
house grouping (i.e. their mixed ability groups) in which they take
all their other lessons, because they have most of their friends in
those groups: friendships within the mixed ability groups certainly
seem to be influenced by social and academic factors, but by no
means exclusively so. What is more important, however, is their
attitudes towards children different from themselves who are not
their friends. An unstreamed, co-operative school is likely to allow
more positive attitudes to develop: there will be less jealousy,
resentment, hostility, snobbishness and fear. In this context Liam
Hudson has made a point which is worth considering. "My own
suspicion", he remarks, "is that progressive schools do make most
children happier than authoritarian ones; but that they withdraw
from children the cutting edge that insecurity, competition and

145

resentment supply. Here the progressive dream comes home to roost. If we adjust children to themselves and each other, we may remove from them the springs of their intellectual and artistic productivity. Happy children simply may not be prepared to make the effort which excellence demands." This surmise seems to me mistaken, but if such a view is held by some of the staff, the administration must take this into account.

Apart from passes in General Certificate of Education examinations, we have few criteria for measuring our success or failure that will mean much to the parents, the children or even the local education authority; all the other criteria such as 'drop-out' rates, behaviour problems, degrees of participation and co-operation and so on, are beside the point in most observers' view. As schools introduce more Certificate of Secondary Education courses, the question of confidence among clients becomes more urgent. The movement towards unstreaming has gathered momentum in the past five years, during which time the C.S.E. has been established. It remains to be seen whether or not C.S.E. can take its place beside 'O' level, but it is essential for the full success of unstreaming that it should do so. If pupils are to be encouraged to work as individuals they cannot be 'prepared' (i.e. processed) for G.C.E.; the appropriate examination for children educated in unstreamed classes is continuous assessment of work in a Mode 3 syllabus which is in the nature of a statement of intent. In this way teachers are free to move with the pupils' unfolding interests and abilities. But this puts great responsibility on the teacher and requires confidence in the system from parents. Until the good results come in, as I believe they will, parents' doubts about mixed ability groups will be strong and will tend to be reinforced by the reduction of the place of 'O' level. They will see C.S.E. as a 'lower' alternative to 'O' level, as indeed it is in the sense that it is open to children whose range of achievement at 16 is such that an 'O' level syllabus is out of their reach.

There is the further difficulty for parents that with the introduction of mixed ability groups, the formal class order of merit, the actual competitive exams, the prize-giving—all the traditional paraphernalia of school competition—is likely to go. So familiar points of reference that help a parent to chart his child's way through school are no longer apparent. Schools must be willing to provide other information—less definite, more complex, much harder to convey and parents must be willing to grasp this. The school report must be phrased with reference to the child's own standard and the teacher and the parent must co-operate to relate this to the child's potentiality. This may still mean "must try harder", but the objectives will not be the same simple steps up a ladder of marks. Increasingly teachers will accept the child's failures as their own. A fairer comment than "lacks effort" is "I've failed to stimulate him sufficiently", or, even "my errors of judgement have impeded his development; I will try harder"! But even if teachers were willing to report in these terms, I do not think parents are yet ready to use such reports and I cannot imagine that children ever will be.

When a familiar frame of reference is dismantled, however useless or obstructive or null it has been, some people are likely to consider themselves adrift, lacking direction. This is very likely to occur if they have previously been adrift anyway, but have for the first time had to recognise the fact. Close personal links between children and teachers can be the only replacement for the marks, orders, etc. Teachers must really know their pupils as individuals and must be skilled in assessing their needs and potentialities, at least in the short term. Many teachers have been accustomed to seeing their pupils as material for various courses and examinations rather than as individuals; this is most often the case in grammar schools and may account partly for the negative attitudes to themselves and their schools found by Frank Musgrove (1964, Chap. 6) in grammar school pupils, and to a markedly lesser extent in modern school pupils.

The view we have of ourselves as teachers, what we expect of schools as institutions, will have to be changed if we are to enable pupils to work, think and act as individuals. This may well be the most important aspect of all in organisational change in the comprehensive school.

REFERENCES

CLAYTON, BRIAN, 'Mathematics at Settle High School', *Forum* **9**, 40–42, 1967.

HARGREAVES, DAVID H., *Social Relations in a Secondary School*, Routledge, London, 1967.

HUDSON, LIAM, *Contrary Imaginations*, Penguin, London, p. 134, 1967.

JAMES, CHARITY, *Young Lives at Stake*, Collins, London, 1968.

MUSGROVE, FRANK, *Youth and the Social Order*, Routledge, London, 1964.

PARTRIDGE, JOHN, *Life in a Secondary Modern School*, Penguin Books, London, 1968.

PEDLEY, ROBIN, *Comprehensive Education: A New Approach*, Gollancz, London, 1956.

ROSS, J. M. *et al.*, *A Critical Appraisal of Comprehensive Education*, National Foundation for Educational Research, Slough, Bucks., 1972.

CHAPTER 10

CHANGE IN THE SIXTH FORM

H. G. JUDGE

1

SO FUNDAMENTAL have been the recent changes affecting it, that a recognisable institution called 'The Sixth Form'—and even the name itself—will probably not survive the seventies. Description of these changes, analysis of their causes, discussion of responses to them in the fields of curriculum and organisation, speculation upon the policies now to be adopted, may therefore offer valuable insights into many of the problems which administrators, inside and outside schools, have not yet solved. The debate arouses passion, for it concerns a characteristically English invention and adaptation (even the Scots know little of it) which embodies many unspoken or whispered assumptions about academic excellence, or the meritocracy, or responsibility, or even the British Empire. To talk about the sixth form is to talk about the development of public education in England and Wales in the first half of the twentieth century.

Such talk has been given a new urgency in recent years when political, social and economic pressures have been stronger than ever before. The great urge behind comprehensive reorganisation has been the public demand for equality. Sixth forms have not only grown, but grown in some surprising directions in response to this demand. At the same time, the massive reorganisation of the secondary school system in a comprehensive pattern has (for obvious reasons) tended to disperse sixth forms and to raise intricate problems of cost and effectiveness which are becoming increasingly more urgent. The situation of the sixth form is a deeply uneasy one. It provides the main bridge between a system of education

149

which, for pupils up to the age of 16, is broadly comprehensive in its assumptions and one which, for students from the age of 18, is sharply selective in its methods. The sixth form will be, after the imminent raising of the school leaving age, the only part of the maintained primary and secondary system which is 'voluntary' (that is, in terms of enrolment) and is, in this sense, curiously isolated.

Nobody, I think, was very worried about sixth form organisation in the early 1950s. The warm, familiar assumptions still prevailed. The sixth-formers upon whom Arnold lavished his care still had their spiritual successors, in public and grammar schools and in the new comprehensive schools which did not yet dare to be too different. They were, at least in theory, set upon the high road to university; they were, unlike their juniors at home or their contemporaries abroad, engaged in the specialised study of a few subjects; they were expected to undertake a good deal of unsupervised work; they enjoyed a special relationship with teachers who were happy to approach them as honorary equals; they accepted a wide and satisfying authority over younger members of the community of the school. They were a privileged and responsible minority—the few who had the ability, the domestic support and the determination still to be in full time education at the age of 17 or 18 (Crowther Report, 1959).

Where are they now?

2

Their disappearance is more easily detected than explained. The paradox that universities have become, for sixth forms, both more and less important has contributed much to the dissolution of the traditional sixth. Competition for university places has sharpened as the demands of sufficiently qualified candidates have remorselessly outpaced the supply of university places. A binary policy may be economically or administratively desirable, indeed inevitable, but as long as greater public prestige is accorded to universities than to polytechnics or colleges of education (and correspondingly more generous public investments made in them) then there will be a scramble for university places. At the same time, the expanding exercise of university admission and the importance of achieving public fairness have stimulated the elaboration of a national system of university admission, administered by the U.C.C.A. That system depends—and will, for the foreseeable future, depend—upon linking offers of university places to a stated performance in an 'A' level examination yet to be taken. This imposes upon teacher and student the necessity of securing such a result by all fair means, and is deeply hostile to a more generous and relaxed approach to sixth form studies. A digression—and that is what so much of the best traditional teaching was—becomes immoral. For October 1969 113,110 candidates applied for places and some 54,300 were admitted.

But as the objectives of the sixth form are being sharpened (two A's and a B), they are being blunted by the arrival of more students without university ambitions who have to be sheltered under the same umbrella of curriculum and organisation as the most able. The sixth form is becoming, at one end, more specialised (in getting high 'A' level grades) and at the other, more diverse. After all, in the school year 1965/6 only 25 per cent of those who left at the age of 17 or above in fact went to university, and although (taking the country as a whole) only 15 per cent of sixth formers are engaged in courses other than 'A' level, the corresponding figures in areas where comprehension has developed further suggest that here will be a sector of spectacular growth (Schools Council, Working Paper 16). Sixth-form planners are therefore perplexed by the apparent necessity of marching in the two directions at the same time.

This is not their only puzzle. Perhaps, in the currency of educational discourse, no word has depreciated more rapidly than 'specialisation'. Even its defenders have retreated into the more mysterious expression, 'study in depth'. The depreciation can be related to a conviction that an early choice is often an unwise choice, to a belief that in an increasingly comprehensive system choice for all should be kept open for as long as possible, to the doctrine that an educated man or woman must not be allowed to abandon literature or mathematics at the tender age of 15, to the proposition that our economic and cultural need is for generalists and not specialists (up to at least first degree standard) or to the observation that our present system accelerates an alarming flight of the young and able away from science and technology towards the undemanding attractions of the humanities or the social sciences. There is no longer that confident belief in specialisation to serve as a basis for sixth-form planning.

As most new, and some old, universities have advertised their own disenchantment with orthodox specialisation so another element in the traditional understanding of the nature of the sixth form has dissolved. It was possible, until quite recently, to argue that the two years of a sixth-form course and the three years of an honours course together composed one educational programme. Such an interpretation loses force when so many university courses start from the assumption that the subject approach is no longer relevant. 'Continuity' makes most sense for such Gladstonian subjects as mathematics and classics, and least for social sciences or regional studies.

The more the sixth form emphasised its functional identity with university education and university methods, the more it stressed its methodical distinction from the rest of the secondary school. This distinction was often emphasised when sixth-formers were initiated into their novel status by the Headmaster: on the one hand the free inquiry, discussion, independent study of the sixth and on the other the factual, didactic, class-based instruction of the fifth and all that had preceded it. The distinction has become less real as the primary school revolution (disliked or admired, the most significant contribution by Britain to educational development since the war) has profoundly modified theory and practice in the 11–16 sector. 'Subjects' have become less rigidly defined (or even, in an excess of mindless zeal, allowed to disappear); Nuffield and other syllabus reforms have shifted the emphasis from instruction to inquiry; the class, as a perpetually stable teaching group, has been both broken up and enlarged (for example, in team teaching); the new technology (in programmed learning, in television, in audio-visual language teaching) has displaced the teacher from his role as sole dispenser of information; the textbook has either perished or changed its appearance and purposes. The cumulative effect of all these changes has been to soften the transition from main school to sixth form, and therefore to dilute that sense of peculiarity, superiority and confidence, which was one of the undoubted marks of the sixth form of the past.

The associated sense of enjoying a monopoly has also disappeared. The growth of further education has raised new and awkward questions about both the nature and administration of the sixth form. Even the most arrogant Headmaster (and we still have some) can no longer assume that all real education for the 16–19 age group goes on in sixth forms, and that technical colleges exist only to provide a second-rate vocational training for the less clever or an alternative route to 'A' level for the eccentric minority who cannot accept the standards of a sixth form (that is, who wear long hair or smoke), for those whose parents can no longer afford the rising fees of an independent school, or for those of riper years who discover in themselves 'A' level ambitions. For every three 17-year-olds still in full-time education in schools, one is in full-time education in colleges, and as the pressure for a more extended general education mounts, as the need to husband scarce resources secures wider recognition and as the traditional definition of the sixth form is steadily emptied of meaning, so unanswered questions about the relationship of sixth form and of further education will demand resolution.

Other powerful changes have affected the sixth form. The national debate (if a heated exchange of prejudices may qualify for that description) on 'comprehension' initiated in the early 1960s gave way after Circular 10 of 1965 to technical, and possibly more fruitful, discussion of just how the abolition of selection at 11+ could be applied in each area. A sixth form in a 14–18 school is simply not the same kind of institution as one in an 11–18 comprehensive school. The balance between older and younger pupils is adjusted, and questions of both curricular and pastoral organisation placed in a new context. When the sixth form is removed altogether, into a separate establishment such as a sixth-form college where no younger pupils are present, then even more fundamental changes are imposed. Even where major surgery of this kind is neither needed nor wanted comprehensive reorganisation, by dispersing into several secondary schools the more able 11-year-olds previously concentrated in the selective grammar schools, never fails to challenge the traditional sixth form—both by widening, at first only by implication, the criteria of admission to it and by forcing administrators to calculate whether each secondary school can be allowed to have 'its own' sixth form. If some comprehensive schools do not have their own sixth forms (although, in nearly everybody's book, possession of a sixth form was until about 1967 the undoubted proof of scholastic virtue), then what are the implications for them and for the schools who *do* have sixth forms?

Any catalogue of the forces of change must be incomplete, but perhaps enough has been said to define in general terms some of the problems of sixth form administration in the 1970s. The pressure of the universities has, so far at least, been the most influential and most readily identifiable. It has narrowed and corrupted many of the traditional aims of sixth-form education. At the same time, sixth forms have enlarged their objectives by including a steadily growing number of young people who have neither the ability nor the wish to pursue their studies into a university: new courses and new approaches have been needed. That specialisation which has been the defining strength of the sixth form is being deeply criticised both as undesirable in itself and as a contributory cause of a disproportion of arts and science students so serious that our economic and cultural survival is at risk. Change in the universities has dimmed the vision of an underlying continuity between two years of sixth form and three years of Honours degree work, while change in the main school has drained the reality from the contrast between the 'preparation' of forms 1–5 and the 'fulfilment' of the sixth. The growth, in numbers and importance, of the further education sector obliges the sixth form to understand both the similarities and the differences which obtain across the frontier, while comprehensive reorganisation has removed the logistic prop from the sixth form of the past.

These changes demand attention and action (which will be outlined in section 3 of this chapter). It may, moreover, be that observers enjoying the triple advantage of distance, hindsight and a sociological education will relate these challenges to a more profound disenchantment with grammar schools, and *a fortiori* with sixth forms, as the instruments of an unrepentantly bourgeois and meritocratic culture. Sixth forms existed so that the children of the poor and of the lower middle classes could insert themselves, by ability and application, into privileged positions in the social hierarchy. But high academic standards were not (yet) enough and therefore, notably through the prefect system, grammar schools emphasised middle-class values (nice accents, no ice-creams in the street). This caricature of what dismayed the critics recalls Orwell's prophetic attack upon

> ... the outer suburban creeping Jesus, a hangover from the William Morris period, but still surprisingly common, who goes about saying 'Why must we level *down*? Why not level *up*?' and proposes to level the working class 'up' (to his own standard) by means of hygiene, fruit juice, birth control, poetry, etc. (1937).

The argument is given greater subtlety by Professor Hoggart, and dignified by research by Messrs. Jackson and Marsden (1962), but its lineaments are recognisable. In this kind of middle-class missionary enterprise (the extension of the advantages of the public school to the pupils of the grammar school) confidence has collapsed, and the sixth form got buried under the ruins.

Some will accept and like this interpretation; others accept and dislike it; many neither accept nor like it. But if this interpretation of change in the sixth form is rejected with the rest, the statistical facts stand. In 1947, 5·5 per cent of 17-year-olds were enrolled in full-time secondary education in England and Wales. Ten years later, by 1957 (at the time when the Crowther Report was being prepared) the proportion had risen to 9·23 per cent. In 1960, it was 11·09 per cent, in 1965, 13·79 per cent and in 1970, 20·00 per cent (cf. Schools Council Working Paper, No. 45, p. 37). Increases of this scale and pace impose great strains upon the institutions which bear them.

How, in terms of curriculum and organisation, are these institutions responding?

3

In the 1950s, and in a country which prided itself on having no national control of the curriculum, the pattern of sixth form studies was in fact dominated by the G.C.E. 'A' level examination. It still is. An examination which was intended to introduce more flexibility and width into the sixth form had, ironically, the opposite effect. G.C.E. came to be regarded as an examination in two unrelated stages: the fullest possible range of subjects was taken at 'O' level by the student at the age of about 16 and three subjects were then taken at 'A' level two years later. These 'A' level subjects were, moreover, in nearly all cases drawn from one group of subjects—either in Arts or Science. There were eloquent critics of these arrangements, and by a process of national persuasion and local action administrators introduced changes. Students were, in some cases, encouraged to regard the G.C.E. examination in the light of its original intentions and were not automatically required by the schools to take the same subject at both 'O' and 'A' levels; significant resources of teaching and time were applied to sixth-form minority studies, in which interests unrelated to examination objectives could be pursued; many more students were allowed by time-tabling arrangements, and encouraged by counselling, to study 'A' level subjects drawn from both the Arts and Science sides. Administrators within the schools have therefore gone as far as they can within the existing framework to introduce more variety and contrast into the sixth-form curriculum. They have not yet begun, on any appreciable scale, to provide adequate courses for that increasing number of students for whom 'A' level is quite inappropriate. Many of them (and they already number 19 per cent of all sixth-formers) remain in the sixth form for only one year, and spend most of their time mopping up a few extra 'O' levels or otherwise redeeming their misspent youth. The three most urgent questions about the sixth-form curriculum therefore are: What pattern should be provided for the successors to our present 'A' level students? What should be provided for those who, in growing numbers, will be welcomed into the sixth form after taking the C.S.E. examination but without wishing to qualify for higher education, or to spend more than one extra year at school? How should these two patterns be related?

A summary of the attempts now being made to answer these questions must be obsolescent as well as inadequate but one new principle related to the process of discussion and decision does emerge. For the first time, there exists in the Schools Council a body which may claim to represent all the national, local and professional interests which have a clearly defined concern with what should be taught and to whom. In the past, such practical decisions drifted out of some kind of university consensus on what the content of sixth-form education should be, and was mediated through the old Secondary Schools Examinations Council and the University examining boards to be interpreted, with more or less skill, by small-scale administrators operating the curriculum and the time-table of each particular school. Those days are past. The proposals which have emerged from the Schools Council reveal the difficulties which surround the process of framing a new decision on the sixth-form curriculum and illustrate the different assumptions which are made, even in the highest quarters, about the importance of providing *one* framework for all varieties of sixth-form studies or about the value of specialisation. The first publicly proposed reform specifically limited itself to the kind of student already taking a two-year 'A' level course. By implication, some different provision would need to be made for the one-year student, or for the less able. A failure to take the full importance of this point was perhaps the major weakness in Working Paper No. 5 (1966), which proposed that major (not more than two) and minor subjects should be taken together. This suggestion gave offence to those who championed traditional specialisation, as well as to those who disliked the failure to provide for "the new sixth former". Further uneasiness was caused by the realisation that an elaborate pattern of this kind would require even larger sixth forms—which many existing schools would be unable to provide.

The Schools Council proposals were therefore refined to produce, in Working Paper No. 16 (1967), a two-'A'-level pattern, with the addition of 'electives'. Electives were not, indeed could not be, precisely defined since the schools were to be allowed the major part in determining their content. An elective course was to last, in general principle, for one year and would be open to students of modest ability not including 'A' level in their programmes. In the course of 1967 and 1968 the universities, fortified by the Report of the Dainton Committee (1968), urged upon unenthusiastic schools the advantages of a four or five subject course and examination, while ignoring, as they were entitled to do, the whole problem of providing for the growing majority of sixth formers who would not proceed to universities. The Headmasters' Association, in a contribution which admirably summarised all these and other developments (1968), protested at the folly of trying to contain all sixth-form courses within one rigid curricular framework and sought to win freedom by forging more chains in suggesting the introduction of a *third* G.C.E. level, between 'O' and 'A', to be called Intermediate: this would be for some students their final school examination, while for others it could be a stage on the progress to 'A' level in a specialist subject or a final stage in a supporting or contrasting subject. 'O', 'I' and 'A' would provide a variety of examination objectives, among which the student (well advised, no doubt) would choose and for the study of which the school would have to make highly complex and flexible arrangements. Other proposals have been made, at least tentatively: a general examination for all sixth-formers, with an American-type college entrance board examination specially designed for the university candidates superimposed upon it; a final public examination for all those still at school at the end of Grade 6 (the lower sixth) with a final Scottish-type year of pre-university specialisation for a minority of undefined proportions.*

Whichever (if any) of these patterns is adopted, the decision will have immediate consequences for the organisation of the sixth form. Indeed, some of them would make it impossible for many schools to maintain a sixth form at all, while others would make it difficult for any sixth form to be run separately from 11–16 schools. Change in the organisation of sixth forms will be accelerated and schools will continue, as throughout the 1960s, to re-examine the relationship between sixth-form student and lower-school pupil. The expansion of the schools, and perhaps a growing distaste for the more authoritarian versions of responsibility implied in the traditional prefect system, will force teachers to modify the system of responsibility and control. Do we, to express the choice in deliberately naïve terms, want sixth-formers to be a uniformed example to their juniors fully integrated with them in one community? Or do we intend to contrive for them a transition from dependence to independence, with more freedom to define their own social patterns without uniform, and with extensive control over 'their own' part of the school buildings? It is doubtful whether we can, for long, go on having it both ways.

* The above briefly summarises the Q and F scheme, discussed and rejected by the Schools Council in 1970. The debate continues, and is now centred on the revised proposals of the Briault and Butler Working Parties (Schools Council, 1973). A one-year Certificate of Extended Education course is proposed for students of modest ability, and a two-year course of five subjects at Normal and Further levels for the more academic. The attempt to design a single structure, applicable to the whole range of ability, is thus abandoned (*Editor*).

Nor is it easy, once the harmless platitudes about participation have been uttered, to predict just how a new machinery of staff and student co-operation will operate. Sixth-formers will, through councils and committees, be involved in resolving a whole variety of questions about the standards to be expected of them, about the expenditure of funds assigned to social purposes or about the use of their own common-room areas. At present, most Heads would neither wish nor expect them to have any voice in drafting the policy of the school in terms of teaching or examinations. Is it self-evident that a clear and successfully defensible line can be drawn between coffee and curriculum? Heads who move from a generalised belief in the values of participation and involvement towards adopting a machinery for consultation will need to define quite clearly and in advance just what functions are to be assigned to that machinery, if the whole process is not to sink into the agonised confusion which has marked so much of staff/student relationships in higher education during the 1960s. These same Heads will, moreover, need to re-examine the whole process of decision making within their schools, and in particular to redefine (or perhaps define for the first time) the part of other teachers in that process. The demands of sixth formers to be consulted on matters lying within their competence are already being matched by the demands of teachers, with all kinds of responsibilities in schools, to share in the making of decisions lying within their competence. It is an urgent task for Heads to understand these demands, to respond to them and to incorporate them within the framework of government. Any apparent alliance of Head with students against staff will be resented bitterly and with good reason. It is important, simultaneously, to ensure that teachers are properly represented in all places (including governing bodies) where decisions affecting their work are taken, and that sixth-formers are fully involved in those decisions affecting their place within the community.

They must also be allowed, within the given framework of curriculum and organisation, to make proper and well-informed decisions on their own course of studies and educational objectives.

As numbers increase, so the tasks of providing adequate advice become more burdensome and more specialised. Each individual decision has to be enlightened by expert advice, and neither the traditional house organisation of the 11–18 school nor the traditional sixth form master is adequate. Each sixth-form student needs a tutor, concerned with no more than a handful of students in each generation, who is equipped by experience and temperament for the task of advising and informing. Such tutors need the support of a well-staffed and equipped advisory service, offering information on careers and educational opportunities beyond sixth-form age.

This section has discussed the effects of some of the profound changes in the sixth-form situation upon curriculum and organisation. Some of these effects will be sharpened in a sixth-form college, or any institution which deals exclusively with students over the age of about 16. The organisation of courses will have to be self-sufficient, and cannot depend for staffing or facilities upon the provision made for younger age groups. The national popularity of such colleges will therefore depend in considerable measure upon the type of curriculum adopted for this age group. Counselling and pastoral arrangements will need to be highly sophisticated if they are to provide adequately for young people who will be members of the community for only one or two years and who will have joined it at what is acknowledged to be a vulnerable and uncertain age. Administrators will not be able to evade or obscure the issues of participation and consultation, which will inevitably be articulated in the context of student/college and not that of pupil/school. Sixth-form colleges already are, and increasingly will be, the laboratories in which the most fundamental questions of organisation and curriculum will be exposed and attacked.

The last few years have seen a new crop of consultation and co-operation between schools and colleges of further education. There are, inevitably, dogmatists who believe either that all 16–19 education should be in schools or that it should all be in further education colleges, but such flat and noisy contradictions are irrelevant to our present problems: the most urgent administrative task is to mobilise the resources which the public system has available for this demanding and expensive age group. Where colleges and schools exist in partnership (as they now do in many areas of the country) machinery has to be created to make that partnership effective, to ensure that educational plans are held closely in line and that students choose their courses in the wisest possible way, with the fullest possible information. Such machinery has to be sensitive enough to respond to changing patterns of curriculum within the school, to changing demands of industry and the community upon the college, and to a prompt understanding of the shifting division between general and vocational education. It has to include arrangements for joint time-tabling and for the sharing of staff and accommodation.

A study of recent developments may, indeed, prompt the conclusion that the days not only of separate sixth form but of the administratively autonomous school are numbered. The I.L.E.A. Report on 'Sixth Form Opportunities in Inner London' (1968) illuminated the difficulties of continuing to regard every school as 'equal', with an equal right (and even duty) to develop an ever widening range of sixth-form courses at ever greater cost. If schools and colleges need to be grouped, then schools often need to be associated with one another. If these arrangements are to proceed beyond generalised goodwill, awkward but inescapable questions of authority and control will have to be answered. If, to take one simple example, all 16+ courses in a town are to be concentrated in one school (whether or not that school maintains its own classes for 11–16 year olds) what then ought to be the relationship between the educational strategy of that school and all those contributing students to it? Should the head of the mathematics department have no more direct responsibility than the head of a secondary school department has for the teaching and development of his subject in the contributory primary schools? It may well be that the major problems of sixth-form organisation in the 1970s and 1980s will be problems of area management rather than school administration.

4

No educational institution has changed so much in the last decade as "The Sixth Form" and none has presented more intriguing problems of curriculum design or of internal school organisation. The final form of the answer to many of these problems will depend upon characteristically British interaction of decisions, and national non-decisions. A curriculum pattern, or more plausibly a not wholly inconsistent variety of curricular patterns, will emerge at national level from the long negotiations of the Schools Council. The application of that pattern, with all its implications for the size, organisation, and even age range of "sixth forms", will be modified by political decisions about the pace of reorganisation, or the scale of resources to be committed to this one sector of the educational enterprise and to that enterprise as a whole. The form which that pattern will take locally will depend not only upon the imminent and fundamental reform of local government but also upon a network of local demographic, economic, social and cultural factors. The task of the school administrator at the lowest level is to make what sense he can of the changes, to anticipate as well as he can the effects they will have upon the sixth form he knows best, to interpret as carefully as possible the national and local decisions by which his own policy is circumscribed, to refrain from following any policy (however personally seductive) which may be irreversible, and to remember that the most important students are those in the sixth form today.

REFERENCES

CROWTHER REPORT, *Fifteen to Eighteen*, H.M.S.O., London, 1959.
DAINTON REPORT, *Enquiry into the Flow of Candidates in Science and Technology into Higher Education*, H.M.S.O., London, 1968.
DEPARTMENT OF EDUCATION AND SCIENCE, *The Statistics of Education*, H.M.S.O., London. (Published in several parts for each year.)

FLOUD, J. E., HALSEY, A. H. and MARTIN, F. M., *Social Class and Educational Opportunity*, Heinemann, London, 1956.

HEADMASTERS' ASSOCIATION, *The Sixth Form of the Future*, London, 1968.

INNER LONDON EDUCATION AUTHORITY, *Sixth Form Opportunities in Inner London*, London, 1968.

JACKSON, B. and MARSDEN, B., *Education and the Working Class*, Routledge, London, 1962.

ORWELL, G., *The Road to Wigan Pier*, Gollancz, London, 1937.

OXFORD UNIVERSITY DEPARTMENT OF EDUCATION, *Arts and Science Sides in the Sixth Form*, Oxford, 1960.

PEDLEY, R., *The Comprehensive School*, Penguin Books, Harmondsworth, 1963.

PETERSON, A. D. C., *The Future of the Sixth Form*, Routledge, London, 1973.

SCHOOLS COUNCIL, *Sixth Form Curriculum and Examinations* (Working Paper No. 5), H.M.S.O., London, 1966.

SCHOOLS COUNCIL, *Some Further Proposals for Sixth Form Work* (Working Paper No. 16), H.M.S.O., London, 1967.

SCHOOLS COUNCIL WORKING PARTIES, *Proposals for the Curriculum and Examinations in the Sixth Form*, London, 1969.

SCHOOLS COUNCIL, *16–19: Growth and Response 1. Curricular Bases* (Working Paper No. 45), Evans/Methuen Educational, London, 1972.

SCHOOLS COUNCIL, *16–19: Growth and Response 2. Examination Structure* (Working Paper No. 46), Evans/Methuen Educational, London, 1973.

SCHOOLS COUNCIL, *Preparation for Degree Courses* (Working Paper No. 47), Evans/Methuen Educational, London, 1973.

SNOW, C. P., *The Two Cultures and the Scientific Revolution*, Cambridge University Press, London, 1959.

YOUNG, C. and HUTCHINSON, M., *Educating the Intelligent*, Penguin Books, Harmondsworth, 1962.

YOUNG, M., *The Rise of the Meritocracy*, Thames and Hudson, London, 1958.

PART 4

CASE STUDIES

STUDY 1.   NEIGHBOURHOOD SCHOOL

PART 1.   NEIGHBOURHOOD SCHOOL DESCRIBED

A School Teacher

A shortened version of an article which appeared in
New Society *of 23rd June 1966*

Fifty-odd members of staff are squeezed into the library on tiny chairs. The Headmaster is speaking.

"Now, gentlemen. There are three main problems associated with this school which we are now facing in acute form. The first is the fact that we have to work in separate buildings. The second is the low standard of the entry. The third is the discipline of the boys and, it must be said gentlemen, of the staff."

It was said afterwards that he had never spoken so frankly in all his fifteen years as Headmaster; yet somehow he always manages to just miss the point.

The school is a boys' comprehensive school, 900 pupils, in an inner urban area. It occupies two buildings of unequal size, situated in different neighbourhoods three-quarters of a mile apart, with a trunk route running down the middle. A third building, as far away again from the others, is used for some technical classes.

I am a very junior master there, in my second year of teaching, and I know of school policy only what I can see from its results or gain from judicious questions. This is simply a worm's-eye view, and must be judged as such, but it is typical of the view that any worm would get in a good many of our schools.

The Head was certainly right that the starting-point of some of our problems is the physical separation of our buildings. The best of the equipment and of the staff tend to be concentrated in the larger building. This means that if the boys whose base is the annexe are

167

not to miss some of the best things the school has to offer, they must have some sessions in the main building. This itself involves the movement of a considerable number of boys back and forth in the dinner hour and under their own steam; it also means that they have to report on different mornings of the week at any one of three different buildings, widely scattered. One group of 11-year-olds in my first-year class were caught setting light to a rag soaked in petrol underneath a lorry parked on their route; another group called in on Woolworth's for some quiet shoplifting. Undoubtedly a great deal more goes on than we know about, and the possibilities of evasion and petty delinquency open to older boys of 14–15 are even greater.

I am not alone in placing some store by the corporate atmosphere generated by a school. A sense of unity, a sense of loyalty, and a feeling of common purpose can be over-emphasised at the expense of the individuality and self-expression of the individual members of the school. But where the sense of corporate life is fragmented almost to vanishing-point the school's tasks, particularly in a difficult neighbourhood, become almost impossible to perform.

This is not, however, the chief among our difficulties. It was a ludicrous administrative decision to amalgamate the separate buildings of separate schools in separate neighbourhoods into one 'school', and it leaves us with a lot of problems, some of them insurmountable. Nevertheless, the educational shortcomings of the school cannot be blamed on it alone; there are more vital factors still.

The parents of my boys are unlikely to read this article. Some of them are living in new council flats and only just feeling their way; I hope they will gradually become more involved in and knowledgeable about their children's education. Others are waiting in slums until they are pulled down about their ears; a whole area round the building I teach in is at present being demolished. Contact with parents by staff, however, and parental contact with the school are officially discouraged by the school. The analysis that follows is what I would like the parents to know.

168

The 'low standard of the intake' has become the catchword in frequent use to excuse all our failings. In 1964 our entry had been divided into five grades. We had no grade A's, no B's, eighteen C's and the rest of the intake were D's and E's—in achievement. This year, seven grades were divided into three groups, and we were supposed to have an even spread from each of the three groups. We had none from the top group, one from the big middle section, and all the rest from the bottom: 93 per cent of the intake was classed as below average.

There is some doubt in my mind as to whether these gradings give a true picture. A longitudinal study is at present being conducted in our neighbourhood in which a number of our first- and second-year boys are involved. This study suggests that in native ability the boys of our neighbourhood are as good as their contemporaries anywhere in the country, but that in reading achievement 38 per cent of them have failed to achieve a minimal standard exceeded by all their contemporaries apart from the bottom 5 per cent. In other words, they are not stupid, but the grading system makes them look so.

The causes of this disparity between ability and achievement are unlikely to be found only in the school, nor even only in the primary schools; many aspects of the subcultures which make up the neighbourhood militate against education. It must surely, however, be the schools which mount the counter-attack. Ours does not.

Instead we concentrate our efforts on those few boys who may at some time pass an outside examination. To this end there is a rigid structure of streamed classes and subject teaching modelled on the grammar school and more distantly on the public schools. In 1964 one boy achieved one A-level pass; in 1965 there were six A-level passes in four different subjects. In that year also there were fifty O-level passes achieved by rather fewer boys. At the moment there is alarm and disgust because the 'low standard of the intake' will make it difficult or impossible to maintain this improvement; indeed it will.

The investment, which is now paying a few dividends, will turn out to be a dud—yet we hang on to it grimly, as though there were no alternative. It has been costly. The major educational effort of the school has been concentrated on less than a tenth of the school population; some favoured masters rarely see any boy outside that tenth, and heads of departments tend to concentrate almost exclusively on them. The rest of us, 90 per cent and more of boys and staff, are left to contain and occupy each other till blessed release comes at the age of 15.

It is, inevitably, in these lower reaches of the school, where the educational effort should be concentrated, that there is waste and suffering. First- and second-year boys are often a pleasure to teach, and respond well to the variations in curriculum and method which are possible in view of the lack of any kind of academic pressures. By the time they are third year, however, they become dimly aware of their true position; educationally speaking, they have been sold down the river.

Although they could not possibly explain themselves verbally, they respond to their situation as though they understood it perfectly; discipline becomes a serious problem. All that stuff they hear about school being a waste of time was true; they are living examples of it, and cannot escape. "What is the point of our coming here?", asked a fourth former, sincerely, in a class I was trying to teach. There is no honest and constructive reply to give: the truth is too harsh.

This aspect of the school's failure is seen at its worst in the so-called remedial classes. There is one remedial class in each year; each contains about twenty-five boys, few of whom can read. The first and second years are treated like inadequate children. The third year is transitional, as they begin to realise their true position. By the time they reach the fourth year, 14 turning 15, only the toughest available master can cope with them. If we ever have a compulsory fifth year, the logic of our present system will suggest simply that we must find a tougher master still.

The staff of the remedial department, some of whom have a genuine interest in the tasks of remedial education, have no training beyond what they have been able to gain from short courses after they started work in the field. Certainly no remedies are produced. Few boys, if any, are transferred upwards from the remedial classes; many leave illiterate, or with so weak a grasp of reading and writing that they revert to illiteracy shortly after leaving. These classes are simply the bottom stream, the dregs of the dregs; and the secret is not kept from them.

This situation is the result directly of the Headmaster's pre-occupation with those who have already achieved most when they arrive and are accordingly graded comparatively high. It is a pre-occupation which is becoming increasingly irrelevant, and which may be losing him, from the point of view of examination successes, much of the dormant talent in the school.

The Head's approach brings clearly to the surface two important elements in the school's organisation: rigid streaming, and rigid subject teaching, whereby a master is allocated to a subject rather than to a group or groups of boys.

Streaming is done on the basis of reports received from the primary schools. There are six or seven streams on entry, according to the number of the intake. There is virtually no transfer between streams save for a dozen or so boys early on in their first year. The little flock of sheep are separated from the great horde of goats at the start, and kept that way.

Emphasis on subjects, rather than on groups of boys, means that a class may frequently have a form master who takes them for register (or who at least is responsible for their register: sometimes master and class will be in separate buildings, in which case another master deputises and a slip is sent across with the names of the absentees) but for nothing else. The class thus becomes a floating entity of its own, with no one taking a particular interest in the boys as individuals; and it is hardly surprising that some individuals react badly to this—particularly the ones from disturbed backgrounds, of whom there are many.

Some schools overcome this problem with a house system, which has the advantages of providing a social system parallel to that of the classroom but not based on academic achievement, and of providing a person who is actually responsible for the well-being of the boys in his house. We too have a house system; it is resurrected every sports day. There are, however, no housemasters and no house meetings, and the boys do not know what houses they are in. It is not surprising that only a few members of the staff, honourable exceptions, show any real interest in the boys as individual persons.

The basic pattern of the school's organisation and goals does not leap readily to the eye; a school is a confusing place. There may be things that I have yet to learn which might lead me to modify the description I have given. If, however, I am right—as I think I am—a number of other aspects of the life of the school fit the pattern as I now see it.

I remember clearly two incidents early on in my teaching career at this school. The first was when I went to the main building to pick up my form on their first day at secondary school. There was a lot of sorting out to do; a lot of waiting, and a lot of reassurance needed, in the long waits between actual events like going somewhere or shyly giving one's name and being herded into another group. A record number of parents were present, many (about the right proportion) immigrant—new to Britain.

The Head delivered his speech to them, that sunny autumn morning with the sun looking kindly in through the high Victorian windows. "Glad to see you," he said (I paraphrase). "Glad you take an interest in the splendid education your son is going to get at ———— School. But remember, he's growing up now: he doesn't need you hanging on to his harness straps any more. So we don't expect to see you here again. . . ." The words, I know, were better chosen for his purpose, but not much, and that was certainly the message I got; to judge by the results they got it too: "We don't want you here."

The second was a little later when, in connection with an individual problem in the class, I mentioned to the master in charge of the annexe that I was calling round on the parents that evening. He was kind, but firm; we don't approve of that: let the school attendance officer do the visiting (the school attendance officer becomes a kind of policeman). I have consistently disobeyed this injunction, and I reckon all parties have gained from it. But most of the staff adhere to it.

Unfortunately this exemplifies the school's attitude not only to parents but also to the neighbourhood in general. The environment in which the boys live is regarded as alien, hostile, crime-producing. It certainly does produce a lot of crime, but many other things as well, and it is the environment in which the boys spend their lives. No member of the staff apart from myself lives in the catchment area, and most would strongly support the view that it is not merely unwise, but dangerous to do so. "What would happen if my wife and I met X in the street?" My wife and I do, and have not suffered yet. Most of the staff have other profitable part-time occupations; but work in a local youth club in connection with work in the school does not occur.

The neighbourhood is in fact an essential key to the understanding of much that goes on in the school. Both neighbourhoods with which the school is primarily concerned are in transition. One is almost entirely council housing, the mid-twentieth-century's answer to the nineteenth-century slums (what is not council housing is rapidly being pulled down). People are still adjusting, not only to the change in the quality of our environment but also to difficulties like that of bringing up a family on the seventeenth floor. The other is mainly private housing in various stages of decay, with a comparatively high proportion of immigrants. The school, however, is officially not interested.

Immigrants form nearly 30 per cent of the school's population. It goes without saying that there is no official prejudice against immigrants at any point; the schools really are good at this. Some sensible steps have been taken recently, at the instigation of a very good West Indian teacher, to give positive help to a number of immigrant boys who have communication problems. As in so many things, however, if we were tackling the native problem effectively there would be no difficulty for immigrants and no special arrangements

173

would be necessary; they would simply join in with the special arrangements for native boys who have communication problems and move on according to their natural abilities. At any rate, the important case of the intelligent immigrant boy who is held back by language difficulties can now be helped in the school even if he is not always, and this is all to the good.

Discipline in a school of this kind, run in the way it is, is likely to be a problem; so it often is. By and large relationships between masters and boys are friendly, if superficial; a lot of amicable back-chat goes on between classes. A considerable number of boys, however, 'step out of line', and the reaction is invariably repressive. It could hardly be otherwise, considering the educational position of the boys, the lack of contact with their backgrounds, and the lack of personal interest in them. The instrument is the cane, applied to the seat; few days go by without a number of canings. Any member of staff apart from those doing their first, probationary year of teaching, may use the cane, and most of us do, some frequently.

Even if one disapproved of the method, it would be difficult to do anything about it in the school as it is. Order, in many classes, is almost impossible to keep, and without some kind of order teaching or constructive activity of any kind is impossible. Hence the weak master and the newcomer rely heavily on the strong-armed men who are feared by the boys. In my first year in particular (when I was not officially allowed to use the cane and never in fact did) there were situations which I could not control, and in some of them I thought quick, sharp punishment was the only answer. I was grateful to the strong-armed man down the passage, who caned at my request without question.

It helped in the short run, though not at all in the long term. Some of my fourth-year boys, whom I now refuse to cane, remain on friendly terms with me but think I am being very soft with the regular miscreants of the class: "The only thing you can do with that lot, sir, is to cane 'em, hard!" A dispiriting result for ten years of liberal education. And I shall never forget the look of hatred and anger and pain in the eyes of a difficult 15-year-old when I caned him last term.

School ends at 4.10. By 4.15 there is nobody on the premises save the cleaners, one or two bachelor teachers in the staffroom, and perhaps a group of West Indian boys playing cricket in the playground (much discouraged). The rest have gone; the staff to beat the rush hour, and the boys home, if anybody is there, or to devilment in the streets. 'Out of school activities' do not exist for the majority. There are four activities, and they depend entirely on three members of staff. They are very good examples of what can be done by individuals even in hostile circumstances. Their success, though used by the Head on occasions such as speech day, does not seem to have made much impression on the Head or his staff as a whole.

Little interest is shown in modern teaching methods, and less still in research. Much is made by the Head, when visitors come to the school, of the up-to-date workshops for wood and metal, the art room, and the audio-visual aids for modern languages. There is some truth in this display. We have a local authority which is in many ways excellent, and this is one of the ways. Nothing, in some respects, is too good for a school. Unfortunately, this applies to equipment, rather than to attitudes; to materials rather than to quality of education.

Most of the work is done in ordinary classrooms, and much of it is still containment, not education; the television set and the film projector are often an acknowledged escape from the classroom, and much sought after as such.

Before I arrived at the school I had to make it clear that owing to my other commitments to local organisations (youth clubs and the like) I would not be able to play a direct part in out-of-school activities. At the same time, I offered my local contacts if they could be useful. I expected to be the exception, not the rule. I was surprised at the lack of interest in an all-round education, and the school is not interested in my local knowledge. Some of the staff are concerned, but we are rendered powerless by the overwhelming impact of the school's organisation and expressed goals. For the majority, their attitude is summed up in the remark made by the careers master in my hearing and in the hearing of several of the boys to the youth employment officer just before he spoke to them: "They're a real shower, this lot." I nearly hit him. It eats into one, none the less. The cheerful cynicism of members of staff taking a quiet drag in the staffroom during assembly has its effect: gay, amusing, and utterly deadly. "I don't take public-spirited action like that nowadays", I realised to my horror I had just said to a younger master in connection with the blowing of the whistle in the playground in the absence of the deputed master. It jolted me; I am as cynical, as lazy, and as hopeless as any.

We are caught up in a rigid system: rigid streaming which kills the enthusiasm and opportunities of most of the boys, rigid subject teaching, which ensures that no personal interest is taken in them, and a rigid hierarchy, whereby graded posts go to favourites who accept the *status quo*, and where Heads are older men whose attitudes kill the ideas of young teachers from training colleges in a few terms. (This has been well documented recently by John Partridge in his book *Middle School*.) And within this invisible, rigid structure the fluid and fascinating life of the school goes on.

The boys' reaction to this misconceived organisation of goals is generally hostile; among the favoured few it is favourable, and in many others the hostility is often tinged with resigned tolerance—this makes life in the school possible. We are, however, turning out unskilled workers in enormous numbers, of which the country has a decreasing need, and we are helping many on the road to delinquency.

I wish I could think that our school, and our Head, were utterly exceptional, but from what I have read and from what I have heard, they are not.

For Discussion

The following are some of the questions which seminar groups on the Cardiff course were invited to consider, in relation to the alleged 'misconceived organisation of goals' at Neighbourhood School:

1. How might the same school appear from the viewpoint of the Head or of a senior member of staff?
2. Are the Head's objectives, as described in this paper, appropriate to the circumstances of his school—or of comprehensive schools in general? What would be your goals and your objectives if you were similarly placed?
3. The Head refers to the lack of staff discipline as one of his problems. Do you agree? How would Professor Thomason's 'organisational training' approach (Chap. 6) work out in this situation?
4. Would it be realistic to try to involve either the pupils or the parents in formulating, or in implementing, the school's objectives? If so, how would you go about it?
5. What kind of interaction between the school and the community would you wish to encourage?

The mythical sequel in Part 2 was devised to focus attention, in the context of pastoral care, on managerial problems of organisational change.

PART 2. NEIGHBOURHOOD SCHOOL REVISITED

Meredydd G. Hughes

A year or so later, a full general inspection of Neighbourhood School by H.M. Inspectorate took place, the first since reorganisation. The inspectors spent several days in the school; they were thorough and asked many questions.

The report of the inspection which went to the governing body was scrupulously fair. It fully recognised the divided premises and neighbourhood disabilities under which the school was functioning. It paid tribute to excellent work in particular spheres by individual members of staff. It then discussed at length a number of alleged deficiencies in the organisation of the school.

There were three aspects for which the report reserved its most critical comments. They were:

(1) the alleged absence, below the sixth form, of an effective system for the pastoral care of pupils;
(2) alleged deficiencies in arrangements for educational guidance and careers advice to pupils and their parents;
(3) an alleged lack of evidence of any initiative taken by the

177

Head to mobilise staff resources in a joint effort to tackle the acute problems which face the school.

With regard to the first two points the report recommended that attention might profitably be given to recent educational thinking concerning guidance and counselling (cf. Schools Council, 1967; Gill, 1967; Daws, 1967; Moore, 1970). On the third point it conspicuously made no recommendation.

At the meeting of the governing body which considered the report the spokesman for the Inspectorate had little to add. The Headmaster helped to elucidate some apparent discrepancies in the statistics but took no further part in the discussion. Several governors spoke at length. The chief outcome was a recommendation to the L.E.A. that a school counsellor be appointed to the staff of the school to strengthen this aspect of its work. The Headmaster, when asked for his views, was cautious and non-committal.

Under 'Any Other Business' the Headmaster caused a sensation by announcing his resignation. He said that he had been contemplating retirement for the last twelve months or so. He did not mind confessing that he had found the last few years of reorganisation and amalgamation rather trying and he now felt that this was an appropriate time to hand over the reins of office to a younger man. The chairman, like everyone else, was taken aback, but quickly recovered and instantly paid a glowing tribute to the Headmaster's devoted service over sixteen years, to which all agreed. There being no further business the meeting ended—rather abruptly.

In due course two advertisements were published—one for the post of Headmaster of Neighbourhood School and the other, on a short-term basis in the first instance, for a school counsellor who might also, at the discretion of the Headmaster, be expected to do a certain amount of teaching.

From an impressive list of applicants you were selected as the new Head, largely because of your eloquent plea that schools should accept an increased responsibility for the pastoral care of its pupils and your promise that this would be your first priority. A graduate master with seven years' teaching experience, now completing the one-year course in counselling at Keele University, was appointed to the counselling post. The summer holidays have begun and you will both be taking up your appointments in September.

You have received, but have not yet answered, a letter from the new school counsellor asking for a clarification of his duties and his relationship to other members of staff. He adds that he is very much looking forward to working under a Head who is known to favour the deepening of pastoral care in schools.

Your first visit to the school takes place at the end of July; you were not available earlier. You have arranged to meet the acting Head to discuss the time-table and other urgent matters. (The previous Head left at Easter and the second master has been acting Head for the summer term.) Among other things he wishes to know whether, and to what extent, the counsellor is to be available for teaching duties.

The acting Head also reports to you the strong feelings of some members of staff on two matters:

(1) The majority of staff are unhappy at the prospect of being asked to carry out duties of a pastoral nature going beyond normal class teaching. Some of them fear, in particular, that, if tutorial groups are set up which cut across class-teaching groups, substantial additional paper work will be involved for staff when record cards and terminal reports have to be completed.

(2) Many of the staff are deeply suspicious of the appointment of a school counsellor, which has been a subject much discussed in the staff rooms. The hostility has crystallised in a number of specific objections, though there is a wide variation in the emphasis given to the different points. As understood by the acting head the main fears and points of objection are as follows:

(i) Will the position of the careers master be adversely affected?

(ii) Providing reports for the counsellor is liable to involve the staff in further paper work.

(iii) It is anticipated that pupils would be taken out of class for counselling, providing an additional excuse for malingering, possibly depriving pupils of vital lessons and generally giving the impression that lessons do not matter.

(iv) It is regarded as unprofessional for pupils to be encouraged by the counsellor to express themselves freely in confidence about their school difficulties, as the remarks of the pupils may include tendentious statements about other members of staff.

(v) How can a counsellor be a loyal member of staff unless he takes his share of responsibility for discipline in the school—and what happens then to his 'permissive non-judgemental role'? (Gill, 1967).

(vi) Members of staff with few free periods feel that the appointment of a counsellor at the expense of a teaching appointment unfairly increases the teaching load for the rest of the staff.

(vii) It is feared that the counsellor, speaking on behalf of the 'pupil-clients', will come to control the organisation of the curriculum and that he will effectively determine the courses and options to be provided at the different stages.

(viii) In view of the Seebohm Report (1968), will the logical development be to bring social workers into the school, who will be accountable to outside agencies and not to the Headmaster? (Clegg, 1968).

The acting Head admits that he is out of his depth in these matters, though he has recently heard of books which discuss some of the points (Lytton and Craft, 1969; Holden, 1969; Hughes, 1971). It is with a sense of relief that he looks forward to reverting to the post of second master for the last few years before retirement.

Your main problems, as the in-coming Headmaster of Neighbour-hood School are becoming clear to you. Their solution is less apparent.

For Discussion

1. Taking account of the limiting factors, how are you to build up a work-able system of pastoral care in the school? What kind of criteria will you (or you and the staff) have in mind in working through the various possibilities: sections, houses, tutorial groups, forms and year groups, or a combination of two or more of these? Will a management 'organi-sation chart' help to get things any clearer?
2. How do you envisage the role of the school counsellor and its relation-ship to other roles in the school, including the careers master? Might it be useful to try to devise a model to indicate the relationships or areas of responsibility you think desirable in the provision of guidance, counselling and contact with outside agencies?
3. How are you to obtain the willing co-operation of the staff in both these endeavours and in bringing greater flexibility into the organisation of the school?

REFERENCES

CLEGG, SIR ALEC, Seebohm: a sorry tale, in *Education*, 11 Oct. 1968; replies in *Education*, 25 Oct. 1968.

DAWS, P. P. *et al.*, The counselling function: a symposium, in *Educational Research*, Vol. 9, No. 2, Feb. 1967.

GILL, C. J., Counselling in schools, in *Trends in Education*, H.M.S.O., Apr. 1967.

HOLDEN, ALICK, *Teachers as Counsellors*, Constable, London, 1969.

HUGHES, P. M., *Guidance and Counselling in Schools: A Response to Change*, Pergamon, Oxford, 1971.

LYTTON, H. and CRAFT, M., *Guidance and Counselling in British Schools*, Arnold, London, 1969.

MOORE, B. M., *Guidance in Comprehensive Schools*, National Foundation of Educational Research, Slough, Bucks., 1970.

SCHOOLS COUNCIL, *Counselling in Schools*, Working Paper No. 15, H.M.S.O., 1967.

SEEBOHM REPORT, H.M.S.O., London, 1968.

STUDY 2.   WESTWOOD COMPREHENSIVE

Peter C. Webb

PART 1.   THE SCHOOL IS REORGANISED

Situated in a town of some 500,000 population, with a wide range of industries, Westwood Comprehensive has had a varied history. In 1955 it opened as a 5 form entry mixed selective modern school, in new buildings sited in a large council housing estate adjoining a newly developed industrial zone within the town. Its intake was drawn from the new estate plus a section of the older downtown area. The site was a good deal larger than was really necessary, but the local education authority had planned to build a college of further education adjacent to the school. However, early in 1960 a decision of the Education Committee to build a second unit on the site, with the intention of converting the school to comprehensive status, proved acceptable to the Ministry of Education, who allowed the necessary administrative changes to be made in respect of the new use of the site, and the new unit, designed to bring the school up to 9 form entry in size, was opened in 1963. Although designated a comprehensive the school was heavily 'creamed' not only by a direct-grant grammar school but also by several very efficient maintained grammar schools in the town.

From 1963 until 1968, Westwood Comprehensive operated as a selective modern school rather than on a full comprehensive intake. It had, in fact, a smaller proportion than might have been expected from both ends of the ability range, providing a range of examination courses which were its main attraction to parents whose children stood a chance of achieving them, but had not found their way into the grammar schools. Thus, the school, operating as a 'comprehensive' with a creamed, but (self) selective intake, had been under a variety of pressures, some of them severe, to keep up with the grammar schools in terms of 'A' levels, 'O' levels, and other externally appraisable examination results, including those for local technical college entry—the local 15+ leaving certificate. The Headmaster, a modern languages graduate and a good musician, had drive and ambition for his school; he had seized on every chance to create a favourable image, both publicly and professionally, and was eager to compete on equal terms with the grammar schools, for staff and resources, and for prestige. He had assiduously courted local university and college of education circles for various forms of patronage and connections (members on governing body, speech days, and so on); and had made it a matter of his personal concern that local businesses and the technical colleges had looked to his school for a supply of apprentices and juniors for professional entry at a variety of levels. All scholastic achievements were listed in the speech-day report; and exhibitions and public performances illustrated regularly his outgoing, competitive policies in the public relations field. This had many favourable effects for the school; but internally there were hints of restrictions of communications from school to outside world, except through the one channel, and occasionally even of the censor's scissors. In general, many of the policies were successful, and the proportion of pupils staying on into the fifth and sixth forms grew steadily throughout the sixties.

The growth of the school, from these effects, and from its changes of capacity and intake, took it from a population of 680 pupils and 32 staff in 1960 to 1340 pupils and 69 staff in 1968. The large yearly intakes of new young staff produced by this expansion combined with a high turnover rate (18 per cent average loss per annum) allowed the Headmaster a position of considerable personal power, and the school's administration and management became centralised heavily on him, in spite of its size and its increasing complexity. He was thus able to impress his ideas and policies heavily on the school's activities and organisation; and he needed only a deputy head, a senior master and a senior mistress, all supporting him in largely executive roles, to maintain a powerful grip on the school as a whole. Apart from meetings of the whole school staff, there were no formal consultative structure of committees; initiatives generally came from the Headmaster himself, or from a few highly qualified members of staff with a similar sort of drive and enterprise.

In his relations with the local education office, the Headmaster worked closely with two or three very influential members of his governing body, including the chairman, a very powerful local politician; and maintained the same sort of relationship with the Director of Education and his officers. His personal standing in the town was high, and he went to much trouble to maintain good relations with local men and institutions of influence. He was a member of a number of local and national committees, connected with education and social service, a regular churchgoer and former Sunday School teacher, and an active member of a musical society. Together with a particularly enterprising and public-spirited young man on his staff, he had set up a new venture in local community service for his fifth- and sixth-formers, which, from 1966 onwards, had achieved national publicity for its efforts, especially in providing services for old-age pensioners, and others in need of personal help.

During 1968, however, the education committee's plans for complete comprehensive reorganisation were being hammered out; in March 1969, they were agreed with the Department of Education and Science. Leaving out the direct grant school, the scheme envisaged a system of all-through 11–18 schools, in which some of the older, secondary modern schools had to be used as 11–13 partial feeder units, until such time as the larger schools could be extended. The town itself was zoned; Westwood's zone included its new council estate, a large part of the old downtown area, and some smallish middle-class sections.

The reorganisation plans had included a reconsideration of the uses of building programme allocations from the Department of Education and Science, and in August 1968 work had started on an extension of the second building to house a sixth-form unit. This was completed in September 1969; the money had formed part of a project intended to replace one of the older secondary modern schools. As a temporary measure, the sixth-form unit was also to accommodate some of the fifth formers. The aim was to add a fifth-form unit to the sixth-form unit, on the raising of the school leaving age.

The sequence of changeover of pupils planned by the local education office for the period 1968/9 to 1971/2 is shown in Table 1.

TABLE 1.

	1968/9	1969/70	1970/1	1971/2
Form 1	285	180	190	190
2	290	285	180	190
3	285	390	400	420
4	280	375	390	400
5	140	180	200	220
6	60	70	90	120
	1340 (69 staff)	1480 (77 staff)	1450 (75 staff)	1540 (81 staff)

Notes. The growth of the overall total is accounted for by the changes produced by the zoning system, and by the growth of the numbers staying on into the fifth and sixth forms.

Negotiations between the Headmaster and the local education office during 1968 produced a small addition to capitation allowances, and an increase of two typists to the school office staff. But the most important concessions made by the local education authority were those concerned with teaching staff. The details are set out in Appendix A but it is important to mention the decision to appoint a Grade A head of remedial teaching, and a senior tutor. By the time these decisions had been made, however, it was too late to advertise these posts, and the Headmaster decided to appoint a senior tutor from within his own staff, and to leave the other appointment till the autumn term.

185

The Headmaster held two staff conferences during the summer term to explain the new developments in detail, and to outline the new administrative, teaching and, as he called them, social arrangements. The first two remained in essence much as they had been before except that the year groups in the middle school (Forms 3 and 4) were much larger and would include lower ranges of ability, so that new time-table arrangements would have to be made for them (see page 188: Appendix B). The director of studies lower school) would have a newly designated assistant with a scale post, and the same would apply to the director of studies (middle school), as the former head of upper school was to be designated from now on. The newly appointed senior tutor, a specialist, academically highly qualified, was given responsibility for developing a variety of courses for the fifth and sixth formers.

As for the 'social' organisation, the Head expected that the existing house system, which had its impact largely in the lower school, would remain the main channel by which pupils would identify socially with the school. The form tutors would also have a major part to play, in the recording of academic progress, and in collecting data on specially designed forms for all cases which involved any special attention or inquiry relating to any individual child. In other words, the form teacher would remain part of the link with the outside world. The whole system of care of individual pupils through the form system, and social training, involvement and identification through the house system, he would call a 'lattice' structure. The lattice structure would also have to handle normal disciplinary functions. Performance 'stars' and behaviour 'blacks' would count for house marks, as established already; and house tutors would continue to handle detentions and other standard punishment systems, except for corporal punishment which would remain wholly the direct responsibility of directors of studies (lower and middle schools) and their deputies, and senior master, senior mistress, deputy Head and Headmaster group. The part played by form tutors in this disciplinary policy would lie in the collection of information about individual children and in the

Department	Grade	No. of graduates		No. of other teachers		Trans-ferred from other schools	Part-time teachers
		with scale posts	without scale posts	with scale posts	without scale posts		
Religious Education	A	–	1	–	–		1
English	E	2	2	–	3	1	
Drama	A	–	–	–	–		
Modern Languages	D	2	2	–	–		
Classics	–	1	1	–	–		
Mathematics	E	2	–	1	4	2	
History	C	–	1	–	1		
Geography	C	–	1	–	1	1	
Economics	C	–	–	–	–		
Commerce	–	–	–	1	–		2
Art	B	–	1 (equiv.)	–	1		1
Music	B	–	–	–	1		
Physics	D	1	–	–	1		
Chemistry	E	2	–	–	1	1	
Biology	C	1	1	–	2		1
Technical	D	–	–	2	2	2	
Home Economics	C	–	–	2	2	1	1
Physical Education	AA	–	–	–	2		
Remedial	A (not yet appointed)	–	–	4	2		
plus							
Headmaster	HM						
Deputy Head	DH (teaches 10 periods in Physics department)						
Director of Studies (Lower School) (DSLS)	E (teaches 12 periods in Mathematics department)						
Director of Studies (Middle School) (DSMS)	E (teaches 12 periods in English department)						
Senior Tutor (ST)	E (teaches 16 periods in Geography/Economics departments)						
Senior Mistress	SM (teaches 12 periods in Biology department)						
Bursar/Registrar	(APT II)						
						Total Staff	
Totals	23	11	10	6	25	75 f/t	+6 p/t

Notes.—Of those transferred from other schools on reorganisation, some have protected allowances (total number transferred ten).

f/t—full-time teachers. p/t—part-time teachers.

Total number of new appointments twelve (six probationers).

The totals at the foot of the Table do not include the Headmaster.

attention they could pay to individuals' development. The maintenance of order and purpose, and good human relations, were the chief objectives of disciplinary policy, as they always had been, and they were the direct responsibility of all teachers having a part to play in the lattice structure. He reminded all teachers in the school of the importance of the external public image which the school presented as an institution in the town, both for the general attitude of pupils when they arrive in the school and of their parents, and for the influence of the school in the government circles which determine what resources, staffing preferences and decision-making freedoms it could gain in order to do its job effectively. A large part of the responsibility for this external image lay in their own behaviour, and in the behaviour of pupils of the school; in so far as this could be influenced by the school's policies concerning human relations, social care, and discipline, the staff must accept a very important share of the overall responsibility.

In September 1969 the school reopened as a full comprehensive with its new intakes into Forms 1, Forms 3 and Forms 4. The time-tabling group—Headmaster, deputy Head and senior tutor—had spent much time during August constructing their time-table (an outline of curriculum structure is given in Appendix B), and had finally completed staff and room time-tables only two days before the opening of the term. The first three days of term were almost chaotic, especially in the middle school where the third- and fourth-year intakes had to be tested, and allocated to teaching groups. Special traffic duties had to be undertaken by the staff allocated to the middle and upper school building to help in directing children, wandering about aimlessly, to their appropriate rooms and classes. The entire time of the office staff was taken up with typing lists of pupils in classes and sets, and these were distributed daily in all staffrooms. Both staff and pupils began to show distinct signs of harassment and frustration. By the end of the first week, however, there was a noticeable easing of the sense of confusion, and the school began to work with more apparent order and purpose.

Appendix B: Curriculum Structure—Summaries, 1969/70
40-period week

Forms 1

1 A	(34)	E_5 M_6 F_4 L_4 H_2 G_2 S_5 A_2 Wk/He$_2$ Re$_2$ Mu$_2$ ⎱ Pe$_4$ (2 groups)
1 B	(33)	Ditto ⎰
1 C	(32)	E_6 M_6 F_5 H_3 G_3 S_5 A_2 Wk/He$_2$ Re$_2$ Mu$_2$ ⎫
1 D	(31)	Ditto ⎬ Pe$_4$ (3 groups)
1 E	(31)	Ditto ⎭
1 R	(19)	E_8 M_8 H_4 G_4 S_4 A_2 Wk/He$_2$ Re$_2$ Mu$_2$ Pe$_4$

Forms 3

3 A	(32)	E_5 M_5 F_4 H_2 P_2 C_2 B_2 Re$_2$ ⎱ J/JA$_4$ G/A/Mu$_3$
3 B	(30)	Ditto ⎬ Mu/L/Sp/G$_3$ Wk/MkTd/He/Nk$_2$
3 C★	(30)	Ditto ⎰ Pe$_4$ (4 groups)
3 D	(31)	E_5 M_5 F_4 P_2 C_2 B_2 Re$_2$ ⎱ G/G/A/Mu$_4$ Wk/Td/He/Nk$_3$
3 E	(31)	Ditto ⎬ H/H/J/L/Sp$_4$ Mk/Wk/Nk/He$_3$
3 F★	(32)	Ditto ⎰ Pe$_4$ (4 groups)
3 G	(32)	E_6 M_7 F_4 S_5 Re$_2$ A_2 Cr/Td$_2$ H_2 G_2 WkMk/HeNk$_4$ ⎫
3 H	(33)	Ditto ⎬ Pe$_4$
3 J	(33)	Ditto ⎬ (6 groups)
3 K★	(33)	E_7 M_7 S_6 Re$_2$ A_4 H_3 G_3 WkMk/HeNk$_4$ ⎬
3 L★	(33)	Ditto ⎭
3 R$_1$	(22)	E_8 M_8 H_3 G_3 A_2 S_4 B/Hb$_2$ Mk Wk/HeNk$_4$ Re$_2$ ⎱ Pe$_4$ (2 groups)
3 R$_2$★	(18)	(EMHGA)$_{26}$ S_4 Wk/He$_4$ Re$_2$ ⎰

Forms 4

4 A	(35)	Re$_2$ ⎱ E/E/E/E/E$_5$ M/M/M/M/M$_5$ F/F/J/Sp/A$_4$ Ec/J/Sp/F/H$_4$
4 B	(35)	Re$_2$ ⎱ L/L/G/H/H/Mu$_4$ P/P/B/Td/Nk$_4$ G/C/C/B/Wk/He$_4$
4 C	(33)	Re$_2$ ⎰
4 D★	(33)	Re$_2$ ⎰ B/Hb/Mk/A/Nk/Mu$_4$ Pe$_4$ (4 groups)
4 PA$_1$	(33)	Re$_1$ E_6 M_8 S_6 Td$_3$ H_2 G_2 ⎱ Mk/Wk/Mk/Wk$_4$ Pe$_4$ (2 groups)
4 PA$_2$★	(34)	Ditto ⎰ Wk/Mk/Wk/Mk$_4$
4 PN	(24)	Re$_2$ E_6 M_4 G_3 H_3 PC$_3$ Hb$_5$ He$_4$ Nk$_4$ A_2 Pe$_4$
4 Com$_1$	(23)	Re$_1$ E_6 M_5 G_2 (Commercial Studies)$_{18}$ Hb$_2$ A_2 ⎱ Pe$_4$ (2 groups)
4 Com$_2$	(21)	Ditto ⎰
4 K	(36)	E_8 M_8 S_4 Re$_2$ A_4 H_3 G_3 WkMk/HeNk$_4$ ⎫
4 L★	(34)	Ditto ⎬ Pe$_4$ (2 groups)
4 M★	(34)	Ditto ⎭

Notes. ★ forms from other schools (some fifty pupils from Westwood School were redistributed in the zoning).

For Discussion

1. Comment on the table showing the composition of pupils and year groups in Westwood School over the period 1968 to 1972. What do you feel are likely to be the main problems produced? Comment on the quality of the planning of the changeover.

2. In what ways would you think that the historical development of the school would affect its performance as constituted from September 1969 onwards? What are its priorities, and how appropriate are they to the new tasks of the school? What would you say are the new tasks, especially in the social and pastoral contexts?

3. Evaluate the Head's philosophy, and educational aims, the organisation of responsibilities within the school (especially in the senior staff echelon), and the overall structure of organisation.
   What are the likely results of the increase in its size?

4. Comment on the school's policy for external relations. How does it affect what goes on inside the school, especially in terms of its academic, and social functions and organisation?

5. Comment on the Head's speech at the staff conference. What do you think of his 'lattice' theory?

6. Make a forecast of the likely discipline problems of the school. What steps would you take to anticipate, and deal with them?

7. What would you think will be the likely difficulties of the form tutors in carrying out the pastoral tasks required of them, as set out in the Headmaster's speech? How would you (a) redefine them, (b) provide guidance and support for the teachers concerned?

8. There seems to be a tendency for the planning of the school's operations, especially in its curriculum structure, to divide the pupils into groups receiving different general treatment. If you agree with this observation, what effects would you expect to find on the attitudes of the children concerned?

9. In what ways would you have attempted to redesign the balance of the staffing of the school during 1969? How would you plan the development of the staff during the coming two years? See Appendix A for details.

10. If you had to create a small committee to work on the school's disciplinary and social/pastoral policies for the next three years, who would you have on it, and how would you define its terms of reference?

PART 2. A DANGEROUS SITUATION EMERGES

During the rest of the term the appearance of order and purpose in activities and behaviour was maintained effectively, but at a cost which eventually became very noticeable in the middle school. Both pupils and staff began to display indications of tension, these affected the middle school staff, in particular, and there was a marked increase of absenteeism, especially among younger staff. The director of studies (middle school), announcing his resignation for the following April (he had been appointed to a headship elsewhere), took the opportunity to report frankly to the Head that he was glad to be getting away from what he considered to be a dangerous situation. He hinted strongly that he felt the school was not far from losing control of a section of the pupils. The deputy Head, consulted about this by the Headmaster, declared that this was somewhat alarmist, but admitted that there had been a considerable increase in the detention lists, and in the number of cases of appeals for help with cases of discipline from the younger members of staff. He himself complained about the failure of the caretaking staff to cope with the increased problems of keeping the middle school clean, and dealing with damage to furniture and fittings. The senior mistress had also noticed that women members of staff were working under difficulties of indiscipline and insubordination and were showing signs of strain. She felt that this was due to the problems of teaching the type of middle school groups which the school had not experienced before.

The Head, the deputy and the senior mistress agreed that they would have to impose newer and severer disciplinary measures, and that there would have to be increased corridor, dining-room and playground duties for the staff; a new system of detention was devised. All these were announced to the various school assemblies and to a full staff meeting during the early part of November. By the end of the first week of December, it had become clear that these measures were not succeeding in containing the growth of disciplinary troubles, and there were some outbreaks of vandalism, and a noticeable increase of truancy. Signs were observed of the formation of gangs, accompanied by deteriorating standards of dress and behaviour, among girls as well as boys. It was with some sense of relief all round that the term closed without serious incident.

The new term had hardly begun, however, when the local newspaper, usually so favourably inclined toward the school, began to run a series about the town's young people. One of the articles, about gangs and their behaviour, contained very strong, hardly concealed, hints that it was Westwood's pupils which had provided the worst examples of gang behaviour; it described their standards of behaviour and dress, the truancy, the vandalism—in and out of the school—and even mentioned delinquency. The Head was deeply hurt and annoyed, but failed to find out who had leaked information from inside the school; he called for immediate reports from his senior staff. The following are brief summaries of these reports.

Deputy head. Placed main responsibility for disturbances on the failure of younger staff to keep control. Indiscipline was largely centred in the middle school, staff were not taking detention system seriously as a punishment; there were also signs of staff turning a blind eye to 'internal truancy'. Difficulties over the pastoral role of form/house tutors had not been adequately worked out, or understood. Much of the trouble appeared to be stemming from a small group of about twenty near-delinquents; who were occupying an increasing amount of his time.

Senior tutor. Had found it difficult to assess the problem—there was little or no trouble in the fifth or sixth forms. Had found much support for school's social activities in its clubs, though there were some which had got off to a good start, but then failed—one instance was the '15+ Club'.

Director of studies (middle school). Much of the trouble came from groups in the middle school, mainly those in the lower reaches of the fourth form who had been transferred from the small secondary modern in the town. He felt that there was real danger of a break-down of discipline, partly as a result of failure of control on the part of some younger men and women in the middle school staff; but mainly arising from the activities of a core group of real trouble-makers on whom all attempts at discipline and persuasion had failed. He feared that the types of punishment available to the staff would ultimately fail to have any impact on the worst cases. Even the cane, which he had had to use more in one term than he could remember in twelve years of teaching, was beginning to lose its effect in certain forms.

Senior mistress. Felt that the girls showed much the same charac-teristic disturbance patterns as had been described in the boys. Indeed, the problem was worse, for two reasons—one, that, in a virtually all-male hierarchy, girls' problems were less understood; two, that there could be no recourse to corporal punishment, so that disciplinary methods were comparatively restricted. This gave the less experienced men teachers some trouble. She too had her small core of thirty or so intractable cases; she estimated that she spent an average of three hours a day solely on disciplinary matters associated with these girls—four in particular who, she felt, were emotionally disturbed to a serious extent. There was no help for her in this job—she could not find a trainable deputy who would be willing to accept the additional responsibility. She felt that the situation was almost out of her control, and getting worse. Her own health was beginning to suffer. Two other matters she felt should be reported. One was that while the major trouble area was in the fourth form which consisted of pupils transferred from other schools, the effects were being transmitted to some of the already disturbed, or easily led, girls of other forms. Secondly, she was concerned at the palpable signs of stress in some of the younger women staff, including the probationers. (This too was taking up much of her time.) Several were in such trouble that they appeared to be staying away from school.

The outcome of the discussions was a policy of increased emphasis on effective control and discipline, and the Head decided to hold another staff meeting to announce the new measures. These would include a new set of paper controls and routines in respect of detention and corporal punishment, and increased supervisory duties for the staff.

A few days later the Head was invited by the Director of Education to meet him, together with his chairman of governors, to discuss the newspaper articles, and their implication. At this meeting the Headmaster reported on the internal situation, repeating some of the information given by his senior staff and outlining the new policies he had decided on. The Director, however, was not inclined to let the matter rest there; he was disturbed at the notion of increased emphasis on corporal punishment, and upset to find that the newer members of the staff were experiencing such difficulties. The Head said that he felt that the school should be given time to settle down to a routine, undisturbed by the emotional and other difficulties of the pupils transferred to the fourth form for only their final year's schooling. He felt that the way the reorganisation had been arranged had been largely responsible for producing many of the school's behaviour problems.

The Director of Education agreed with this, to an extent, but said that what he was concerned about was that the school was not developing positive policies aimed at correcting these disturbances. He felt that there was more to it than a temporary disturbance; there might indeed be longer-term problems associated with the size of the school, and the lack of definition of pastoral objectives and organisation.

He had been concerned recently with the development of social worker courses in the social administration department of the local university and had been much impressed by some of the work they had developed on the managerial problems associated with the increased size of hospitals and on the policy-defining problems of social care agencies in local government. He would like to propose that the Department of Social Administration be asked to allow one of its specialist research staff to carry out a survey of these two aspects of the school's problems during the Easter and summer terms. The chairman of governors agreed, with enthusiasm; and the Head rather reluctantly accepted the project.

A fortnight later he was invited to a planning meeting at the university. It was agreed at the meeting that the Survey would be set up, possibly as part of a longer term research project in the town's larger schools. The local education authority agreed to help support the project as a piece of consultancy in the field of social education, or possibly compensatory education. Final decisions would await the first report on Westwood School, which would result from an extended visit in the school by an experienced research worker. This preliminary report would be made available only to the Director of Education and the Head.

For Discussion

1. Comment on the first term's difficulties, especially those experienced by the new young members of staff. Could anything have been done to help them to cope better?
2. Comment on the school's disciplinary policies and the processes within the school by which they have been worked out.
3. Comment on the agreements and the divergences between the reports of the deputy Head, the senior tutor and the director of studies (middle school).
4. Comment on the senior mistress's report. Has she correctly analysed her own position as senior mistress, the problems of girls' discipline, and the priorities of her job? Should she spend so much time on a hard core of thirty difficult girls? How would you redefine the senior mistress's job? What support would you organise for her?
5. How do you feel that the school's pastoral organisation is coping with its problems under the new regime? What should be the pastoral objectives of Westwood School? In what ways would you attempt to redefine both objectives and policy for the school's new situation?
6. Comment on the meeting between the Director of Education, the chairman of governors, and the Headmaster. Was the Director of Education right in his evaluation of the school's problems, and in his proposal to bring in a research investigator?

7. If you had been the Headmaster, what would you have done? What policies would you have set out for coping with the school's new problems, both immediate and longer term?
8. Could this situation have been foreseen at an earlier stage? If so, what should have been done about it?

PART 3. A REPORT AND ITS REBUTTAL

The investigator's first report, dated June 1970, set out in some detail an analysis of the school's organisation and the ways in which it coped with a variety of problems. Its main conclusions were that the increased size of the school, the changes in its pattern of intake of pupils, and hence of its policies and objectives, had taken it beyond the stage at which one man, supported by a small group of 'executives' could effectively manage it.

The overall management structure was faulty, in that there was no intermediate level of responsibility formally set out, down to which the Headmaster could devolve a substantial amount of decision-making. A potential structure was there, in that the heads of departments could be said to embody such a 'layer', as in the diagram below (the SM, DSLS, DSMS, ST layer is mainly a 'staff' layer rather than being part of the "line" structure):

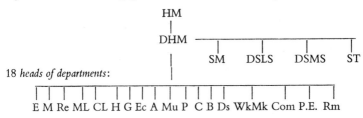

But the 'span of control' in this structure (the line part, that is) was much too great for effective delegation and control; the quality of the heads of departments was too variable. And, in any case, these heads did not all accept that they had a managerial role—many felt that their responsibility allowances were simply a payment for teaching in the sixth form, or represented merely a Burnham grading with no other implications.

A further difficulty was that these departmental units were conceived strictly in academic terms, and could have little to do with other functions of the school. In particular, there was (a) a house system which was stated to be designed for pastoral care and discipline, and (b) co-ordinators for these functions, careers and contacts with parents, in person of the senior tutor, and the two directors of studies.

The most obvious result of all this was that there was confusion over functions and responsibilities, in the minds of both staff and pupils. The lack of definition of roles, tasks and duties, coupled with the failure to organise a formal consultative structure of committees, had led to omissions; in particular in that planning, identification of objectives and definition of policies appropriate to the increased size of the school and the range of its intake, had not been undertaken explicitly by any body of the school's staff, but had been left to the day-to-day reactions of the Headmaster, in consultation only with those near to him, including two or three influential governors. This in turn had led to some alienation of the staff's loyalties and involvement, particularly in those (especially newer, younger members of staff) who had only limited access to senior people in the organisation, and hence felt remote, undirected and unconsidered. There was a distinct lack of corporate feeling and involvement, of identification with the school as a community of interests, values and purposes.

In the pupils, especially those in the middle school, the investigator found that there was the same sort of alienation. Many of them appeared to have no awareness of the house system as a form of organisation for pastoral care—i.e. of their individual needs or problems. Many do not know to whom they should turn for help and guidance, and many of the rank-and-file members of staff would not have been able to help much if they had been approached since there was no detailed guidance available. Some children did not even know the name of their house master, in the middle school. The house system had, for many children, become identified with retaliatory discipline, and so, in the middle school, had the director of studies. As a result, most children would reject the house system, the deputy head and the director of studies as channels of pastoral care. They would simply not be approached.

The report concluded with two major recommendations.

(a) That the school needed a more formal structure of instrumental organisation, authority and delegation, coupled with a system of consultative committees. The most important committee should be one concerned with policy, planning and organisation, and should consist of not more than twelve senior members of staff, each to have two or three overlapping areas of functional responsibility—for example, an academic sector, a pastoral sector, an administrative sector, a professional sector (concerned, for example, with the induction and in-service training of young, especially probationer teachers), a sector concerned with curriculum innovation, and so on.

(b) It would be useful for the school to consider a redefinition of its pastoral and social policies, with the object of setting out an organised framework for coping with problems of individual children's welfare and discipline as one integrated rational structure combined with an effective system of records and documentation. With this redefinition should go a detailed investigation of the possibilities that pastoral organisation in this school (which had become, under reorganisation, a 'neighbourhood' school) should be extended to cover some of the needs of the district for a more complete and integrated channel for social care and education. There appeared to have been an increase in the number of children in the school suffering various forms of disturbance and deprivation. Hence the school needed to develop policies towards compensatory education. The whole function and purpose of discipline needed to be redefined.

On reading this report, the Headmaster was incensed. He wrote a very critical letter to the Director, declaring that he felt he had been unfairly treated. The letter made the following points:

(i) The investigation had been imposed on the school at the worst possible time, when it had suffered very severe strains, both personal and organisational, consequent on rapid expansion, change of function and intake, and switching of children from one school to another at the most difficult time for them, and leaving many of them with only a year or less to go in their new school. All this had been imposed on the school with great haste, at very little notice. What the school had needed was time to get over these difficulties, and settle down to its new organisation and routines.

(ii) The report was much too 'short-term' in its viewpoint. It concentrated on the immediately obvious symptoms and problems resulting on change. Nobody had previously suggested that the school had been badly organised, or unhappy, before reorganisation —indeed it had had an extremely good public image and had achieved national press reporting on its efforts in community service, as well as very good academic results. Given time and encouragement rather than criticism, it would get over its temporary difficulties—which were in any case confined to only a minority of its pupils.

(iii) He objected strenuously to the use of the word 'alienation' in the report. It was insulting to him and to his senior colleagues on the staff, and it was a gross misrepresentation of the attitudes of the great majority of his colleagues. He had been closely involved in their selection, and knew them all well, and he challenged the Director to come to the school and seek out for himself any members of his staff who were 'alienated'. The same applied to the children. More than two-thirds of them had been at the school before reorganisation, and it had not been suggested then that the school was having an alienating effect on its children. Quite the reverse in fact, since many children's parents had been opting for the school, and the numbers staying on into the fifth and sixth forms had increased continuously throughout the sixties.

(iv) He objected to the use of meaningless sociological and managerial jargon in the report. It was obvious that the investigator knew very little about the real problems of running a school. A school was not a factory with a physical output which could be measured in terms of efficiency of production; nor could it be organised as if it were a commercial company with boards of directors, works committees and the like. He did not know what 'span of control' meant in a school—what control, what decisions, functions, responsibilities, planning was the investigator talking about? It was always generalisations, with very little factual evidence. A school had clear educational purposes and tasks, easily understood by professional teachers—they did not need a social worker to tell them how to organise a school to educate children. They also knew what discipline meant in a school—it must always have retaliatory aspects, otherwise the first requirement of running a school successfully—order and purposeful activity—would not be met.

(v) He disagreed completely with the idea of a 'cabal' of twelve senior men to form the central policy-making committee in the school. It was the Head's job to make policy, in consultation with the Director and the governors. He could always consult with his senior staff members—he always had done so, and with junior members too, and had never previously heard any complaints. He also thought that the idea of functional organisation for this committee was quite fatuous. A school's organisation was not divided into 'sectors' in this way, and this proposal would produce artificial divisions and destroy its very valuable flexibility. If there was a unit for innovation, why should anybody else bother to innovate? The same applied to all the other 'sectors'. A 'cabal' would also divide the staff into those who were 'in' and those who were not, and would militate against unity.

The letter concluded by demanding that the Director withdraw the report unconditionally.

For Discussion

1. Was the report fair and balanced in its analysis of Westwood School's shortcomings? Was it too critical? Did it give enough weight to the school's positive achievements? Was it too 'short-term' in its evaluation?

2. Comment on the general idea, expressed in the report, that large schools need a more complete, explicitly defined structure of organisation and consultation than small schools, in which much can be left to informal contact and intimate personal knowledge. How far does what happened at Westwood School support or deny this idea?

3. Is it correct to link disciplinary with pastoral policy, needs and organisation, or can they be independent of each other? What measures would you adopt in respect of pastoral and disciplinary problems in Westwood School?

4. What do you feel about the use of words like 'alienation', 'involvement', 'identification', 'line and staff', 'span of control', 'instrumental organisation'?

5. Comment on the idea of the growth of pastoral needs resulting from the new functions of Westwood School as a neighbourhood school. What do you see as the implications of the investigator's comments on cases of disturbance and deprivation, and of the extension of these comments into the idea of compensatory education?

6. Do you agree with the links postulated in the report between pastoral organisation and effort and an effective records system?

7. Comment on the first of the investigator's recommendations. In particular what do you think of the idea of a central policy committee organised functionally? Do you agree with the Headmaster that the use of managerial analysis is inappropriate to a large school's organisation?

8. How do you react to the Headmaster's letter? What points in it do you feel were justified?

9. If you were the Director, what would you do?

CHAPTER 11

REACTIONS
TO THE CASE STUDIES

1. DAVID HOWELLS

BEFORE attempting to discuss either case, it may be illuminating to try to look at the background of Neighbourhood School and Westwood Comprehensive as the historian of education of the early twenty-first century might see it.

Our historian will have noted the rash of reports from Hadow to Norwood and will mark the milestone of the 1944 Education Act. He will see the rise of meritocracy following the Second World War, with its consequent accent on qualifications. He will note the rise in popular and governmental interest in, and demand for, the means of providing these qualifications, starting, of necessity, in schools. He will be able to see more clearly the conflict between the pursuit of knowledge for its own sake and the craze for the provision of 'tickets'. He will take into account the efforts made to implement the Act within a tripartite framework, and the increasing lack of confidence in methods of selection for the different categories. Perhaps a political influence will be apparent in the controversies of the sixties, but there must certainly be some amazement at the attempt to overcome the difficulties so quickly and with so little expenditure, while the demands of the Robbins Report on Higher Education take a large slice of the Exchequer cake for education.

Perhaps our historian will be standing in a school of the future. Will it be a very temporary structure capable of being reorientated without undue difficulty? It should have the most modern means of communication and equipment for learning which a rapidly developing technical age can supply. He will doubtless wonder how any Headmaster could have made a time-table without a computer. He will be amazed that Heads were able to take over administrative duties in large establishments without previous staff college learning. He will be aware of the jargon fully accepted by management course participants. The Professor Thomasons of the future will have less difficulty in persuading Headmasters that a comparison between monocratic bureaucracy and a professional organisation with a broad influx of expertise at the base has a relevance to headmastership. Headmasters will be skilled, and will know that they are setting objectives and implementing them by calculated decisions. They will assess the effect of a decision and, by comparison, modify their means of directing when the required goal is not reached. The science of assessment will take account of qualities which we now like to think are intangible.

We are overworking our historian! He will have a better overall view of the vast shift of moral and social standards of the fifties and sixties. He will see clearly the influence of mass media and note that a body of young people was growing up without, but with the fear of, being decimated by war, and without the discipline of either the economic stringencies or the national service of their immediate predecessors. Fifty years hence it will be easy to see the results of the decline in the influence of the Church, while noting the comparatively high standard of material living, brought about in the main by the existence of two sources of income to the family, at the heavy cost at times of consequent change in the mode of family life. This placed an added load on the teaching profession previously borne by the parent.

How does our Neighbourhood School look now? The very fact that an abortive attempt is made to carry out a system of comprehensive education in three widely separated buildings can be attributed to an effort to make haste too fast. The buildings had probably not had time to cool off from their part in what was to be another 'final' system hardly twenty years of age.

The process of education involves a mass entanglement of human relationships, of pupils amongst themselves, boy with girl, boy and girl with parents, pupils with staff, staff with parents and each other. Change of emphasis in these relationships needs time for adjustment.

It is possible, indeed it seems highly probable, that the time element was such that it forced inadequate planning to precipitate a situation where it was impossible to provide even a temporarily adequate solution to a very complex problem. Here are a few of the questions which need to be asked and answered:

Has adequate thought been given to training administrators and staff to tackle what is virtually a completely new job?

Are the sources of new staff sufficiently aware of the new problems facing schools—or are their products still being trained to meet an old and outmoded system?

Does this place an unbearable load on in-service training?

Are we trying to produce by revolution something which can only be achieved by the process of evolution?

Whatever the answers, our Neighbourhood School finds itself in circumstances which make it necessary to attempt to change from a system with accent on the provision of *instruction* for the few to one with a broad base of effective *education* for the many.

The Headmaster, with the preservation of his sanity and hope of daily survival in mind, had spotted *some* of the major problems. In his anxiety to preserve some continuity of known standards—and in this 'ticket' age this was probably expected of him by parents—he had obviously decided to sacrifice the good of the many for the success of the few.

He had failed badly in certain directions through not appreciating the enormity of his task. He had not sought to make lines of communication clear to his staff. He had not defined his objectives specifically. There had been no attempt to re-educate staff, pupils and parents on long-term policy, and there does not seem to have been any arrangement for continued consultation. There is no mention of advice sought or given by the Inspectorate.

One of the major problems, probably common to all schools, of which the Head showed awareness, was that of trying to create some measure of discipline. The school had little ethos or sense of community. One may well ask, how much did the neighbourhood help in disciplinary problems? One often hears of the effect the school should have on the community—there is little discussion of the role the neighbourhood should play in the school.

In Part 2 the Headmaster resigns, having given sixteen years of devoted service to the school (do they say that at every resignation?), obviously overcome by the problems he had to face. (One may ask, in parentheses, how many Heads and staff are finding themselves in similar circumstances but are denied resignation for one reason or another?)

The new Headmaster will, doubtless, find himself beset immediately with the same problems as his predecessor but will, one hopes, not be worn out with the task. He will surely be anxious to delegate authority along clear lines, and find a means of building up a community spirit in the school, in staff and pupils alike. He will aim to educate the whole school without neglecting the few. His system must provide pastoral care for all, with arrangements made to see that the neighbourhood community is both aware of what he is trying to do and is willing to play a full part.

The new Head is saddled with an experimental appointment, though he may think that every teacher ought to be a counsellor. It may well be that to place responsibility for counselling on one member of staff will add to difficulties with staff already not amenable to discipline, according to the previous Headmaster. It might be better to combine the role of counsellor-in-chief with that of careers master, who, like the heads of department, will have some influence on curricular arrangements. The resulting time-table should then reflect the explained and accepted policy of the school.

Let us now turn to the problems of Westwood Comprehensive. Under the caring eye of the doting father, 'like Topsy it grew'. This Topsy grew too fast and had growing pains which all mistook—and, most of all, the press—for something far more serious. Topsy would have grown up strong and healthy without calling in the consultant—and in any case the wrong consultant was called.

In the first part of the case study this was a selective modern school "under a variety of pressures" in the academic sense, and there is comment on the assiduity of the Headmaster in competing "on equal terms with the grammar schools for staff and resources and for prestige". Is criticism to be detected here? If so, I would question whether the Head's efforts were incompatible with achieving a socially viable internal organisation and a good public image. He seems to have been able to cope with the problems; his relationship with staff, pupils and public were those you would expect from a man obviously living his school.

The Headmaster's troubles began with the influx into his community of those who felt inferior. The previous organisation was no longer adequate. Unless each child in a school has a feeling of belonging, and there are purposeful courses for each one, disciplinary problems are bound to result. We now see the Head as a man willing to consult, to make decisions and to be ready to be responsible for them, but perhaps not to seek the external advice which is at his disposal.

But why bring in a research team? There is no mention of a relationship with the Inspectorate or of the comments of Her Majesty's Inspectors on the research report. One is prompted to wonder whether the Director of Education knew of the existence of H.M.I.s!

While Westwood School is designated specifically as coming within a large city complex, its problems are relevant for schools in all urban or industrial conurbations. One would therefore again have been glad to see some comment on the effects of the community on a school, a comprehensive school being by its very nature a microcosm of the community which engenders it.

It is in this context that the problem of discipline must be considered. If discipline is not used in its narrow sense of maintaining law and order but in its full significance of both mental and moral training, it is important to develop an awareness—and not only among the pupils—of the claims on each of the public good. How this can be achieved without sacrificing the needs of the individual raises large issues of the seemingly inevitable conflict between the ethos of the school and practical living, between the ideal and the possible, between the desirable and the expedient.

One thing is certain—more thought has to be given to objectives and priorities, leading to more opportunities for those who find themselves in the midst of change to find help and guidance. In this respect the group discussion of case studies and simulation exercises on the Cardiff course, which showed up many differences of viewpoint, helped tremendously—partly through identifying these differences—to make more specific the "management approach" of the lectures given by Professor Thomason.

2. H. ELUNED JONES

NEIGHBOURHOOD SCHOOL

Three buildings, three-quarters of a mile apart, with a main road to contend with! From the facts given it is difficult not to conclude that hasty and ill-considered reorganisation in unsuitable premises has accentuated the educational and social handicaps under which Neighbourhood School is struggling, while providing none of the benefits which a large, but purpose-built, school could offer.

Recognising the acute difficulties, however, it is disappointing to see so little evidence of any attempt either to develop a corporate spirit in the school or to ensure that each child has an effective, sympathetic link with at least one member of staff. Meaningful contact with parents is also important, particularly in a setting such as this, but it seems to be actively discouraged.

In our discussion groups many of us came to feel that at the heart of the situation lie the inadequate educational aims of the school, which do not cater for the needs of the vast majority of the children. The Headmaster mistakenly seeks for academic results from a school population extremely unlikely to achieve them. Why does he not experiment with the Certificate of Secondary Education, using the school-based Mode 3, or seek other educational goals? One of the difficulties is that nearly all practising teachers were themselves brought up in grammar schools—those Ordinary and Advanced levels are the goals they know and admire—so they need to be actively encouraged, stimulated, cajoled, even perhaps driven imaginatively and diplomatically to see that the real heart of the educational challenge today is to achieve significant progress with the less able children. Are colleges of education and university education departments equipping students adequately with the necessary skills, and do they, by their own enthusiasm, impart and encourage right attitudes?

In this school some academic success at Advanced level has been obtained by the few, but at what a cost to the school as a whole! A transfer at 16+ to a sympathetic and understanding school with a larger sixth form and a wider programme is here, I think, the only possible answer for such pupils. There is then a need for bold curriculum planning and a wind of change among the staff. New approaches and methods, academic groupings, pastoral care arrangements and career opportunities—all need to be explored on the initiative, or with the encouragement, of the Head. It is easy to be critical from the outside, less easy to see yourself and your school objectively, but the Head needs to take a New Look, and someone must help him to do so. Will it be the Director, the inspectors? They are partly responsible for landing him in this mess, and should take some responsibility for him in it!

I also believe—as has been argued by Raymond Long of Tulse Hill School—that management training is essential for the successful planning and effective running of schools of this kind. At our Cardiff course Professor Thomason applied to the school situation theories of organisation worked out in the context of industry, having recently performed a similar service in relation to Cardiff's new hospital system. Clear responsibilities, effective delegation, good personal relationships and constant care to see that aims and plans are communicated and really understood and acted upon—these are some of the ideas which we subsequently discussed in seminars and group meetings.

In Part 2 we have a new Headmaster and the appointment of a counsellor. I believe it would have been wiser to appoint the Head and let him get the feel of the situation, get to know his staff and help to choose the counsellor. There would then be time to work out his role with care, and quietly, but purposefully, prepare the ground for his advent.

But the appointment is made and the counsellor is there, ready to start. So the new Head must concentrate in the immediate future on the task of developing new personal relationships, all the while planning furiously to introduce some radical changes in aims, courses and programmes for the next school year. He can tackle the need for new patterns of responsibility in pastoral care and decision-making; in the meantime he can 'work in' the new counsellor, enabling him to get to know, in smallish groups, the pupils of the middle school and, later, the first-formers. In addition to his part, with others, in vocational guidance (including careers talks, visiting speakers, visits to factories, etc.), the counsellor might be encouraged to develop courses in personal relationships in the lower and middle school. It will be vital that there should be good understanding between the counsellor and the head, and also with the staff. A talk by the counsellor to the staff on problems encountered and possible solutions would be a good idea. In order to dissipate some of the fears and prejudices which exist in the staff common room he must somehow 'get over' his work and himself and enable the staff to see that he is an effective and helpful colleague. The counsellor must also establish himself with the parents—it is essential that they come to know him and trust him.

For the school as a whole I suggest the provision of generous auxiliary help, particularly clerical assistance, to relieve staff of tasks which others can do and so release their energies for the new responsibilities—preparing reports for counsellors, learning new methods, working together on new projects, perhaps even developing team teaching approaches. If the provision of secretaries, dinner supervisors, laboratory technicians and metal-shop assistants can help to encourage experiment and innovation, banish cynicism and kindle enthusiasm, for heaven's sake let us not hesitate. There may be some mistakes, but there will be new life and vision, I hope, and new zest.

WESTWOOD COMPREHENSIVE

In many ways this too is a tragic situation, and it grieves me to see so much that is good and admirable in purpose and policy defeated by an unwise throwing together of schools, involving the transfer at 13 and 14 of so many children, a large proportion of whom will have only one, or at most two years in the school. My immediate reaction is that a scheme which inflates size while posing such intractable educational and social problems should never have been sanctioned.

Nevertheless, I feel I must also criticise severely the educational aims of the school and, therefore, of the Headmaster. Public esteem, effectively rivalling neighbouring 'more fortunate' schools, good results in examinations, worth-while public occasions—none of these in themselves are wrong, but they should follow as a result of a deeper, more idealistic purpose which would, I hope, exercise just that twist which would deflect these aims from the possibility of bad effects.

As it is, the school has grown rapidly, the necessary rethinking does not seem to have taken place and there is no effective sharing of responsibility or clear-cut delegation. The biggest problem is the sudden influx of new staff, with no real guidance for the younger members. When the crisis comes the senior mistress is aware of this problem, but seems to be struggling with it in isolation. One asks, why has this issue not been brought forward? What effective 'talking over' with his senior staff does the Head have? Why does the senior mistress not have a 'trainable deputy'. There is something radically wrong here.

The situation is tense but the Head only moves when the Head of middle school hands in his resignation and then, and only then, reports frankly to him. Why not before? Did the Headmaster have no consultative procedure involving his senior staff? It is apparently only when the press steps in that he calls for a report from them all.

Ensuing discussions, leading to a tightening up of previous disciplinary measures, reveal a lack of positive, creative ideas and also how little had been done to help the staff to cope with the new situation, particularly the difficulties of handling adolescent boys and girls in our permissive society. How skilfully did the Head deploy his staff? Did he, as far as possible, place senior and experienced staff with the more difficult age groups, the third and fourth forms, while using his young and inexperienced teachers in the first two years and with the fifth and sixth forms? Did he discuss with the more experienced staff, who must also have come to him by transfer, where they might be used to best advantage to integrate the incoming youngsters into the receiving community?

Alerted by the press, the Director of Education and the chairman of governors consult with the Headmaster. It is fair to ask whether the Director had initiated any consultations on the inherent problems in the previous year: did he help the Headmaster and staff to prepare for this new and difficult situation? He has an interest in social worker courses at the university; he might also have arranged lectures and courses for the staffs of the schools on the obvious problems ahead as a result of reorganisation. The research scheme he now suggests is not likely to be successful unless the Headmaster is in sympathy and is convinced it can be helpful.

The consultant investigates, but we are not told whether this is done in a friendly and helpful atmosphere. I agree with much of his report—the school has grown too large too suddenly and now spans too wide a range to enable one man to hold all the reins. Delegation of authority and sharing of decision-making is essential, involving heads of department in new managerial responsibilities. Many heads of department, harking back to a period when additional payments were a recognition for sixth-form teaching, do not appreciate that their role carries wider and quite onerous responsibilities in the framework of the school. It is the Head's task to educate them into this, and it needs to be done with tact and understanding as well as with determination. In fact we should all have been doing this, as Heads, for some time.

While largely agreeing with the recommendations, I would have couched them in different and more traditional terminology, in the hope that in this way they would be less likely to offend and, thereby, be more acceptable to the Headmaster. He could then, without losing face, build more adequately on what he had already achieved, for it is only fair to recognise that there is an element of truth in his reaction. It also seems a fair comment that he is not the only one who has shown a lack of awareness of long-term and short-term difficulties.

Case studies such as the above proved of considerable value to Heads and senior staff on the Cardiff course, leading to frank and helpful discussion of fundamental aims and how to achieve them. Might they not also be profitably discussed at County/City Hall and in Curzon Street?

PART 5

EVALUATION

CHAPTER 12

A FRAMEWORK FOR EVALUATING OPERATIONAL ORGANISATION IN SECONDARY SCHOOLS

PETER C. WEBB

A. INTRODUCTION

We are concerned here with the operational organisation of schools, especially comprehensives. At this level, that is at the level at which the task is done, through the contacts made between teacher and learning groups or individual pupils, effectiveness is a matter of the design of the system, and the quality of personal involvement it induces.

In neither case is the operational organisation's effectiveness autonomously determined. As a system it is usually (as in other organisations) not fully aligned with non-operational organisation; thus the structures of academic departments, determined largely by Burnham considerations, and of management, determined by administrative and institutional systems at school/L.E.A. level, often have little alignment with the operational structure of teaching or pastoral groups and their programming. But there is interaction between them in that, for example, the structure of academic departments may stand in the way of development of integrative curricula, or of the full development of pastoral organisation with appropriate responsibility payments and statuses.

Similarly the quality of personal involvement in the operations at classroom and staffroom levels is itself part of a wider pattern of human relationships stretching through from the inside to the outside of the school. Attitudes of L.E.A. committees, officers and governors tend to be transmitted inside and to affect internal relationships. Thus the patterns of attitudes, perceptions and relationships are not wholly autonomous, though they may be discontinuous as between groups and levels. Not infrequently, for example, the children's perceptions of the structure and quality of pastoral responsibilities turn out to be at variance with those of their designers.

Such failures of alignment in design of systems and in perceptions, attitudes and involvement are to be expected in all large organisations. But while they will never be eliminated in any organisation, it is obviously profitable to reduce them below the threshold levels at which they become obtrusive. It is also obvious that some schools manage to achieve better designed and integrated functional organisations, and that some (not necessarily the same) schools achieve better involvement of staff's and pupils' loyalties and efforts than others. The interesting questions are concerned with what we mean by better, and with how the schools achieve it.

The basic criteria we shall use in this chapter for evaluation of operational organisation in schools will, then, be design effectiveness and human effectiveness. We shall set them out in more detail, and use them for some tentative generalisations of types of operational structures. This would be a much more difficult task without the analytical notation and classifying systems for school organisation developed in North Wales by a team of H.M. Inspectors under the direction of Dr. T. I. Davies (1968). Building on this work, it is possible to present a framework of evaluatory suggestions for the different categories and divisions of operational organisation.

B. BASIS OF ANALYSIS

Grouping systems in schools are constructed on the basis of three major purposive elements; these are pedagogic, social and pastoral. They are, of course, strongly interactive and also not simple objectives in themselves, but compendia of sometimes quite diverse, but also overlapping, values. This is particularly true of social education, for example, which can be limited to the (supposedly) cohesive effects of 'houses' set up for competitive activities; or it can be extended to include learning to live effectively, in a social sense, with individuals or groups of a wide variety of abilities, outlook or class; or to understand and accept the tensions between the need to conform and the desire to satisfy and develop oneself as an individual; or to understand and accept the complexities and responsibilities of living in a modern community. At these points it overlaps both the pedagogic (in social or community studies) and the pastoral, in providing links between an individual and a tutor responsible for supervising his development in the school.

The result of these overlaps is that most schools fall back on the device of merging the social component partly with the pedagogic, and partly with the pastoral. This allows even quite large schools to manage with a two-dimensional organisational design, based on

(a) pedagogic/social, i.e. *curricular*, and
(b) personal/social, i.e. *pastoral*, operations.

The first functions through the setting up of time-tabled classes or teaching groups, the second through the creation of 'reference' groups such as house groups, form tutor groups or year tutor groups, as discussed in Chapters 7 and 8. These reference groups may identify with certain of the teaching groups where the form, or the house-group, is taught as a group for a significant part of the week. This system of teaching groups and pastoral reference groups forms the basis of the analytical approach used in this chapter.

But before we go on with this analysis, it will be as well to remind ourselves that it is, in a very significant sense, artificial. Analysis of complex systems of activities and objectives is a necessary stage in the design of organisations. It is arbitrary, however, in that what to the pupil is a single network of experiences, set in programmes of contact, work and locations, has to be split up into sectors designed for no other reason than to make setting up a system of responsibilities, tasks, functions and controls possible in each one of them. In general the larger the school the greater the formality and arbitrariness of this design of structures, and the greater the need for exposition and communication in terms of these separated out aspects of the same thing. Thus the idea that a school has separately definable, if over-lapping, organisations for curricular functioning on the one hand, and pastoral care on the other, is only valid from a managerial point of view. In the eyes of the children, particularly the younger and the less analytical ones, what happens to them in school is a largely continuous experience; it would be unnatural and super-fluous for them to have a strong sense that what is happening to them is 'pastoral' as distinct from 'social' or 'pedagogic'. It may indeed be confusing to children, and even to some staff, to stress this analytical distinction; however elaborate the Head may make the design of the organisation as a response to the range of his school's objectives it should not be a complex task of analysis for a pupil to work out who to go to to have any particular problem solved.

C. EVALUATORY

These words of caution uttered, we may now go on to set out some evaluative categories for curricular and pastoral organisation. In the system proposed here, there are five of them:

(a) mechanical, or design;

(b) economic, in the sense of efficiency of resource deployment;

(c) judgemental, concerned with decision-making; and situa-tional, in terms of local or specific needs;

(d) human or social, concerned with grouping effects and perceptions;

(e) dynamic, in the sense of coping with educational and social change, and the development of staff and their capacities.

(a) *Mechanical or design*

A time-table or curriculum structure has certain purely mechanical characteristics—it is in fact a complex honeycomb of allocations, in which the total of possible combinations is immense. Only a few of them are free from mechanical defects such as double periods for Latin, as in this fourth form option set for examinations in a comprehensive school,

$$L/G/G/A/C/Mk/Ds$$

4 periods

or this, in a grammar school in Wales,

$$(W/F + F/L/Re)/(P/P + C/C)$$

5 + 5 periods

designed so as to make it feasible to set single-period against double-period subjects, and allowing Welsh to be taken in addition to French, but in doing so forcing a massive choice into or out of science at the age of 14.

At a more basic mechanical level, it is worth giving some attention to the relative advantages of the 8×35-minute period day as against the 7×40 (this is partly a matter of the disposition of rooms, and the decision whether to move children to teachers or vice versa), of the 5:3 or 4:4 layout of eight periods (important in relation to getting the most out of labs. and practical/craft rooms), or even of the more flexible arrangement of the nine- or ten-period day with the middle two or three periods used for a staggered lunch break.

To generalise, the principal features governing mechanical or design effectiveness in a curriculum structure are its balance (some schools allocate so many teacher periods to the fourth, fifth and sixth forms that the second and third are 'squeezed' into very standardised programmes, sometimes in over-large groups—a self-defeating arrangement if ever there was one), its freedom from defects of the sort mentioned above, its richness in terms of devices to open up opportunities while preventing wrong choices, and its flexibility in allowing a variety of educational treatments to be made available to each group.

On the pastoral side, mechanical or structural effectiveness is a matter of allowing and programming direct contact between each individual child and a tutor having pastoral responsibility for him. This implies a designed set-up with links to records, disciplinary systems and academic organisation, with enough flexibility (combined with good communications on the teachers' side) for children's unprogrammed contacts—when they have a problem to be dealt with, either informally or by referral to the relevant pastoral/welfare specialist—the counsellor or careers teacher, for example. Pastoral structures are usually one of three types:

(a) extra-curricular—for example houses or tutor groups not set up for teaching purposes;

(b) curricular-aligned—in which pastoral responsibilities are added, as a function, to the duties of those in charge of primary teaching groups (forms, as distinct from sets), co-ordinated by year-tutors, or heads of lower/middle/upper school;

(c) intra-curricular—for example, house groups or tutor groups —usually mixed ability—used as teaching groups for some part of the week, but whose main basis of definition is social.

For quantitative evaluation of mechanical aspects, perhaps the most satisfactory approach is through the analysis of case loads. It would take too long to go into this in detail here, but it may provide a sufficient hint to outline an example.

An eight-form entry school with a type (b) structure may by this means be compared with the same sized school with a type (c). The specifications may be set out as in Table 1.

By making assumptions as to how often each tutor should interview his pupils (twice a term minimum, for example), how often children may be expected to make unprogrammed contacts, and what proportion of cases need to be passed on to supervisory staff,

Type	Years	No. of pupils	Primary divisions and tutors	Careers/ counsellors, etc.	Supervisory staff	Total staff involved
(b) Form tutor	1 – 4	240 each yr.	Form tutors (32)		Lower (2) Middle (2)	36 2
	5+	240 altogether	Form tutors (8)	2	Upper (2)	10
Totals		1200	40	2	6	48
(c) 4 houses House tutor system	1 – 4	240 each house	House tutors (32)	+ 3 remedial group tutors 2	Lower (4) Middle (4) + 8 over all	43 } 10
	5+	240	House tutors (8)		Upper (4)	12 }
		1200	40	5	20	65

Notes. (1) Remedial group tutors in type (b) will be within form system, but outside house system in type (c).

(2) Supervisory staff will consist of head of each house in type (c), together with head and deputy of each house overall. (These types are not necessarily only specified in this way, and should not be taken as typical—for example, type (b) could additionally have a co-ordinating year tutor for each year.) It is remarkable that, as specified, the house system involves virtually the entire staff of the school, while the type (b) structure involves about two-thirds to three-quarters. This will make the problems of co-ordination and communication greater in the former, though it may improve overall supervision; and, of course, the house system may have social purposes to do with its situation, location, or environment—in other words, the count of staff involved is not the whole basis of the decision.

L/M/U division of each house in type (c), plus their deputies in type (b); but head of house in

221

it is possible to work out an expected case load for each tutor/ supervisor involved, and use this to compare the two systems. In each, given reasonable assumptions, the tutors would average between three and five interviews a week, while supervisory staff would have two to three in type (b) but about two in type (c) (not counting purely disciplinary cases, or visits from parents and social welfare agencies outside the school); careers/counsellors might expect in either set-up some ten, or more, depending on how they are programmed.* It is important to stress that this is only a hint at the possibilities of structural case load analysis—in practice it is difficult and often arbitrary, and is more suitable, as it stands, for use as part of planning and decision-making processes than for direct evaluation. But some consideration of mechanical design effectiveness is obviously necessary as a first step, in this section; other considerations will come in later sections.

(b) *Economic*

The school time-table is the mechanism by which the various resources (teachers, teaching spaces, equipment, subjects—in so far as these have economic 'value') are deployed or distributed among the teaching groups set up. To the extent that the groupings of children reflect, say, ability (which may be correlated with home or class background), or worth in terms of potential, this allocation of teachers and resources may be said to reflect a valuation of the economic importance, or need, of these groups or their activities (learning science, for example). Again, an important characteristic is 'balance'; any squeeze on some groups resulting from excessive allocations to others would be defective in this context (it is sometimes produced inadvertently by the sequence in which the time-table is constructed—though this in itself can be taken as an indicator of priorities). The reciprocal of the teacher allocation is the size of the teaching group, also an indicator of

* In outlining this approach, I am drawing heavily on the (unpublished) work of my colleague H.M.I. Mr. P. F. Smart.

economic balance—as between one year group and another, for example, or as between subjects.

A second type of design defect expressing itself in terms of economic losses occurs in systems involving early options, by which pupils in Latin, for example, are offered a chance to drop it, as an option against some other subject, after only a year; for those who do so, their year's work may well have been something of a waste of time and effort.

An important use of teacher periods, or subject classes in the T. I. Davies (1968) notation, can be made by attributing a cost to them. This is useful in planning ahead, where the costing of different structural models—streamed, unstreamed, setted in various ways—can be obtained by attributing an average or standard salary. Costing systems such as this could become a very useful feature in the planning of schools, and systems of schools.

The discussion of pastoral organisation, under (a) above, has already given quite a few hints about the economic and costing aspects of different forms of pastoral organisation. In the two examples given (which may not, of course, be wholly typical of their categories) the house system appears to be rather costlier in terms of allocation of people to pastoral functions. Care needs to be taken in interpreting this, since the case load divided among them is not assumed to be significantly changed; but the intercommunication problem, the records work, and the decision-making may need greater capacity. Since economic analysis is concerned as much at least with effectiveness as with costs, the question of the two systems' relative effectiveness also needs to be taken into account.

(c) *Judgemental—situational*

The curriculum or time-table structure is really a system of interlocking decisions—for example, on what basis to divide a comprehensive intake of, say, 280 children into groups for teaching, what subjects to give the groups, and in how many periods; how to define, group and allocate children into remedial units, and what to provide for them; what arrangements of options to set up for examinations groups in forms 4, 5 and 6, and whether to separate O level from C.S.E. groups; what programmes to provide for non-examination leavers, including the ex-remedials; which groups should have access to the science laboratories (in some cases, remedial children are not time-tabled into the laboratories at all). And so on.

Since the whole time-table is fixed overall in respect of its finite numbers of pupils, teachers, spaces and periods, these decisions inter-lock with, and act as constraints on, each other. The whole decision system, involving the grouping process and the treatment some groups receive, can be taken as a direct reflection of the school's actual working policies and priorities—and hence its philosophies—as they apply to the different groups of children it has set up (con-ditioned, of course, by the Headmaster's skill at manipulating this rather complex honeycomb—a skill whose distribution in the population could be a rather interesting investigation). The judge-ments and decisions embodied in the time-table system are social as well as educational, only sometimes made explicitly as a response to consciously defined objectives and priorities (which is partly why the sequence in which the time-table is constructed is so significant). One might, for example, look at the position of art, as an indicator of the relative importance of aesthetic as against academic priorities for the more, and the less, able groups; or investigate the number of languages offered to more able groups, and what other subjects, at what stages, may be dropped to make way for them—non-academic subjects, and sciences are often affected. Also signi-ficant are the inconsistencies inevitable to some extent in all 'honey-comb' allocations, which occur especially along the long section of the school. A good example is the case of the small comprehensive which finds itself rather short of modern language capacity, but manages to keep a sixth form going by allocating only three periods of its teacher's time to each of the second and third forms, thus constricting the supply of pupils who can reach the sixth-form stage in the subject. Or, again in modern languages, the policy of providing them right across the ability band in the first two years which in simple logistics can mean that the great majority of the pupils *must* give them up after that.

Local considerations are often very important factors in these decisions, and the system's effectiveness can be judged to some extent by how well it copes with specific situational problems such as separate buildings, intake imbalances (social as well as educational), population growth or decline, L.E.A. policies, and local occupational needs. A particular problem in Wales is the problem locally of bilingual ability—one 6 form entry rural school is using this, jointly with ability-banding, as criteria for grouping in its first two years, but the incidence of C.S.E. as an addition to the range of examination-based classes it must cater for has meant that it is unable to extend its bilingual grouping further.

(One reason why a study of curriculum structure is so interesting is that it can take such local factors into account, and its system of priorities expresses itself, always against a background of limitation of resources. Such a study, based on classifications of size, type, and organisation, is essential as a basis for wider policy decisions, educational and administrative. For example, in the small (3 form entry) bilateral schools of rural Wales, the 2 G: 1 M* basis of organisation has resulted from limitations of size and staffing—1 G: 2 M would cost more teacher-time in small academic subject groups setted in options; but it seems that this has actually tended to result in a larger proportion of the age group staying on into the fifth, and even the sixth forms. Whether this is good or not and whether the right groups of pupils are paying the right sort of price for this is for the policy-makers to decide.)

Much the same sort of discussion is appropriate to pastoral organisation—indeed the proportion of resources to allocate to pastoral care is itself a significant decision, depending on local factors, as much as on calculations of case loads, as in the example in (a) above. Local factors impinging on such decisions will include the nature of the area socially, its urban–rural characteristics, and an evaluation of

* i.e. two "grammar", one modern, streams.

compensatory and cultural needs. But the difficulty is that the effectiveness of a wide variety of alternative models in the operational context of all these local environments has not been usefully investigated, and this whole decision area is severely affected by lack of knowledge and operational experience.

It is thus not possible to say that, in a school of such and such a size, or location, or social composition, any specified form of pastoral organisation will tend to work 'best'. The best one can hope for is to be able to set out a reasonably full classification of types, each with certain operational characteristics, and to indicate what conditions, statuses, responsibilities, support, and training are likely to be needed to give each type a chance of working effectively. Choice of set-up is then a matter of matching these characteristics with the school's situation. But implementation is something else still—to do with attitudes, communication and involvement.

(d) *Human or social*

If comprehensive schools, set up to try to offset the social divisiveness of selective systems, are to provide adequately for the full range of ability, they may need to be large and complex. The kinds of dilemma this produces, in public debate, about the human aspects of comprehensive schools are

(a) whether their size is likely to make them less sensitive to individual needs or problems;

(b) whether it does not become too difficult to provide a fair balance of opportunity and access to resources as between the much wider range of groups and interests than in the smaller selective schools (and for this balance to be *seen* to be fair);

(c) whether they can expect to receive adequate management and leadership, in the same sense as can be given by the head teacher of a small school, in a selective system;

(d) whether their aim and objectives, educationally and socially, have not been extended too greatly for a single organisation to cope with them.

As expressed, however, these are too crude. There is no continuous increase in insensitivity with increasing size in schools—indeed the number of small schools which can fairly be described as insensitive, or which patently favour certain groups of children as against others, is certainly not small. Nor is good leadership and management confined to small schools, and their reverse absent from them. The fact is that there is much greater variation in terms of human effectiveness *within* the postulated categories of schools in these statements (grammar, modern, comprehensive, small, large and so on), than exists *between* them. Within any one of these categories, the organisational variable is sufficient by itself to produce considerable differences in human relationships; and in any case, the quality of human relationships is not a simple function of type, size, or growth but has complex social determinants. It may even be better treated, analytically, as a moderately independent *causal* variable, affecting individuals' perceptions of and reactions to, relatively neutral organisational features.

This can make it difficult to incorporate each postulated relationship effectively into the organisational structure of a school. For example, a school may aim to offset the 'type-casting' effects of streaming by adopting a wide range of devices—from the elementary trick of not calling its forms 1A, 1B and so on, to the more sophisticated devices of non-streaming, that is, of setting up mixed ability groups to be taught in non-academic, while using setting for academic, subjects. Children can see through them equally; sophisticated some of them may be, organisationally, but the disguised ability grouping hidden away in the setted system (where there is appreciable correlation in set-membership) is quite readily discerned. They, and the staff, too, may still perceive the distinctions between sets, in the different rooms, teachers and resources allocated to them. Again, a small school can be as readily as a large one sufficiently complex and organisationally inconsistent for a child to suffer a feeling of loss of identity and location—all that is necessary is to make it difficult enough for him to work out what group he should be in, and where it is, at any given moment. House-based curricula of type (c)—see p. 220—with a high proportion of setting, seem to be very good forms of organisation for presenting children with such analytical problems. But it does not follow that children in such organisations will necessarily find them hateful or repressive—other factors exist which work on their feelings and perceptions as well.

Not that the organisational factors have no significance at all. In schools, the organisational structures exist to produce the framework for contact between the teachers and the pupils to work in. Hence the need for analytical notations of the T. I. Davies type already mentioned, able to support organisational design decisions. How much setting to have in mixed ability systems, what emphasis to put on year-group as distinct from house-group pastoral forms in setted, streamed or banded structures, what degree of differentiation of curricula is tolerable between bands to allow the various kinds of human and professional problems to be dealt with—transfers between bands, for example; these are all organisation-specific. That is, they demand specific design responses, involving judgement on the Head's part as to their likely human responses in his particular school.

The required pay-off in any organisational design, in terms of human response, is simply involvement, or commitment; their opposites being withdrawal, or alienation. And it is a reasonable proposition that, at the elementary level, what is needed to avoid alienating people too severely are the requirements we have already set out for good organisational design—order and purpose, absence of muddles, inconsistencies and simple design faults, balance and fairness between groups in provision of teacher time, resources, opportunities and access to advice and help, and, for the staff, consistency between tasks and responsibilities on one hand, and clear communication, resources, time, training and rewards on the other.

But this is at the elementary level. It is obvious that these things have their effects through the perceptions of the pupils and staff, and not of those who design them. For organisational design is not to be approached as if it was the same sort of problem as, say, engineering design. As Hughes has observed in Chapter 2, the 'components' have human limitations and a life and a will of their own and these will influence the extent to which their activities will be as specified in the design. Moreover, the setting up of a group for teaching purposes has social side effects in that the group tends to develop an autonomous will and desires of its own, which may considerably influence its members' perception of the organisation and its aims and processes. Groups can thus behave quite irrationally from the point of view of the organisation, which may as a result find itself having to be content with standards of behaviour which are very low indeed, or, to put it another way, will have to tolerate an uncomfortably large proportion of unintended, autonomous, behaviour.

When a group or a class becomes aware that the school is accepting such minimal standards of commitment, this may in itself be a clue to them that the school has no great interest in them as a group. If this reinforces other clues, such as which groups get opportunities and access to resources, it may lead to alienation and the substitution of other cultural and social values to fill the gap.

Obviously in schools which are larger and more comprehensive in the sense of having a wider cross-section of social and cultural classes in their intake, there is more scope for this sort of thing to become significant; but the nature and occurrence of thresholds and the balance in their causation between the longer-term organisational, and the more immediate personal, factors have not really been investigated in various types of school organisation. Consequently there are few reliable rules at these higher-order behavioural levels; each school has its characteristic qualities in its internal relationships which may be favourable enough to offset a poor organisational or pastoral design or unfavourable enough to stultify a good one.

It is against this background of group effects and perceptions that policies concerned with grouping for school work need to be viewed at the design and evaluatory stages. The grouping of children wholly or largely on the basis of achieving ideal or homogeneous classes to teach is an over-simplification. What needs to be looked at in addi-

229

tion is the likely human and social reactions in various sectors of the school, and the supporting system of pastoral care, clerical and educational resources, and the insight, involvement, knowledge and skill of the staff in social as well as academic matters. This is a matter of leadership, and training programmes.

(e) *Dynamic*

The previous section has already hinted that rapid change of task or composition in a school lowers the thresholds at which it may lose significantly its control over the loyalties and involvement of some of the individuals and groups among the pupils and staff.

External change in ideas, knowledge and techniques in education is rapid; so are the changes in the demands society sees fit to make on its schools, especially on the new comprehensives, as several contributors to this volume have noted. Reorganisation involves risks—for example, that design of the new organisations will be too difficult, or that increase of responsibilities and changes of skills needed will be too large and too rapid—in other words, that the organisation will not adapt or 'learn' quickly enough.

Rate of learning or adaptation in an organisation is a complex variable, itself dependent on a number of other complex factors, some human, some organisational. It is not a simple combination of the rate of learning of the individuals who make it up; in the cases of the individuals and of the organisation itself, there is a considerable gap between their inherent capacity to react and the capacity of the organisation to allow them, and itself, to do so. In other words, the constraints on organisational learning are factors of at least equal significance.

Some of the most important constraints are external. Especially in local educational administration, the constitutional requirements that decisions be referred to this or that agency (D.E.S., H.M.I., examining body, successive L.E.A. committees), the institutional procedures (standing orders, limitations on ancillary office staffing, controls on expenditures and estimates), the often limited resources of the L.E.A. and other offices themselves to take on new work; all these are constraints on adaptability in the schools, particularly at times, such as reorganisation of secondary education, when rapid and effective adaptation is needed.

But inside the school, the time-table—changed only once a year, if that, and the structure of pastoral and tutorial responsibilities, also unlikely to be changed more often than once a year—both result in a fairly static situation with respect to adaptability. They represent, in other words, an inherent constraint. Others are the examination system, the tendency to accept fairly rigid subject-from-subject demarcations, and the lack of incentives in the salary/responsibility structures, which are all associated with status distinctions. In consequence, schools do not change rapidly, and tend to adapt slowly even to quite pronounced externally dictated changes in their constitution. At times of considerable change, this is a disadvantage.

Adaptive change needs to be purposive; that is, designed. This is, in the first place, the responsibility of the Head teacher; but in today's larger and more complex schools he can do no more, and perhaps no better, than to generate necessary change by inducing it in his teaching staff's attitudes towards their work in the changing situation. They need to be encouraged to take part with him in formulating policies, planning ahead and evaluating results; and be given opportunities to initiate, and involve their colleagues in, developments in their own and related fields. The creative and adaptive capacity of a school staff can be increased by leadership of this sort, which develops people by providing them with opportunities to develop themselves, and which provides a source, hitherto largely lacking, of on-the-job training experience for those who will have the job of managing future schools (cf. Webb, 1973).

Given that schools tend to be over-centralised and relatively inflexible at the operational level, it may be useful to hint at techniques for opening out some of the in-built constraints. The most promising may be the associated ideas of block time-tabling and team teaching, in which large groups of children are handed over for blocks of time to groups of tutors, and given blocks of resources.

The tutors, normally under a 'team' or 'faculty' leader, then make the decisions themselves about how to group the children, time-table the activities and deploy the resources, and set out the learning requirements for evaluation. This kind of arrangement gives week-to-week flexibility in both grouping and the allocation of teachers. Similar approaches can be made to pastoral grouping. The variations possible on this kind of arrangement are very considerable and there are organisational implications in respect of academic structure and responsibilities; but it is technically feasible to time-table an entire school on this basis, at least as long as it is not too small.

D. IMPLICATIONS AND CONCLUSIONS

1. There is a need for much subtler, more complex structural, or organisational considerations—grossly defined alternatives, such as streaming/unstreaming are an over-simplification.

2. It is not a matter of mere mechanics—what really counts in determining the effectiveness of an organisation is the quality of what goes on in the classroom. The organisation determines who gets there in the first place, and what they expect, and what opportunities they have, when they get there. But the key factors lie in the attitudes, the perceptions and the expectations of the teachers and their pupils, as affected by their immediate situation, and the degree of control they have over it. These are the realities in this discussion.

3. The technical nature of the curriculum/time-table structure is such that in the large, complex school, it remains a powerful factor tending to inhibit autonomy and change, and to over-centralise control. In any large organisation, the problem of human involvement demands a solution in terms of devolution of authority, decentralisation of control and decision-making, and a sense of responsibility for one's own development. Hence the need, in constructing a curriculum organisation, to leave significant areas of flexibility, opportunity—to seek stability as well as change—and decision-making autonomy. New forms may be needed.

4. There is a special need in the large new comprehensives for

analysis, evaluation and development work, in terms of structures and organisational possibilities, in terms of infrastructures; a new analytical language may need to be developed.

5. The skills, insights and sympathies needed to make a success of curriculum construction in a large comprehensive are clearly very considerable. The indications are that they are not abundantly available, and that help may be needed, especially at the planning stages. The same is true of the educational administrators who have to plan systems of schools, and create the new units often out of existing resources. The strong implication is that training in this field is urgently needed.

REFERENCES

DAVIES, T. I., *School Organisation: A New Synthesis*, Pergamon, London, 1969.
WEBB, P. C., Staff development in large secondary schools, *Educational Administration Bulletin* (2.1), Autumn 1973.

CHAPTER 13

ASSESSING THE ROLE OF THE HEAD*

Meredydd G. Hughes

School headship, it has been suggested, is an obsolete institution, which should be transformed, dismembered or abolished (Corbett, 1971; Stanton, 1972). Teachers' organisations are engaged in debating the greater participation of teachers in school government which is widely thought to be desirable (N.U.T., 1971; N.A.S., 1972), while rival groups compete in making similar claims on behalf of pupils. A Bow Group publication suggests that the head should be a managing director, responsible to a school council of L.E.A. representatives, parents, teachers and co-opted members (Watts, 1971). Heads themselves, in formulating their own views, have given consideration to 'the claims of assistant teachers, parents and pupils to share in the exercise of authority and in the processes of decision-making in schools . . .' (H.M.A., 1971).

Until recently the role of the Head, in both primary and secondary schools, was regarded as an invariant, the fixed point which could be taken for granted while other aspects of the educational system were subject to change. The Headmaster was, as Professor Baron (1956) put it, 'in a very real sense, the focus and pivot of his school', a remark which could equally be applied to headmistresses.

The transplantation into the maintained secondary schools, after the 1902 Education Act, of a concept of headship derived from the highly esteemed independent schools has been described by Professor Baron (1952, 1955, 1956), and further discussed by other writers (Bernbaum, 1970; Musgrave, 1968; Rée, 1968; Westwood, 1966).

* Based, by permission, on the writer's article, School headship in transition, *London Educational Review* (1.3), 1972.

The emphasis was upon the Head as a leader (Hoyle, 1969). He had considerable independence, had undisputed authority within the school, and frequently took the initiative. Heads were also considerate; they did a substantial amount of teaching, particularly of seniors, and adopted a paternalistic, pastoral relation to assistant staff as well as to pupils (Bamford, 1967).

Less attention has been given to the not dissimilar stern paternalism of the Victorian elementary school 'principal teacher' in relation to pupils, pupil teachers and inadequately trained staff. In industrial areas this tradition carried over into the higher grade schools, whose Heads established an association which briefly rivalled the Headmasters' Association of Secondary Schools (Baron, 1952).

The autocracy and the benevolence, common to the public and elementary school traditions, are two aspects of the accepted stereotype of school headship which lie uneasily together. In relation to his staff the Head is simultaneously 'the boss' and 'the senior colleague', which can create difficulties, as Watson (1969) noted. In different guises the distinction has been discussed by social scientists in several contexts. Bennis (1959), for instance, distinguishes between the hierarchical superior as 'an instrument and arm of reality, a man with power over the subordinate' and the superior as an agent of growth, 'a helper, trainer, consultant and co-ordinator'. The two aspects are potentially in conflict, and there is need for a 'double reference' and a 'commitment to maturity' on both sides in order to activate the two simultaneously.

In practice the double reference is difficult to achieve, and two styles of leadership tend to emerge, which are typified in the contrasting advice given to their young colleagues by the two senior Headmasters previously quoted in Chapter 1 (Thomas and Bailey, 1927). Thomas advised the probationer Head to keep his distance from staff, and added:

> You will be lonely, but that is one of the inevitable penalties of chief command. The compensation is a far easier and far less resented exercise of the authority which you must exercise unless you intend to be only nominally Head Master.

Similarly Professor Musgrove (1971, p. 118) suggests that the good Headmaster is aloof and 'will make of loneliness an effective tool of command'. The view is broadly supported by Fielder's finding (1958, p. 44) that, in a variety of contexts, social distance between leader and led is positively associated with certain measures of effective leadership, though it should be noted that Fielder's treatment has subsequently been extended to take account of limiting situational variables (1967).

A markedly different style of leadership is recommended by Thomas' co-author, Bailey:

> Frankly I believe that the Head Master's main duty is to give a lead to his colleagues, really to teach them. He should be the most keen teacher on the staff. . . . My strong advice to you is to resist your natural inclination to govern and to try to be the friend and counsellor of your staff.

The informal, 'senior colleague' relation to staff, advocated by Bailey, is in harmony with the 'participative leadership' and 'job enlargement' concepts developed by Argyris (1957), Likert (1961), and other writers in the human relations school of management theory. It is also the aspect on which the Gittins Report (1967) puts its main emphasis in a chapter on the role of the primary school Head: the Head is to be the leader of a team, who works alongside the staff in 'a democratic situation of ordered freedom' (p. 532).

The actual behaviour of Heads of similar schools shows wide variation (Bates, 1971), and there is much flexibility in the enactment of individuals, which is related to the different modes of authority which may be exercised (King, 1968). Thomason has noted in Chapter 5 that the Head's role is *extensible* in the sense that he has considerable freedom to mould it to his own personality, and that in this he is similar to a top business executive. The extensibility is subject, however, to the responsibility laid upon the Head by Articles of Government or Rules of Management to 'control the internal organisation, management and discipline of the school', which exposes him to an onerous common law duty, particularly in relation to the law of negligence (Barrell, 1966, 1970). Correspondingly the law grants him considerable authority, so that the oft-quoted analogy of the captain of a ship has a firmer legal basis than is often recognised (Anderson, 1971).

Critical appraisal of the Head's behaviour, a popular staffroom pastime, frequently naïvely implies a unidimensional continuum from 'bad' to 'good', which is loosely related to Lewin's 'autocratic–democratic' construct (Lewin and Lippitt, 1938). Other classifications, such as 'task-oriented–person-oriented' and 'instrumental–expressive' (both of which can be linked with the familiar distinction between means and ends), may be more relevant, and have been effectively used in analysing an administrative role in education (Taylor, 1964). Care is needed in handling such dichotomies, however, lest one make the unwarranted assumption that the instrumental task specialist is necessarily insensitive to the value of persons and human relations.

Constricting alternatives may be avoided by using a two-dimensional model of leadership behaviour, in which 'initiating structure' and 'consideration' are regarded as independent measures of leadership (Halpin, 1956). 'Initiating structure' refers to endeavours to establish 'well-defined patterns of organisation, channels of communication, and methods of procedure', and 'consideration' to 'behaviour indicative of friendship, mutual trust, respect and warmth in the relationship between the leader and the members of his staff'. Numerous studies in differing educational and other contexts confirmed the common-sense expectation that the effective leaders, as perceived by work associates, are those whose score is above average in *both* dimensions. They are task specialists and also human relations specialists.

Because of the independence of the two dimensions, the strong initiator of structure may be an aloof martinet or an approachable senior colleague, a Thomas or a Bailey. The leader's successful initiation of structure, however, makes it more feasible for him, and provides him with more time, to show consideration if he is so minded. This is in accord with the point made by Davis (Chap. 8), arising from her own experience, that a cardinal objective in streamlining the organisation in a large school is to allow more time for personal contact. 'Far from being de-humanised and remote, if the chain of communication is working efficiently [the Head] should be relieved of the burden of administration in order to be seen and known as a person, not dismissed as a business manager' (p. 133).

An alternative strategy is for the Head, as task specialist, to concentrate on instrumental problems, encouraging his deputy to be the social–emotional human relations expert who provides expressive leadership to staff. A division of labour along these lines was advocated by Burnham (1964) in a study of deputy headship. Support is provided by research on behaviour in experimental small groups (Bales and Slater, 1955), but hardly—as Burnham (1968) seems to claim—from Halpin's work. Dual leadership may well be a convenient arrangement where it matches the personalities of the persons concerned, but the case for its general adoption is less convincing, in spite of Etzioni's advocacy (1965). In larger schools the managerial structure is more complex, as Burnham also recognises, and some specialisation of function among senior staff is likely to be structured in terms of academic and social organisation.

The Heads themselves differ in their emphasis on the two aspects. Some large-school Heads argue for a recognition that their roles are increasingly managerial (Bruckshaw, 1971; Conway, 1970; Poli, 1969). Recent research suggests, however, that Heads are reluctant to relinquish the traditional 'human relations' aspect of their work (Bernbaum, 1970). A study of the role conceptions of primary and secondary school Heads (Cohen, 1970) showed the Heads of the larger schools (defined as having over 300 pupils) to place more emphasis than the smaller-school Heads on rules and regulations (i.e. they *initiated structure* to a greater extent), but there was no corresponding increase in their impersonality (i.e. their *consideration* was undiminished). 'The data', states Cohen, 'showed the large-school Head to exhibit a degree of concern for the individual child, the individual teacher and the particular parental request equal to that shown by his small-school colleague.'

A study of comprehensive school administration defines a large school very differently (Bates, 1971), but arrives at similar conclusions. In large schools 'there was a perceptible reluctance on the part of Heads to break with the main sources of direct contact with pupils' (p. 99), and there were few areas which Heads delegated completely as schools increased in size. A University of Bristol investigation, the broad scope of which has recently been described (Lyons, 1972), may be expected to provide specific information in this area, based on an analysis of the desk diaries of senior teachers, while a study at Cardiff University College explores the interpenetration of the organisational and professional aspects of the Secondary School Head's role (Hughes, 1973).

The latter study, which involved the extensive interviewing of Heads, school staff, L.E.A. officers and chairman of governors, under grant from the Nuffield Foundation, revealed relationships between aspects of internal school organisation and the discretion and status given to the Head by external authority. It also showed that the interpretation given to the claim of Heads to be leading professionals, rather than simply managers, is closely related to the achievement of effective co-ordination between the sapiental and organisational authority systems, as described by Thomason (Chapter 3). In particular, the analysis identified the 'innovating Head' as a well-defined and significant sub-category: the innovating Head tends to be professionally active outside his own school, but also finds it possible to interact frequently with his own staff, encouraging them to take the initiative in trying out new ideas and media (Hughes, 1972).

The evidence provided by recent research of a need to reassess both the instrumental and the expressive aspects of the Head's role is thus cumulative and unmistakable. For the primary school the case can be made out, as in the Gittins Report, in terms of new methods which require collective planning and a sharing of responsibilities. Because of greater organisational complexity, the problem is even more acute at the secondary level. The attempt to cover both major aspects has been described as a cause of 'the stress and strain which is undermining the health and morale of many Heads of large comprehensive schools' (Conway, 1970). The point is confirmed by two independent observers: 'All too many of these Heads are carrying far too big a burden of their school's success on their own shoulders—because of their desire to live up to traditional ideals of being a "good Headmaster" ' (Benn and Simon, 1970).

Looking to the future, there are at least two directions in which alleviation of the role strain and role overload of Heads of schools might be sought. The first possibility is for the Head to concentrate. exclusively on managerial problems, adopting a highly specific, instrumental, task-oriented style of operation. Such an emphasis is not unfamiliar outside Britain, and would presumably be acceptable to those who would argue, like Lieberman (1956), that the professionalism of the teacher can only be enhanced by sharpening the distinction between the teacher and the administrator. A necessary corollary of this line of reasoning is that previous teaching experience is less important for the Head than that he should have had managerial experience in other organisations. A number of managerial appointments have been made to independent school headships, but little is known of their organisational consequences, or whether the persons appointed absorb, or remain aloof from, the dominant ideology of their professional teachers. One American study is tangentially relevant; Gross and Herriott (1965) found a lack of professional leadership from elementary school principals to their staff to be associated with adverse effects on the schools.

The alternative strategy, which may be more congenial and more realistic in the British context, is to strengthen the colleague relation to staff, while seeking redefinition within both the instrumental and the expressive role sectors. The traditional, person-oriented, consideration-giving image of headship is remodelled rather than discarded, but the operation is unlikely to be easy or painless. It requires something of the 'double reference' advocated by Bennis, and implies a more open, and a more egalitarian, interpretation of the Head's colleague relation to other teachers (Hoyle, 1972; Williams, 1972).

In moving towards a collegial system, it may be more realistic in the first instance, as the NUT (1973) finally decided, to place the emphasis on staff consultation rather than on staff participation in decision-making. When the consultation is seen to be 'for real', so that two-way communication occurs as a matter of course, there is professional growth on both sides, and the nature of the staff involvement undergoes a gradual change. Even though the final responsibility is with the Head, it frequently becomes difficult to distinguish in practice between the processes of consultation and of participation (cf. Tucker, Chap. 9).

Collegial authority is seen in a more radical form at Countesthorpe College in Leicestershire, which is seeking to live up to the claim of its first Warden that it is a 'wholly participatory democracy' (McMullen, 1972). Such schemes make strenuous and time-consuming demands on staff at all levels, requiring them to have the maturity to be able to integrate the managerial and professional aspects of their roles, so that they work effectively as a team, collectively and severally initiating structure and showing consideration. If the faith and enthusiasm of the pioneering participants is matched by the manifest achievement of organisational objectives, the objections of the critics will appear less valid, and the indirect effect on the governance of more conventional schools may be considerable (cf. H.M.A., 1972). In the long term, other ideas, such as management by a team and the circulation of the headship position among senior staff, may come to be recognised as possibilities for serious consideration.

Whatever the distant prospect, it seems likely that, in the foreseeable future, enduring and effective structures of participation will require imaginative and resourceful leadership at the centre to encourage, as well as to sort out and harmonise, the influential acts of other organisational participants. Co-operation, rather than leadership, will be recognised as the creative process, but we may agree with Barnard (1938, p. 259) that 'leadership is the indispensable fulminator of its forces'. Though a general conclusion cannot be drawn from a single case, information concerning

Countesthorpe College (Corbett, 1971) is consistent with the proposition that, when the Head of a school divests himself of formal authority, his staff leadership role as co-ordinator of the implementation of joint decisions and integrator of the varied contributions of organisational members is no less crucial than in a traditionally governed school. While the Head's apparent authority diminishes as procedures become more democratic and participation becomes widespread at all levels, his personal influence could well be greater. The Head who is able to respond in a positive manner to the challenge of democratic leadership will still have an inestimable contribution to make. In the midst of educational change he will, paradoxically, continue to be 'in a very real sense, the focus and pivot of his school'.

REFERENCES

ANDERSON, H., The Headmaster's authority, *Headmasters' Association Review* (69), 1971, pp. 173–8.

ARGYRIS, C., *Personality and Organization: the conflict between the system and the individual*, Harper, New York, 1957.

BALES, R. F. and SLATER, P. E., Role differentiation in small decision-making groups, in PARSONS, T. and BALES, R. F. (eds.), *Family, Socialization and Interaction Process*, Free Press, Glencoe, Illinois, 1955.

BAMFORD, T. W., *The Rise of the Public Schools*, Nelson, London, 1967.

BARNARD, C. I., *The Functions of the Executive*, Harvard Univ. Press, Cambridge, Mass., 1938.

BARON, GEORGE, *The Secondary Schoolmaster, 1895–1914*, Ph.D. Thesis, University of London, 1952.

BARON, GEORGE, The origins and early history of the Headmasters' Conference, *Educational Review* (7), 1955, pp. 223–34.

BARON GEORGE, Some aspects of the "headmaster tradition", *Researches and Studies* (14), 1956, pp. 7–16.

BARRELL, G. R., *Teachers and the Law* (3rd ed.), Methuen, London, 1966.

BARRELL, G. R., *Legal Cases for Teachers*, Methuen, London, 1970.

BATES, A. W., *The Administration of Comprehensive Schools*, Ph.D. Thesis, University of London, 1971.

BENN, C. and SIMON, B., *Half Way There: report on the British comprehensive school reform*, McGraw-Hill, London, 1970.

BENNIS, W. G., Leadership theory and administrative behaviour: the problem of authority, *Administrative Science Quarterly* (4), 1959, pp. 259–301.

BERNBAUM, G., The role of the headmaster: final report, Duplicated Report to the Social Science Research Council, London, 1970.

BRUCKSHAW, B., The changing role of the Head, *Welsh Secondary Schools Review* (57), 1971, pp. 34–35.

BURNHAM, P. S., *The Role of Deputy Head in Secondary Schools*, M.Ed. Thesis, University of Leicester, 1964.

BURNHAM, P. S., The deputy head; in ALLEN, B. (ed.), *Headship in the 1970s*, Blackwell, Oxford, 1968.

COHEN, LOUIS, School size and headteachers' bureaucratic role conceptions, *Educational Review* (23), 1970, pp. 50–58.

CONWAY, E. S., *Going Comprehensive: a study of the administration of comprehensive schools*, Harrap, London, 1970.

CORBETT, ANN, The school bosses, *New Society*, 15 April 1971, pp. 627–30.

ETZIONI, AMITAI, Dual leadership in complex organizations, *American Sociological Review* (30), 1965, pp. 688–98.

FIELDER, F. E., *Leader Attitudes and Group Effectiveness*, University of Illinois Press, Urbana, 1958.

FIELDER, F. E., *A Theory of Leadership Effectiveness*, McGraw-Hill, New York, 1967.

GITTINS REPORT, *Primary Education in Wales*, H.M.S.O., London, 1967.

GROSS, NEAL and HERRIOTT, R. E., *Staff Leadership in Public Schools*, Wiley, New York, 1965.

HALPIN, ANDREW W., *The Leadership Behavior of School Superintendents*, Ohio State University, Columbus, 1956.

HEADMASTERS' ASSOCIATION, The government of schools, *Headmasters' Association Review* (69), 1971, pp. 178–80.

HEADMASTERS' ASSOCIATION, *The Government of Schools*, H.M.A. Report, 1972.

HOYLE, ERIC, *The Role of the Teacher*, Routledge, 1969.

HOYLE, ERIC, Educational innovation and the role of the teacher, *Forum* (14), 1972, pp. 42–44.

HUGHES, MEREDYDD G., *The Role of the Secondary School Head*, University of Wales Ph.D. Thesis, University College, Cardiff, 1972.

HUGHES, MEREDYDD G., The professional-as-administrator: the case of the secondary school Head, *Educational Administration Bulletin* (2.1) Autumn 1973.

KING, RONALD, The Head Teacher and his authority, in ALLEN, B. (ed.), *Headship in the 1970s*, Blackwell, Oxford, 1968.

LEWIN, K. and LIPPITT, R., An experimental approach to the study of autocracy and democracy: a preliminary note, *Sociometry* (1), 1938, pp. 292–300.

LIEBERMAN, M., *Education as a Profession*, Prentice-Hall, Englewood Cliffs, N.J., 1956.

LIKERT, RENSIS, *New Patterns in Management*, McGraw-Hill, New York, 1961.

LYONS, GEOFFREY, Patterns of administrative work in secondary schools, *Educational Administration Bulletin* (1.1), 1972, pp. 22–28.

MCMULLEN, TIM, Countesthorpe College, Leicestershire, *Forum* (14), 1972, pp. 48–49.

MUSGRAVE, P. W., *The School as an Organization*, Macmillan, London, 1968.

MUSGROVE, FRANK, *Patterns of Power and Authority in English Education*, Methuen, London, 1971.

NATIONAL ASSOCIATION OF SCHOOLMASTERS, *Management, Organization and Discipline*, N.A.S., Hemel Hempstead, Herts., 1972.

NATIONAL UNION OF TEACHERS, *Teachers' Participation: a study outline*, N.U.T., London, 1971.

NATIONAL UNION OF TEACHERS, *Executive Report on Teacher Participation*, N.U.T., London, 1973.

POLI, P., Administering a large school, *Headmasters' Association Review* (66), 1969, pp. 30–40.

RÉE, HARRY, The changed role of the Head, in ALLEN, B. (ed.), *Headship in the 1970s*, Blackwell, Oxford, 1968.

STANTON, M., School management, *Forum* (14), 1972, p. 85.

TAYLOR, WILLIAM, The training college principal, *Sociological Review* (12), 1964, pp. 185–201.

THOMAS, W. J. and BAILEY, C. W., *Letters to a Young Head Master*, Blackie, London, 1927.

WATSON, L. E., Office and expertise in the secondary school, *Educational Research* (11), 1969, pp. 104–12.

WATTS, R., *Parents in School*, Bow Publications, London, 1971.

WESTWOOD, L. J., Re-assessing the role of the Head, *Education for Teaching* (71), 1966, pp. 65–74.

WILLIAMS, T., Staff involvement and participation in decision-making, *Headmasters' Association Review* (70), 1972, pp. 27–30.

EDITOR'S CONCLUDING COMMENTS

1

THE various sections of the present volume display a diversity of perspective and of approach to secondary school administration. The editor, either initially in 1970 or in reviewing the contributions some four years later, has not regarded it as his function to iron out the occasional differences of view or of emphasis which appear within the text. The six practising Heads, who have written on operational aspects or reacted to the case studies, are unlikely, in their thinking about the administration of their own schools, to have made explicit use of Webb's analytical categories or of Thomason's classification of decision roles. There are naturally some differences of outlook among the practitioners themselves, as there certainly were on the Cardiff course, on such matters as the organisation of pastoral care, the appointment of professional counsellors and the school's response to community influence. Again it may be surmised from Webb's broad survey of curricular arrangements that his approach to non-streaming for academic subjects would differ from that of Tucker, who, as a committed non-streamer, has provided a perceptive case study of a specific organisational innovation. Judge, in a contribution on the sixth form which appears even more relevant in 1974 than when it was first written, found it desirable to deal with substantive issues which call for administrative decision both within the school and in a wider context.

It will be noted, however, that, underlying the diversity, the later contributions, in their treatment of administrative process in relation to specific issues in school administration, are entirely compatible with Thomason's theoretical formulation. At several points they illustrate his basic distinction between bureaucratic and professional authority systems, each having its distinctive control system. As first pointed out in Chapter 2, professionalism is a special issue in educational administration, and—as some organisational theorists have pointed out—it has even wider implications. Blau and Scott (1963), in discussing what they call the dilemma of bureaucratic discipline and professional expertness, have noted that the work of professionals is increasingly carried out in bureaucratic organisations (note also Thomason's reference to scientists in industry, p. 50), while operations in bureaucracies are becoming increasingly professionalised. Studies of school administration are thus potentially of general interest in the development of a comparative approach to organisational theory.

Writing of schools in the United States, Bidwell (1965) has conceptualised their functioning as the outcome of complex interactions between structural arrangements involving clear role definitions (representing a degree of bureaucratisation) and the attitudes and orientation of staff (representing degree of professionalisation), with other variables also intervening. Practitioners will know of the tension between the two systems; but the professional aspect is strengthened in the United Kingdom by the fact that, contrary to the position in most other countries (Stones, 1963), the Headmaster is still regarded, and regards himself, as a practising teacher. As Bailey (1927) put it, in *Letters to a Young Head Master*, "I cannot conceive a great Headmaster who is not a fellow craftsman of his colleagues." A common professionalism unites the administrators and the staff who are administered, which should provide a favourable climate for the growth of the participative procedures suggested by Thomason and Webb and described by practising Heads in the present volume. As noted in the previous chapter, the concept of *profession* held by the professional-as-administrator is thus of crucial importance.

Whether increase in size militates in practice against the fellow craftsman and colleague approach is an issue on which the research evidence is inconclusive. In Chapter 4 Thomason surmises that the development of larger schools will decrease reliance on professional commitment in favour of a greater dependence on impersonal 'closed-loop' control. Webb, however, having raised the question whether the size of a comprehensive school is likely to make it less sensitive to individual needs or problems, comes to the conclusion that the quality of human relationship is not a simple function of type, size or growth, but is better regarded as a moderately independent variable.

In a small school, under stable conditions, the Head, if so inclined, could make all the main decisions. Major organisational change—such as unstreaming—or a substantial increase in the size of a school makes an autocratic style less tenable. Tucker, in Chapter 9, has shown how an innovating Head, to achieve his goal, has to share many of the consequential decisions with relevant professional staff. In Chapters 7 and 8 Jones and Davis discuss in detail how the sharing of decision-making can be effectively organised in a large school, involving junior as well as senior members of staff. While both writers make it clear that larger schools require greater clarity concerning role definitions and the processes of communication and decision-making (and are, to that extent, more bureaucratic), this clarity can be achieved in a way which gives ample scope for the professional assumption of responsibility at all levels in the organisation. It may well be that it is in the larger school that the process which Thomason has called 'organisational training', and which provides a specific model of staff development, is most easily recognisable. It is certainly true that the larger school is better placed to adopt the block time-tabling and team-teaching approaches suggested by Webb (p. 231) as measures to reduce over-centralisation and inflexibility.

Both Jones and Davis make brief references to student participation, and Judge points to some of the difficulties that can arise in reaching agreement as to the area in which such participation is acceptable. Expressing a personal view in *The Headmasters' Association Review*, D. A. Frith, Headmaster of Archbishop Holgate's School, York, suggests (1969) that, while Heads will still be responsible for final decisions,

Schools need to prepare their pupils, in ways suitable to their age and development—and that means treating them in as grown-up a way as they can possibly take—for understanding in practice what honest consultation means and can achieve, so that they will have faith in the process and have some idea of how to make it work. It needs to prepare them to be as open as possible, not to be primarily concerned to achieve and cling to personal power.

The complexity of client involvement when the clients are, in Thomason's words, naïve persons in process of being transformed into mature persons, is only the latest of the challenging managerial problems with which today's Heads have to deal, and which require further discussion and careful study.

2

A basic and essential feature of the management approach to school administration, which is evident to some degree in all the contributions, becomes explicit in Professor Thomason's discussion of the managerial concept of a 'control loop'. It is the control loop which relates the identified objectives of the system to (1) decisions concerning means for achieving the objectives, and to (2) comparison processes which weigh up what is achieved against what was proposed. The perception of a discrepancy between the reality and the intention frequently leads to further decisions concerning means, e.g. the Head of Westwood School, in Part 2 of the Case Study, proposes to tighten disciplinary controls even further when the comparison process shows that the previous measures have failed (and incidentally risks slipping into the stalemate condition of 'cycling', whereby the problem runs round and round the loop without having any effect). In many cases the cycle will be successfully completed, the adjustment of means progressively bringing performance into closer alignment with the agreed objectives.

An alternative, or additional, course of action, when changing the means proves to be ineffective or only partially effective, is to scrutinise, criticise and modify the original objectives in the light of the organisation's lack of success in achieving them. The implications of a change of objectives are likely to be far-reaching, and will need to be worked out at all levels of the organisation. This, in effect, is what is attempted for Westwood School in the investigator's report (Westwood Comprehensive, Part 3).

Management by objectives (MBO in the management literature) is a phrase which occurs on a number of occasions in Thomason's treatment, and which basically refers to a focus of attention on objectives, identified and agreed at the various levels of the organisation, as a prerequisite for collaborative decisions on means and evaluation. The concept has also been given prominence in a number of other recent discussions of educational management (Glatter, 1972; Davies, 1972, 1973; Light, 1973; Webb, 1973), and it may therefore be of interest to note briefly the markedly different interpretations given to it over the years.

Originally expounded by Drucker (1955) in an industrial context, the MBO construct was further developed by McGregor (1960), of 'Theory X' and 'Theory Y' fame. Not surprisingly in view of its originators, it included a strong emphasis on the participation of subordinates, both in defining objectives and in working out the consequent implementation and assessment procedures. In the 1960s it was taken up and packaged by management consultants (Miller, 1966; Humble, 1967), becoming a highly sophisticated, and highly regarded, system of organisational control. Widely adopted as a panacea for organisational ills, it has also been criticised as a device for manipulating the workers (Sofer, 1972) and as a bureaucratic form-filling exercise (Wickens, 1968). According to Molander (1972), in practice it "frequently lapses into a bureaucratic ritual or worse still produces results for which the technique was not intended". Such statements provide grounds for caution in considering the application of MBO principles to education, though it may also be urged, with good reason, that degenerate outcomes are not inevitable.

A careful assessment by Davies (1972) of the reasons, publicly stated or inferred from observation, which have resulted in the adoption of MBO in educational authorities and institutions gives little cause for reassurance. It seems that teachers and administrators, as they begin to explore the cybernetic world of organisation and management, need to be better prepared for the occasional charlatan or witchdoctor—the people who "offer magical solutions to profound problems through mastery of special techniques", as Birley (1972) aptly puts it. Glatter (1972), referring to the content of training courses, warns of the danger of creating inaccurate expectations by "selling" techniques or sets of techniques, rather than realistically facing up to the problems likely to be encountered in using them. Similarly Light (1973), in an analysis of MBO as a strategy of staff development in education, urges its merits as an approach or a learning process rather than as a programme or set of procedures.

The writings cited above may fairly be claimed to provide support for the standpoint adopted in the present volume, as reflected in its sub-title: a management *approach*. In studiously avoiding the over-emphatic claims of the managerial technocrats, one does not need to deny the value, in many and varied contexts, of the formidable battery of techniques available to the educational administrator today—though it is sometimes insufficiently recognised that they are obsolescent phenomena, liable to be superseded (like the programming languages of the computers themselves) by more sophisticated models, as they prove insufficiently flexible to respond to increasingly complex demands. One may legitimately have misgivings, however, about a general transfer to schools of management techniques and systems (cf. Taylor, 1973), some of which may be illfitted to the requirements of complex and highly specialised, professionally staffed, service organisations. Their indiscriminate adoption, leading—almost inevitably—to disenchantment, might well hinder the growth of the systematic thinking about objectives, decision-making and evaluation, which is urgently required in schools, as it is in other institutions. A healthy scepticism about management systems may, paradoxically, almost be a necessary pre-condition to the development of a management approach which recognises, and takes account of, the complex and varied demands of the school organisation.

3

In his final chapter Professor Thomason gives an encouraging indication of likely future development, as he describes a more open and collaborative approach to control procedures in schools, which replaces the mechanistic closed loop model of traditional management theory. The thesis gains support from the emphasis placed by the practitioner contributors in later chapters on staff involvement and participation, an emphasis which has recently been echoed by the professional associations, as noted in the previous chapter.

The case for participation may be stated in terms of the increased complexity of school life and the increasing size of school units, in terms of curriculum development and teaching methods which call for a sharing of effort and responsibility among colleagues, and in terms of the speed of educational change which causes anxiety and uncertainty (N.U.T., 1971). Further factors are the development of formal procedures of participation in further education and teacher training, arising from the Weaver Report and Circular 7/70, and a changing climate within society whereby people generally wish to participate in decisions affecting their working lives and their community.

The Headmasters' Association has responded to such views by recommending that "all Heads should establish procedures by which their teaching colleagues can be consulted fully about matters affecting their work and the life of the school" (H.M.A., 1972).Some would go further, and Parkes (1973) has suggested, on the basis of his initial impressions of the FE experience, that there is little difference in practice between a decision-making structure and an advisory one. This is a matter which clearly deserves further study.

The greater professional involvement implicit in the twin concepts of organisational training and staff development may not be without difficulties both for Heads and staff. Writing in an Australian context, Bassett (1967) notes that "some staff have such poor morale and are torn by such internal dissension" that a proper working relationship is difficult, while some Heads may not have

251

"the professional maturity to create a proper relation with their staff". It is not to be supposed that such difficulties are confined to the Southern Hemisphere.

There is a natural presumption that staff, in general, wish to have greater participation in school government, but there appears to be some ambivalence in staff views. The N.U.T. Working Party on Teacher Participation (1973) found that opinions were divided, and that "in some areas there is an apparent lack of interest in the whole question". In an American study which obtained responses from over a thousand teachers, Seeman (1960) found that, on four out of ten items requiring a preference between leadership of a directive nature and a non-directive group-centred approach, a majority preferred the more authoritarian style, while the position was reversed on the other six items. The writer has similarly noticed that, in a number of schools with well-developed consultative procedures, some members of staff participate enthusiastically while others complain about added responsibility and the amount of committee work involved.

Ambiguous responses to participation have similarly been noted in industry in a survey by Dubin (1965). He quotes Likert (1958) to the effect that to be involved in a substantially greater amount of participation than expected produces a negative reaction because of the threatening nature of the situation to the subordinate. According to Likert, "the best results obtain when the amount of participation used is somewhat greater than expected by the subordinates, but still within their capacity to respond to it effectively". Blumberg (1968) points out that it would be unwise to conclude from the above that worker participation should be limited to some small and fixed amount. A more constructive interpretation of Likert's findings is that participative processes should be introduced gradually, with plenty of preparation at each stage.

The above discussion has implications for the training of personnel which may be taken into the school context. They reinforce the proposal made by Raymond Jones (p. 122) in relation to the preparatory training of secondary school teachers, and also the suggestions concerning inservice training made by David Howells and Eluned Jones in Chapter 11. In addition to formal presentations on topics related to school organisation and management, it is suggested that simulated situations and role-playing exercises, involving participation in work groups and the joint planning of projects and activities on a departmental and a non-departmental basis, should be an integral part of such training. The membership of our Cardiff course felt strongly that something of this kind is urgently required.

Similarly, consideration has to be given to the new demands which the organisational training approach makes on the Head, his immediate deputies and the 'middle management'—heads of department and heads of houses. The old procedures and patterns of thought are no longer helpful as they work with groups instead of passing down instructions to be followed by staff. Much is to be learnt from the emphasis on interpersonal and intergroup relations of courses on the human problems of leadership which are arranged, in the United Kingdom, by the Tavistock Institute and other bodies (Rice, 1965; Gray, 1972). It is questionable, however, whether the psychologically strenuous sensitivity training through the analysis of direct experience in groups, which such courses provide, is a universally appropriate means of developing the relevant skills.

At the cognitive level the insights of the group dynamics theorists have much to offer in working out the implications in practice of the basic proposition that participatory leadership, rather than supervisory leadership, results in greater changes of opinion (Preston, 1949; cf. Cartwright, 1968, Part 5). The implications of another proposition, stated by Cartwright (1951), need to be worked out in schools as in other institutions: "Changes in one part of a group produce strain in other related parts, which can only be reduced by eliminating the change or by bringing about readjustments in the related parts." On the other hand, a definition of leadership as "a process by which an agent induces a subordinate to behave in a desired manner" (Bennis, 1961) gives a clue to a possible danger of an excessive preoccupation with this kind of approach. More

253

specifically Seeman warns that human-relations training in general "may degenerate into training whose major outcome is skill in calculating the motives and vulnerabilities of others" (1960, p. 95). Nevertheless, if such limitations of the approach are clearly understood, it would appear that an understanding of social processes and a modicum of skill in social interaction are desirable managerial attributes in a change of emphasis from a bureaucratic to a more participative and professional mode of organisation.

The above discussion leads naturally to the important point that participation must be more than a tactical ploy to secure support for predetermined policies. Unauthentic participation will be seen for what it is and will be quickly discredited. As Lane (1966) has observed, "representative administration has a propensity to turn into a sham at precisely the most crucial moments of decision". The Headmaster of Nailsea School, D. W. John (1969), has written in similar terms: "Nothing is more degrading or unacceptable in consultative processes than the impression that one is being manipulated. This remains true when it is only an impression and not the reality." John argues that, though the Head must retain the power to take decisions, he needs to convince his colleagues that, in devising machinery—such as a study group—to influence staff opinion, he himself is willing to maintain a mind open to conviction by the argument of others.

In the application of management concepts to schools our final emphasis is therefore on authenticity in leadership and a correspondingly open response from staff, as they accept the responsibility which accompanies participation. A management approach to school organisation thus implies, not a set of manipulative techniques for social engineering, but a sustained attempt by Head and staff to understand the principles of social interaction within, and in relation to, the school—which may be regarded as a complex organisation with its own special characteristics—leading naturally to co-ordinated action, involving also the co-operation of clients, to achieve the formulated goals of the organisation.

REFERENCES

BAILEY, CHARLES W., in THOMAS, W. JENKYN and BAILEY, CHARLES W., *Letters to a Young Head Master*, Blackie, London, 1927.

BASSETT, G. W., CRANE, A. R. and WALKER, W. G., *Headmasters for Better Schools*, Univ. of Queensland Press, Brisbane, 1963; 2nd ed., 1967.

BENNIS, W. G., Leadership theory and administrative behavior, in BENNIS, W. G. *et al.*, *The Planning of Change*, Holt, New York, 1961, p. 440.

BIDWELL, CHARLES E., The school as a formal organisation, in MARCH, J. C., *Handbook of Organisations*, Rand McNally, Chicago, 1965, pp. 972–1022.

BIRLEY, DEREK, *Planning and Education*, Routledge, London, 1972.

BLAU, P. M. and SCOTT, W. R., *Formal Organisations*, Routledge, London, 1963, pp. 244–7.

BLUMBERG, PAUL, *Industrial Democracy: The Sociology of Participation*, Constable, London, 1968, p. 102.

CARTWRIGHT, D., Achieving change in people: some applications of group dynamics theory, *Human Relations* (4), 1951, pp. 381–92; also in CHARTERS, W. W. and GAGE, N. C., *Readings in the Social Psychology of Education*, Allyn and Bacon, Boston, 1963.

CARTWRIGHT, D. and ZANDER, A., *Group Dynamics: Research and Theory*, Tavistock, London, 3rd ed., 1968.

DAVIES, JOHN L., Management by Objectives in Local Education Authorities and Educational Institutions (1), *Educational Administration Bulletin* (1.1), Summer 1972.

DAVIES, JOHN L., Management by Objectives in Local Education Authorities and Educational Institutions (2), *Educational Administration Bulletin* (2.1), Autumn 1973.

D.E.S., Government and conduct of establishments of further education, *Circular 7/70*, H.M.S.O., London, 1970.

DRUCKER, P. F., *The Practice of Management*, Heinemann, London, 1955.

DUBIN, R., *Leadership and Productivity*, Chandler Pub. Co., San Francisco, 1965, p. 40.

FRITH, D. A., Student unrest in relation to the schools, *Headmasters' Association Review* (66), July, 1969.

GLATTER, RON, *Management Development for the Education Profession*, Harrap, London, 1972.

GRAY, HARRY, Training in the management of education: an experiental approach, *Educational Administration Bulletin* (1.1), 1972, pp. 1–9.

HEADMASTERS' ASSOCIATION, *The Government of Schools*, H.M.A. Report, 1972.

HUMBLE, J. W., *Management by Objectives*, Industrial Educational and Research Foundation, London, 1967.

JOHN, D. W., Policy decision and decision making, *Headmasters' Association Review* (66), July, 1969.

LANE, W. R. *et al.*, *Foundations of Educational Administration*, Macmillan, New York, 1966.

LIGHT, A. J., The search for a strategy, in PRATT, S. (ed.), *Staff Development in Education*, Councils and Education Press, London, 1973.

LIKERT, R., Effective supervision: an adaptive and relative process, *Personnel Psychology* (11), 1958, p. 329.

McGREGOR, D., *The Human Side of Enterprise*, McGraw-Hill, New York, 1960.

MILLER, E. C., *Objectives and Standards: An Approach to Planning and Control*, American Management Association, New York, 1966.

MOLANDER, C. F., Management by Objectives in perspective, *Journal of Management Studies* (9.1), 1972, pp. 74–81.

NATIONAL UNION OF TEACHERS, *Teachers' Participation: a study outline*, N.U.T., London, 1971.

NATIONAL UNION OF TEACHERS, Final Report of the National Working Party on Teacher Participation (Appendix to the Executive Report), N.U.T., 1973.

PARKES, DAVID L., Circular 7/70 and the government of schools, *Educational Administration Bulletin* (1.2), Spring 1973.

PRESTON, M. G. and HEINTZ, R. K., Effects of participatory versus supervisory leadership on group judgement, *J. Abnormal and Social Psychology* (44), 1949, pp. 345–55.

RICE, A. K., *Learning for Leadership*, Tavistock, London, 1965.

SEEMAN, MELVIN, *Social Status and Leadership*, Ohio State University, Columbus, Ohio, 1960.

SOFER, C., Social control in organizations with special reference to appraisal schemes, paper prepared for NATO symposium, 1971, quoted by GLATTER R., in *Management Development for the Education Profession*, Harrap, London, 1972.

STONES, E., The role of the Headteacher in English education, *Forum* (6.1), 1963.

TAYLOR, WILLIAM, *Heading for Change*, Routledge, London, 1973.

WEAVER REPORT, *Study Group on the Government of Colleges of Education*, H.M.S.O., London, 1966.

WEBB, PETER C., Staff development in large secondary schools, *Educational Administration Bulletin* (2.1), Autumn 1973.

WICKENS, J. D., Management by Objectives: an appraisal, *Journal of Management Studies* (5.3), 1968, pp. 365–79.

INDEX